THE TRIGGERMAN

THE TRIGGERMAN

John Ragusa III

A Division of Shapolsky Publishers

The Triggerman

S.P.I. BOOKS

A division of Shapolsky Publishers, Inc.

ISBN 1-56171-335-X

For any additional information, contact:

S.P.I. BOOKS/Shapolsky Publishers, Inc.
136 West 22nd Street
New York, NY 10011
212/633-2022 / • FAX 212/633-2123

Manufactured in Canada

10 9 8 7 6 5 4 3 2 1

Dedicated
to
Mr. & Mrs. John Ragusa, Jr.
and
Ann Wilson

PROLOGUE

AT THE LOUISIANA STATE PENITENTIARY, ANGOLA, LOUISIANA, USA

The mirror laughs.

He looks down at his hands.

The palms, the backs, the liver spots.

Once so vital, now so impotent.

He raises them to his face and traces the lines on his cheeks.

A three-day stubble roughs his fingertips as they wander the course of age from jaw to eyebrow.

He lowers and cups them, enabling him to collect water from the basin.

He splashes the fatigue from his mind in one cold, wet, forceful stroke, feeling the quiver of uncirculated blood as it rushes to his brain.

The hands of a hero?

No.

The hands of a patriot?

No.

The hands of a God?

No.

The hands of an emaciated, old, dying man?

Maybe.

The hands of evil?

Yes.

The mirror laughs again …

IN SAINT CECILIA'S CATHOLIC CHURCH AND SURROUNDING NEW ORLEANS, LOUISIANA, USA

The threat of hurricanes in November never phased Father Joseph Prio.

As Parish Priest for St. Cecilia's, his concerns nested elsewhere. Even though St. Cecilia's stood a mere six blocks from that dangerous, tempestuous body of water known as Lake Pontchartrain, he feared not. For he had faith. Faith in himself, faith in God. Humankind's soul, however, had escaped his confidence. Never more so than now as he listened to the garbled transgressions of a young, newlywed confessee.

"I hit her, Father. Once, twice, in the face—I don't remember. Then I squeezed her crotch as hard as I could. I wanted to cut it out of her, cut it out! God, I'm so sorry. I'm so sorry, but, Father, it was my best friend, my best friend she was sleeping with, and after only six weeks of marriage!"

The man-child before him was like a frenzied, emasculated beast. "My son! My son!" Father Prio snapped, jolting the boy out of his madness.

"Pray with me ... dear God, you have before you a man filled with hatred. Hatred for the woman he loves. She has hurt him deeply, terribly. So we ask you to enlighten us. Should he forgive and reconcile or should we nullify his marriage in your eyes? Their marriage is young; there are no children. Answer us, Lord."

The confessional booth was silent except for the faint scrape, scrape of Father Prio's fingernails scratching the underside of a large crucifix hung around his neck. The scratching stopped. "Call me tomorrow. We'll arrange an immediate session of marriage counseling. If that fails, then we'll nullify. But dammit, under no circumstances—and I mean no circumstances—are you to strike her or any other woman again. If you do, I'm going to personally bust your ass! Do you understand?"

"Yes, Father."

"For penance—five Hail Marys and five Our Fathers," Father Prio made the sign of the cross, "Ego te absolvo—Go with God now and remember what I've said!"

Father Joseph Prio was, at middle age, a man first, a man of the cloth second. He was soulful and basic, without grandeur or theatrical self righteousness, devoted unselfishly to the benevolent apportionment of his parishioners' lives. He sported a tough, gray-black beard drooping below brown-black eyes interlinked with a receding gray-black hairline. The space between his two front boyish teeth was set off by a pair of wire-rimmed glasses. They tilted on the nose of his five-foot, ten-inch, one hundred seventy pound hunter's build.

He was a dedicated street savvy priest and a hurricane of a man.

St. Cecilia's Catholic Church, constructed in 1965, was the pride of all New Orleans Catholics, a great many of whom were of Italian descent. Located on a block of West Esplanade known locally as Church Row, St. Cecilia's served as a spiritual getaway for those area Catholics who shunned the world famous, more tourist oriented St. Louis Cathedral in Jackson Square.

For Father Joseph Prio, St. Cecilia's had been more than just a magnificent haven over the years—it had been, to the priest, a luxurious prison. One in which he had been sentenced to life, without parole.

He stepped into the Rectory, closed the door and shook the bite of a Pontchartrain November from his thoughts, remembering, as he warmed the day's mail lying unopened on his desktop. He decided to attend to it now, foregoing his usual afternoon snip of white wine and cheese.

His footfalls were silent on the Rectory hallway floor as he moved past the outer desks into his inner office. Its decorative peasant simplicity added a tiny delight to his world. The bishop of the diocese had strictly forbidden him to entertain outside guests here, so its purpose was confined to that of a private study. He loved the contrast, being church administrator for a beautiful modern facility, then spending his quiet hours here. He flipped on his flea market desk lamp and sat briefly motionless as he read his favorite plaqued inscription on the wall to his left:

Peace within the cell: fierce warfare without
Hear all; believe a few; honor all
Do not believe everything you hear
Do not judge everything you see
Do not do everything you can
Do not give everything you have
Do not say everything you know
Pray, read, withdraw, be silent, be at peace.

Father Prio imagined the future Pope John XXIII, Angelo

Roncalli, reading this verse as a boy. A verse, allegedly spoken by St. Bernard, that had appeared inside young Angelo's presbytery in Sotto il Monte, Italy. He smiled, redirecting his thoughts and posture to present day, feeling on his bottomside those familiar cigarette burn holes in the center seat of his Salvation Army desk chair. Being reminded of cigarettes encouraged him to light one up as he commenced to work.

The junk mail appeared first. Then the bills and contributions, then a few bits of correspondence addressed directly to him. One of these bits caught his immediate attention.

No return designation. Labeled only to:

Father Joey Prio
St. Cecilia's
New Orleans, Louisiana

Father Prio twitched, shuddered, the back of his neck hairs suddenly at attention.

Joey.

He removed his confessional robe, revealing a pair of tight blue jeans and blue denim work shirt. He slipped his brown loafers off and rubbed his bare feet together. He looked down at the letter again.

It had been more than 25 years, more than 25 honest years since anyone had addressed him as Joey. Leaning back, shutting his eyes tightly, he began to pray, "Please, Lord ... have mercy on me ... for I am not the same man I was then." With that and a penknife of fortitude, Father Prio—Joey—slit the letter open.

> Joey,
>
> Buon Giorno, Amico mia.
>
> I hope your days are well and prosperous. With all due respect, I find myself in need of a favor considering the nature of our past relationship, I'm sure you will assist. An old friend I haven't heard from in quite a while is in despair. He contacted me recently and requested that I arrange a priest's visit for him. I invite you to dinner to discuss this matter.
>
> Friday 8 p.m.—Mama Maria's
>
> Ciao,
> C. C.

Father Prio folded the letter back into its envelope and again rested his eyes, only now shutting out prayer.

C. C. was Carlo Cefalu.

Carlo was an ex-schoolmate of sorts. A teenage friend who had helped Joey graduate from a curriculum of violence, treachery, and advanced New Orleans hustle.

Father Prio rose from his chair and walked to the age-encrusted wetbar in the corner of his sanctuary. He took a shot glass and bottle of vodka from it and continued to his moth-eaten, spring-showing couch, with the gait of a man burdened, feeling, as he sat, like a lost puppy under the wheel of a huge car—careening backwards ...

1959

"Joey, what the hell do ya think ya doing?"

Boy Joey felt two coarse weather-scratched paws around his Adam's apple. Solidly connected to two tubes of pure steel disguised as forearms.

Carlo was big for his age. Mean, too. He ran his little ferocious French Quarter gang with all the finesse of a mud-stuck hippopotamus.

"Damn, Joey!" Carlo bellowed, releasing Joey's body, letting it collapse to the ground.

"How many times I got to tell ya? When ya partner is in the score, don't keep ya car parked and running. Ya idiots should have the fuckin' thing timed to where ya can make the block, then pick him up. Ya can't sit in a fuckin' car where cars ain't supposed to sit, wait ten minutes while ya bud's making off with the goods. Ya gonna get nabbed and that's that!"

Joey didn't appreciate being embarrassed by Carlo. He was good at this shit and he knew it. Carlo might be the *capo*, but he was also an invective, sarcastic bully, way too big for his britches, Joey decided. So Joey stood up and knocked the piss out of him. Carlo gave an inch, back stumbled, felt his mouth and nose for busted cartilage or teeth or just membranes, smiled real slow, then put his hand out in a gesture of truce. Joey retreated, kneecaps weakening, sized up the offer, then warily clutched Carlo's hand for all he was worth.

They shook on it and from that icicle-gray, freezing New Orleans afternoon, Carlo never got back in Joey's face. Never.

Salvatore "Toto" Prio, Joey's father, owned a grocery store in New Orleans, off Carrolton Avenue, called Prio's Square Deal. He was the typical Sicilian immigrant—silent, stoic, hardworking. Lucia, Joey's mother, worked at the grocery store, too, with her husband. She served counterpoint to Salvatore's every wish, unquestioning. They were quiet, busy people with little time to be parents, allowing Joey the gift of leisure. He ran the rough crescent city streets unattended.

Early on Joey began noticing the resident Sicilian hustlers with their flashy cars and jewelry. He was attracted to them and to their seemingly carefree, fun-filled lifestyles. Thus, the first major ambition of Joey's life was simple—to have diamond stickpins, maroon Cadillacs, and Bourbon Street blonde whores.

With Carlo and his friends, Joey Prio became just another misguided voice in a chorus of delinquents.

Glory, Prison or Death, man.

Glory, Prison or Death!

PRESENT

Father Prio was dizzy. He lifted himself to a sitting position on the couch and gazed out the stained glass window on the opposite side of his office, momentarily enthralled by the sunsetting magnificence of St. Cecilia's. The cedar trees surrounding the church and the gardens of hibiscus lining its walkways lay placid beneath the wallow and bubble of the day's stunning November cloudset. In his mind's eye Father Prio could see the distant expanse of Lake Pontchartrain rumbling its way to nowhere safe, as were the cities of Slidell and New Orleans.

To hell with it! He was a priest. He had made a career for himself doing God's work. Atonement, penance for a tragedy, the tragedy of Whiskey Bay ... 1963 ...

Enough!

Carlo was a human being, which made , in turn, Carlo's despairing friend a human being. Not Sicilian scum, but human beings. He had to do his duty. Slightly drunk, Father Prio went back to his desk, lifted his pen and scribbled a hell-bent notation on his calendar:

Friday—8 p.m./Mama Maria's

The hurricane began to cry.

Mama Maria's was a spicy, informal, Italian-Cajun restaurant two blocks off Prytania Street in the Garden District of New Orleans. Serving dishes like crayfish and spaghetti boiled in olive oil—otherwise known as hot pasta crawdads—qualified it as a popular hangout amongst the immigrant Sicilian trade. It was a popularity that had held fast for nearly sixty years.

Mama Maria's also served as a generally accepted "sit down" location for important underworld players. It was serving as such on Friday at 8:00 p.m. Father Prio, dressed in cleric black, bid a polite "Evening" to the hostess and seated himself at a small red and white checkered table in the corner of the dining room.

Carlo Cefalu, minutes later, strutted in. He was a dressed in a Nino Cerruti suit, custom tailored, an expensive pair of Bruno leathers, and was greeted by several people at the door who ushered him in like a celebrity. Carlo's muscle had turned to middle-aged fat, unaffecting his sneering mouth and beaten nose. His only redeeming physical trait was a lock of platinum hair in the front of his pompadour.

"What say, *Paisan*," Carlo said, grabbing Father Prio's hand, giving it a seemingly sincere shake, similar to the shake back in 1959 that had cemented their youthful truce.

"How are you, Carlo?"

"Good to see ya, Joey. You don't look a day over forty five. Me? I'm good, bad, rich, poor, fucked, unfucked, constipated and running—ya name it."

"You always did have a way with the language," remarked the priest facetiously.

Carlo's New Orleans accent was heavy, a rough verbal mix of Brooklyn and Dixie. He seated himself opposite Father Prio in the wooden chair.

"Ah, I'm sorry, Joey. It's been a tough month. The old stiletto in the nuts routine ... you ordered yet?"

"No, but the manicotti looks good."

"Yea, with ricotta, extra tomato sauce, Marsala—that's for me."

"Me, too."

Their waitress hovered nearby, anxious to be of service.

Father Prio found it hard not to notice this unbridled display of respect Carlo was being shown. He had obviously moved up in his world.

After they ordered Father Prio dove, with characteristic aplomb, into unknown waters. "What's this about, Carlo?"

Carlo's mouth sneered diabolically as he took out a pack of cigarettes in a gold cigarette case, offering one to the priest. Father Prio accepted both cigarette and Carlo's offer to light, inhaled deeply and waited.

"Well, first off," Carlo began, "I see that ya not exactly overjoyed with this quarter century or so reunion. I respect ya for that. In fact, I want ya to know I've always respected the move ya made back in '63 ... I mean becoming a priest and all. Still, we've got some heavy secrets between us. Secrets I've never hurt ya with ... ya know that ... right?"

"Yes, Carlo, I know that."

"And the favor I need now falls right in line with your profession, okay?"

"All right."

Carlo hesitated, glaring directly into the center of Father Prio's eyes.

"Here, read this."

A creased sheet of paper materialized out of Carlo's suit pocket, coming to land in Father Prio's grip. He read it.

Carlo,

I heard about your troubles. Give them hell, kid. You can stand to lose a round or two, just don't let them win the whole bout.

Listen, Carlo, speaking of troubles.

I found out the other day that I'm living on marked time. The big "C", I think. The doctors say my insides are pretty fucked up. I've been down too many years this time and I guess it's just taken its toll.

But look, you got to do something for me. I got something on my mind. Something heavy. I got to make peace with God before I go. So I'm asking you to send a priest by here. A priest we can trust.

I'm just an old man now, so my mind ain't as clear as it once was, but I know it's only right to come clean. I got to.

He can come anytime. I'm in Angola.

Thanks and good luck,

V.A.

Father Prio looked up.

"Who's V.A.?"

"His name is Vince Angeletta. He's a made guy who was traveling a lot during our heyday, '59 - '63, but later became pretty big around here. He was real tight with the Top Man—Charlie Nuccia. Took me under his wing in '65 and groomed me. Gave me and a lot of other young guys breaks. In 1973 he just vanished. Strangest fuckin' thing, like he never existed. Didn't hear anything till he got busted on a state murder rap in '75. Then all I heard was some rumors. Been in ever since. He was a good guy. I just want to help."

Father Prio squinted.

"That's crap, Carlo. What's the angle? You guys have got priests all over the place—why me?"

Carlo looked like he could cut Father Prio's throat that very second. He folded his beefy arms threateningly close and did what he had done, only once, when they were kids. He got in Joey's face.

"Awright, Joey. This is the fuckin' angle, ya fuckin' hothead. Ya were a hothead in '59 and ya still one. But see, I don't forget. I saved ya ass in '63. That chick died in Whiskey Bay. Remember, Joey ... she died. Bigger than shit and I covered for ya. Took a lot of shit on that to protect ya, so you're gonna play this just like I fuckin' say. There's no statute of limitations on homicide, murder, voluntary, involuntary, manslaughter, first, second, accessory, so just keep ya fuckin' mouth shut and listen close." Carlo paused for effect. "Vince Angeletta knows where all the bodies are buried. All of them. That guy was into some heavy moves. Him and the Top Man were almost like brothers. Not too many people know that, but I know it 'cause I was really fuckin' tight with Vince. And see,

I do have some troubles right now. Big troubles. The Federal Task Force is coming after the whole New Orleans group and I'm one of their targets. So I want you to take the old fart's confession and tell me everything he says. Who knows, maybe I can use some of the info to save my ass. That's it."

Father Prio felt a violent surge of old street rage flare, the same as on that icicle-gray afternoon, so long ago.

"You're crazy, Carlo. That goes against everything I've lived for, everything I'm committed to," he argued.

"Well then, just imagine the headlines in the Times-Picayune. 'Respected Priest and Church Administrator Arrested on Ancient Missing Persons Case Now Believed To Be Homicide,' 'cause if I go down hard, I'm taking ya and every motherfucker I can get my hands on with me. *Capisce*? It ain't like the old days. There ain't no honor anymore. It's just one big fuckin' free-for-all and I was always tougher than any of them. I know what it is to eat shit and you're gonna know, too, 'cause you're gonna do this for me one way or the other. Misery loves company, fuckface."

With that, Carlo rose.

"Fuck the meal. I'll see ya here next week, same time. I'll be expecting a report, so get ya holy ass up to Angola and talk to Vince. Do ya job and don't forget one fuckin' word he says."

Carlo slithered out the back door.

Father Prio sat, stunned—a pus-like adrenaline rush racing through him. He stood, removed his wire-rimmed glasses, then as calmly as possible walked to the men's room, found a toilet, kneeled and proceeded to throw his boiling, acidic guts up.

God forbidden and sick as an unwormed Louisiana dog! Father Prio chose to do the devil's duty and had to switch glasses for driving to do so. He replaced his regular wire-rimmed ones with a darker, sportier pair.

Driving gave him an opportunity to think. For all his years as a priest he had used road travel almost exclusively. He hated planes and trains and buses. The feel of the highway always called him home. He would reminisce about his parents, Salvatore and Lucia, and all the joyous travel experiences he had had as a child. He distinctly remembered the drive once a month from New Orleans to Alexander to visit Lucia's family.

His father never saying a word, his mother humming soft pretty melodies. Then once every six months to Torbert to visit the Prios. He remembered his Uncle Sam Prio killing a rattlesnake in the family house once. Cussing in Sicilian the whole time about the "Godda Damma Shitta Snakea!" and his ancient Sicilian grandfather trying to say cemetery on the phone. His broken English screaming Seminary! Seminary!—where the dead people are!

Today was no exception. Memories of his life as a preteen made him serene in the midst of this chaos. Father Prio had decided to use a tape recorder to take Vince's confession. It sat next to him in a satchel on the seat. He had to figure out a way of dealing with Carlo. It had to be fistless and legal, but taking Carlo down, a pubic hair at a time, would surely be a pleasure if he could do it.

Once the stain of Carlo crossed his mind, the rest of his memories flattened.

An aerial view of Whiskey Bay, 1963, came into temporal focus as Father Prio descended into the single most horrible memory of his life. Damn Carlo. Damn him!

1963

Whiskey Bay was the most forbidding swamp in the state of Louisiana. A surreal, haunting, vaporous quagmire where creatures lurked, crying for release, where animalistic sex became natural and inhibitions misplaced. It was a famous getaway for teenagers, a South Louisiana lovers' lane splintered off a web of Atchafalaya back canals, one hundred fifty miles west of Lake Pontchartrain. Carlo Cefalu indeed loved it. He, Joey, Alicia, and Scarlet had arrived at its main launch early morning.

"Carlo, where in the world did you get this boat?" asked Alicia.

"Big T in Harvey. Got a bunch of these DV skiffs. Why? Does it tickle your fancy?" teased Carlo.

"You tickle my fancy. Nothing, nobody else."

"Sure, right," concluded Carlo, unbelieving.

Alicia Jordan was a teenage bombshell. She had hair the color of doeskin and wore thickly applied makeup She had the look of being available, easy and none too bright. To Carlo, though, she was terrific. The other teenage girl was Scarlet

Leblanc. She was a classic Creole, very dark, very tall, and very French. One could almost taste the etoufee seeping from her womanhood and the cider dripping from her breasts. Her hair was dyed red but Joey imagined her lower bush to be black.

Scarlet and Joey had just met that morning and had spoken little on the drive up.

Carlo pumped the engines and the small pleasure craft was off.

"Joey, come over here," Scarlet said, patting the spot next to her. Joey moved to her side.

"Isn't this nice?" she whispered in a rich chocolatey voice barely audible over the engine nose.

"Yea," he answered toughly.

A water current swoshed underneath the DV hull. She grabbed him for support.

"I like the way you touch me," she said.

"I like to touch you," he returned.

She put her tongue in his ear, circling the edges of it, whispering again.

"Kiss me, Joey, kiss me."

They kissed. Like wildcats, like kitty cats. They kissed several times.

"Hey, you guys, think you can come up for a breather? I mean, what is this? Do I look like a taxi driver?" protested Carlo, laughing.

Carlo anchored the boat in a shallow area away from the mosquito swarms, not far from where the swamp met land.

He turned the engine off, came from behind the wheel and opened an ice chest. He grabbed two Jax beers and threw them to Joey. Joey popped one and handed it to Scarlet, then popped the other beer for himself.

After a mock toast, Scarlet set her beer down. She looked over to Alicia and gave a thumbs up sign. This, obviously, had been a prearranged signal as both girls began to take their blouses off. Scarlet was wearing a pink and black blouse with a tight black skirt and penny loafers. Alicia was wearing a pair of pedal pushers with a white blouse. Her last name initial J was on the pocket.

Even the hard cases of Carlo C. and Joey P. were mesmerized.

Carlo smiled and reached down into the ice chest again, this time for a bag of pot and fifth of bourbon. He began to roll a joint. Suddenly Joey cracked up laughing. A nervous, contagious laugh that infected the naked girls and Carlo. They all began to laugh and laugh and laugh, uncontrollably. Chirping like sex-starved whippoorwills before an erotic magnolia sunrise ...

PRESENT

November and he was sweating. Drenched!

Father Prio pulled off the road on the outskirts of Baton Rouge. He reached into his jacket for a handkerchief and began to wipe his forehead and upper lip frantically. His gray-black beard was soaked.

Whiskey Bay '63 was a memory that had mutilated his senses again and again, but today it was a memory he couldn't afford. Slamming a fistful of futility into the dashboard, punching the accelerator, Father Prio drove on.

The Louisiana State Penitentiary at Angola, surrounded by the heavily wooded Tunican Hills on one side and the Mississippi River on the other, was referred to by experts as 18,000 acres of central Louisiana killing ground.

It was referred to by its convicts as wide open ... full tilt ... anything goes. Vince Angeletta referred to it as home. Home ... shit ... home.

By noon he had made at least five trips within his housing unit, Satellite Camp H, to the latrine, to the mirror, to look at himself. At his hands, at his face, then splashing cold water on them brutally.

He had failed! He had failed!

He returned to his bunk and reached underneath it. There were two photographs. A taped, wrinkled, but still lovely photograph of his late beloved wife. She was smiling so clear that he could hear the echoes of her laugh even now, and the photo of another girl, younger, dressed in shorts, smiling, too, as if tomorrow would last forever. He closed his eyes and kissed them both.

Memories. God help the inmate who ran out of memories.

God help me, Vince thought. He put the photos back in place and stretched out on his mattress. He began to sing softly.

Laughing Mirror, laugh—laugh at my ugliness
Laughing Mirror, laugh—laugh if you must
Pretty Angels love me—they swallow me sweet
So laugh, mirror, laugh—in hell we will meet.

It was then that he heard the loudspeaker, "Attention on the compound ... Vince Angeletta, Vince Angeletta, report to the visiting room. Vince Angeletta report to the visiting room ... immediately."

Hopping from his bunk in a spry uplift, the old criminal grinned. For God had heard him, acknowledged him and was now going to save his pathetic fucking ass from darkness.

Amen. Amen. A-fucking-men!

Father Prio felt like a virgin-in-waiting. Legs spread, mouth open, body tensed, praying for a quick, bloodless, first penetration by this stranger, this Mafioso-named Vince Angeletta. A shiver had erupted through him when he heard the page. The satchel with the tape recorder laid next to his chair. He punched the recorder on.

Vince entered the visiting room minutes later, dressed in a khaki uniform and black utility shoes. His face was striking with a defiant nose, romantic lips, sunken cheeks and two incredible character lines arching down into a stubble of new whiskers. He was taller than most southern Italians and seemed relatively fit. His silvery, brown-blue eyes were clear.

"I'm Vince Angeletta," he rasped.

"Mr. Angeletta, Vince, I'm Father Joseph Prio. I think you've been informed of my coming."

They shook hands.

"Yes, Father, I'm very glad to see you."

"I understand you wish to make a confession?" asked the priest.

"Yes, Father."

Father Prio motioned Vince to sit in the chair next to him. He wanted to make sure the recorder could pick him up. He then carefully hung his large confessional crucifix around his neck and bowed his head.

"Name of the Father, the Son, the Holy Ghost. Vince, I'm ready."

Vince tilted his face upward and looked to the ceiling, wondering if he knew, in God's name, what the fuck he was doing. He lowered his face slowly, decrepitly, realizing as he did that he, Vince "Angler" Angeletta, didn't know a motherfucking thing about anything.

"Forgive me, Father, for I have sinned."

Phone Calls To and From New Orleans, Louisiana and New York, New York, USA

"Nick, damn I'm glad I got a hold of you. Look, something's brewing down here. Does the name Carlo Cefalu mean anything to you?"

"Yea, isn't he one of the boys we're cooking?"

"That's right. Okay. He just called and wants to offer some goods. Will not, I repeat, will not speak to anyone but you. He says he heard you were the only straight shooting fed around here. Wants to meet next Sunday."

"Where?"

"Gulf Coast, Mississippi. Will confirm the details once you green light it. He's calling back in an hour. The only condition is that no one, repeat, no one but you, a helper and him at the meet."

"Did he allude to what he's got?"

"No, but he said it should be substantial."

"What do you mean, should be substantial?"

"Well, it sounded like he was checking some things on his own. I don't know, but it's worth a try, don't you think?"

"Yea, isn't he that big fat bozo?"

"Yep, that's him."

"Hmm ... okay, it's a go. Nobody but me and you and him, but you tell him if he wastes my time, I'm going to mess him up."

"Understood. Call me in two hours. Should have it all set. By the way, how's Annie?"

"Fine, enjoying the Big Apple. Look Mike, one other thing ... keep this under your hat. If he is for real, and if he does want to deliver, we don't want to scare him, okay?"

"You really are a straight shooter, aren't you?"

"Yea, I guess so. Thanks, Mike, and mums the word. See ya."

"Mike McKinney here."

"McKinney, this is C.C."

"I understand, been waiting. Talked to the man and it's on. I need details."

"Sunday, 5 p.m., Broadwater Beach Hotel, Biloxi, Mississippi, Room 1-0-1-1. Tell him and his to expect to be searched. I don't want any bullshit."

"Neither does he. He says he does not want his time wasted."

"It won't be."

"Mike, this is Nick. What's the deal?"

"It's all set. Sunday, 5 p.m., Broadwater Beach Hotel, Biloxi, Mississippi, Room 1011. He was pretty nasty on the phone, Nick. Said for us to expect to be searched."

"He must have something serious."

"Don't know. He sure scares me and I'm not ashamed to admit it."

"Okay, Mike. Stay on top of it. Call me if the least bit of anything develops. Got it?"

"Yes, sir."

"Later."

"It's been about sixty years since my last confession ... " Vince choked, "I'm all right, I'm all right," he insisted, waving off Father Prio's assistance.

Vince's tongue lapped his mouth, old age spittle dropping on his chin as a frown of pure misery spread across his face. His hands ... once so vital, now so impotent, lay flat on the table.

"Father Prio," he confessed, hesitating to clear his throat again, " ... it was called Legerdemain." Vince looked down and began wringing his hands, "which means sleight of hand

... and I doubt you have anything in that bag that will help." Vince nodded towards the satchel, unaware that it contained a tape recorder.

He stopped wringing his hands and began staring at them.

"Sleight of hand ... ha ... what clever sons of bitches they were."

He became perfectly still.

"Assassin's hands, priest ... my hands!"

BOOK ONE

Pre-November 22, 1963

Little Baby's toes severed
so little baby can't walk
Little Baby's eyes poked
so little baby can't see
Little Baby's arms tied
so little baby can't go free
Little Baby's mouth cries
"My name is truth ... "
Little Baby dies in me

Vince Angeletta

July 15th, 1960

Biltmore Hotel
Los Angeles, California, USA
Early Morning

... he's flying to be with Mr. Luce in New York tonight. That's just like him.

My father ... not wanting to steal the star from his son ... but he's done so much—New York City, New Jersey and Chicago. Those delegates he's won—not me.

Johnson ... hummm. City bosses like him, but most unions don't. As speaker of the House he could've been dangerous. Keep your enemies beside you ... don't know what's 'bout with him.

They say there'll be close to eighty thousand people in the Coliseum, and something like 35 million watching on TV. Mother and the Sis's will be there.

God, I look awful.

One year it's taken ... Hyannisport to Los Angeles.

I'm tired.

And Nixon ... he'll probably underestimate me.

Good!

This is a nice hotel, the Biltmore. A hundred years from now, probably won't be here.

But I will be ... in history, immortal.

John Fitzgerald Kennedy ... Democratic Presidential Candidate ... 1960.

Do I have the will?

Do I have ... the ... will?

Chapter One

July 16, 1960

"LEG-ER-DE-MAIN."

The Chief Pentagon Liaison Officer for Military Personnel/Detached Services, Lieutenant Colonel Warren Bear, was writing as fast as he could. With pen and pad in hand he sat in the Pentagon Office of Special Operations (OSO).

It was 9:30 a.m.

Major General Marion Armstrong III, deputy director of the OSO resumed dictation.

"Take the best F++ team leader and two of the most aggressive team members from White Star. Their enlistments cannot end any sooner than 1964 and it's best if they have no living family ties. Black page their records completely. Get them on the first plane out of Laos. They're to report to Brigadier General Mancus at Ft. Bragg. This is an alpha crypto priority order."

"Is Program Evaluations CIA Laos aware, sir?"

"They're aware. Have the three men at Bragg in seventy two hours, Warren."

"Yes, sir," Colonel Bear said, suppressing a descriptive expletive as he exited.

"I'll be a bastard ... Alpha Crypto Priority Order ... Wow!"

General Armstrong then buzzed his aide.

"Corporal Forrestol ... get me Plato Smith with the CIA's Directorate of Plans (DDP)-Western Hemisphere Division on the phone ... and Corporal, identify yourself only as calling for Mr. Ratchet with the Office of Defense Mobilization."

"Yes, sir, General Armstrong."

Within minutes his aide buzzed back .

"Plato Smith is on the line, sir."

"Plato, this is Ratchet, we've mobilized Contingency LED-1. They'll arrive in seventy two hours."

"Good, Ratchet. Thessalonian is briefed. He'll meet them at Bragg in five days at seven hundred hours. That'll give Mancus time to cover the basics. After that, Thessalonian is scheduled to meet the elements of Contingency LED-2 in Miami, then on to Guatemala with the elements of Contingency LED-3. Is that acceptable?"

"Acceptable."

"And Johnson as VP, we've secured that?"

"Correct."

"So we're insured if the kid wins?"

"Yes, but we'd prefer the other."

"I take it they've refused to push him?"

"Too risky."

"Then, Ratchet, we'd better be ready for any eventuality."

"Correct. That is what Legerdemain is all about ... curtain time, Plato."

General Armstrong replaced the receiver and moved to a maple cabinet a few feet from his desk. He unlocked the cabinet, reached inside, and pulled out another phone with the digits 030601 imprinted on the dial. He lifted the receiver and listened. Thirty seconds later a gruff voice answered from what sounded like a tomb thousands of miles away.

"030601."

Armstrong replied, "030601, this is Intercept Eagle, Legerdemain Contingency LED-1, Contingency LED-2 and Contingency LED-3 mobilized. Repeat Legerdemain Contingency LED-1, Contingency LED-2 and Contingency LED-3 mobilized. Over."

The gruff voice responded, "Intercept Eagle ... received. Legerdemain Contingency LED-1, Contingency LED-2 and Contingency LED-3 mobilized. Acknowledged. Clear."

Major General Marion Armstrong III breathed a sigh of relief, exhaling the breath that he had been holding in since Kennedy had become the Democratic presidential contender on July 13th.

Legerdemain was afoot.

Chapter Two

July 20, 1960

His hand petted her womanhood. He could feel the hardness and wetness of her fold. That slippery nirvana he craved. She purred, nuzzling his ear and his mouth, loving what his strong masculine hand was doing between her legs. She repositioned herself to her knees at an odd angle then took his erection hungrily into her mouth. Both of his hands now stroking her skull-cap poodle hairdo as she caressed him with her tongue.

She whimpered, "Mmm, baby, Ralphie, I love you."

Vincenzo Angeletta, a.k.a. Ralph Bosco, usually disliked being called Ralphie, but with his Chicago girlfriend, Mona Spazek, he didn't mind.

"Me, too, *mia amore*."

At that she began sucking with even more intensity. He had taught her that "*mia amore*" meant "my love" in Sicilian, and she loved it when he spoke Sicilian to her. It was romantic. She also loved the salty taste of his manhood inside of her mouth, its shape, its texture. She slowly, almost painfully brought him to climax.

Mona loved Ralphie. He treated her with respect and tenderness. He was a very, very nice guy. Mysterious, but nice.

Vince cared for Mona, too. She was the first woman in six years that he had had any real affection for. The first woman since Rosalie. Mrs. Rosalie Ann Sedoux Angeletta, his wife, who had died in 1954. Even so, he refused to break security and tell Mona his real name.

Vince used his aliases geographically. If he was in Las Vegas, it would be Tom Phillips. In Miami, Tommy Nunez. In Detroit, Ray Boscetti. In Chicago, Ralph Bosco. Anywhere else, "Angler" or Vince would do.

He was in Mount Prospect, Illinois, near Chicago at 5 p.m. this July 20, 1960 to receive $500,000 for transport. New Orleans banked a lot of Chicago's money and Vince was the Nuccia family's principle money courier or *spalloni*. He was responsible only to the Top Man himself, Calogera "Charlie" Nuccia, boss of the New Orleans underworld.

One of Vince's job requirements was to maintain a low profile. In his clothes, in his cars and in his choice of accommodations. Today, however, Vince was at Mount Prospect's finest hotel, the Excaliber.

The reason for this exception was that Vince had been instructed, in addition to his courier pickup, to check out the progress of a Chicago-New Orleans joint venture construction project called the Sandhurst Shopping Complex.

The Sandhurst Center was two miles from the Excaliber. A July storm lashed the balcony of his hotel suite, clattering the outdoor lounge chairs savagely against the balcony rail as his afternoon playtime drew to a close.

"Baby, I've got some meetings. Here ... here's some money for dinner," Vince reached for his wallet on the nightstand. "And the room key. Why don't you come back around ten or so and keep it warm for me."

He curled his legs around hers, again feeling the moisture between them.

"Oh, Ralphie, whatever you say, honey. Will you teach me some more Sillya?"

"Sure, baby. It's *Sicilian*, not Sillya." He looked at her shrewdly, humorously. "You know, I bet you don't even know where Sicily is."

She slapped him softly on the arm, protesting, "I do, I do! It's in Italy around Rome, right?"

He grinned, "Close, but no cigar, baby. I'll tell you what, I'll make a deal with you. You be back here in a new nightgown and I'll give you another lesson in Sicilian, the likes you'll never forget."

"Oh, baby, I can't wait!" She kissed him joyfully. "I love you, Ralphie."

"I love you, too, Mona—now scoot."

He watched as she wrapped herself in the purple bed sheet and slid off the bed, then picked her clothes up off the floor as she made her way to the bathroom. Man, was she a looker, Vince thought. With her silky thighs and perfectly tapered legs supporting a face as alluring as Jayne Mansfield's.

Mona stepped out of the bathroom minutes later in a pair of red shorts with rolled up cuffs. Vince was becoming aroused again.

"Now, get out of here before I forget my business. And be careful in this weather."

She sashayed over and kissed him, "Bye, Honey, see you at ten."

As the room door was closing behind her, Vince's bedside phone rang. He inhaled a last whiff of her lingering perfume, then answered.

"Whoever this is, you got great timing. Ralph Bosco at your service."

"Ralph, buddy, this is Carmine. I take it you're not busy?"

"Hell, Carmine, I've been up—get it—up, all day. Lots of fun. What's shaking with you?"

"Swell. Look, Ralph, the property on Cartel Street needs to be examined. Fire gutted the whole place. We need a damage assessment. How about around 8 p.m.?"

"Sure. Partial or full?"

"Full."

"I'll be there with bells on, Carmy. Bye bye."

"So long, Ralph, you fuckin' comedian."

There was no Cartel Street, had been no fire or damage. What there was was $500,000—in full—waiting to be picked up.

Publicly, Vince operated as a claims adjuster for the Four Seasons Insurance and Credit Corporation out of Atlanta, Georgia. He received a salary, paid into a pension and even serviced a few accounts, most of which were labor unions. The Four Seasons did business on an international level, so Vince's trips could be explained if the need ever arose. The State of Georgia's corporate registration listed Soccer Clothing, Inc. of Camden, New Jersey, principle stockholders of the Four Seasons company. Soccer Clothing, Inc., was owned by Fleur de Fleur Novelties, Inc. of New Orleans. The nuts of Fleur de Fleur Novelties, Inc. were held firmly by Bartello and Jacobs Law Firm in Lake Charles, Louisiana. Anthony Bartello, counselor-at-law, was first cousin to Frank Bartello, step-brother of Johnny Sincelli—Mr. Nuccia's private attorney and *consigliere*.

Johnny Sincelli's son, Jake, had been the linchpin in Vince's success. They had met in Huntsville Penitentiary in Huntsville, Texas in 1938 and had formed a close friendship. Upon his release in '41 Vince had gone directly to Sincelli Senior for a job. The attorney had put him to work. Five years later Vince met "Top Man" Charlie Nuccia when Charlie formally initiated him into the Nuccia family as a made and qualified Mafioso. Vince and Rosalie were married that same year, 1946, and lived happily until Rosalie's death in 1954. Vince had an extraordinarily difficult time dealing with Rosalie's passing, so much so that he finally had to seek Charlie Nuccia's counseling.

"Vincenzo," the Top Man had said, "living alone is so incredibly hard, without a soft woman to cushion the pitfalls of your life. To adore, to have children with. I'll help you, my friend. I'll help you through this hardship."

Charlie Nuccia had fulfilled his promise to Vince, and in doing so had created a bond invulnerable. Vince owed the Top Man his life. Don Nuccia had put wings on his soul and had taught it to fly. It was flying in Chicago.

Vince picked his shaving kit out of his suitcase and began to clean up. The Excaliber suite was lavishly adorned with real oak dressers and several half-length mirrors in gold coated frames. Vince stood in front of the mirror in the bathroom and focused.

His face, at middle age, was stunningly handsome. Character lines that would be striking as he got older were even more irresistible now. A nose that would dwindle to aged defiance later was still rawly arrogant and those infirm romantic lips at 73 were at 45 lubricating more panties than Sinatra. Add silvery, brown-blue eyes, furry eyebrows and sinking—not yet sunken—cheeks and you had human Sicilian artwork Michelangelo could have sculpted.

As he shaved, he hummed.

Laughing Mirror, laugh—at my ugliness
Laughing Mirror, laugh—laugh if you must
Pretty Angels, love me
They swallow me sweet
So laugh, Mirror, laugh—in hell we will meet.

This oft repeated ditty of a Sicilian tune had stayed with Vince since he was seven years old.

Vince's mother, fresh off the boat from Messina Province,

Sicily, had died birthing Vince in Opelausas, Louisiana. His father, though, an accomplished butcher, had well compensated for her absence in Vince's early life.

In fact, his daddy had sung the tune Vince was singing now many a morning in their Opelausas butcher shop.

Laughing Mirror, laugh—at my stupidity
Laughing Mirror, laugh—laugh till you cannot see
Pretty Angels love me
They swallow me sweet
So laugh, Mirror, laugh—in hell we will meet.

Vince's father had spoken to Vince often of the old country, Sicily, and of its active volcano, Mt. Etna, its picturesque coastal lowlands, Palermo, Catania, Messina, and of its history—the Sicilian Vespers in 1282 and Garibaldi in 1860—also of the Sicilian secret society known by various names as the Unione Siciliano, La Cosa Nostra, Mafia—and what he considered to be its permanent place in the scheme of modern Sicilian culture—even in America.

Vince had not been the most attentive of students, though, and little of what his father had said had impacted him. At least not until that fateful afternoon in December of 1937 when a 32-year-old Vince had walked into the butcher shop only to find his father lying on the floor bleeding to death. Discovering, with his father's dying breath, that a group of bigoted and jealous local businessmen had been responsible.

Vince had always sensed a certain prejudice from their neighbors in Opelausas, but had never taken that prejudice seriously, attributing it to the common folk suspicion of a motherless home. Besides, in spite of it all, Vince's father had created a brisk pre- and post-depression era trade at his meat market, offering lower prices and better quality than his competitors.

The murdering businessmen, who Vince could only term "rednecks," had, by killing his father, simply eliminated their competition. After his father's funeral Vince began to track the redneck boss he held most responsible for his father's death, finally cornering the man in Texas. He could not bring himself to kill the man, but did beat the man to pieces and demanded money from him. Due to Vince's inexperience, though, in matters of this ilk, he was arrested in Texas for extortion and sent to Huntsville Prison. There he had met Jake Sincelli, a made and qualified Mafioso with the Sicilian Secret Society or Cosca or family in New Orleans.

By becoming friends with Jake, Vince had paved the way for himself to join the Nuccia family. Charlie Nuccia, for fifteen years now, had been like a replacement father to Vince, even more so since Rosalie's death in 1954.

Vince slipped his monogrammed bathrobe off and in naked fluency went for a cigar. His five-foot-eleven-inch muscular frame puffed twice, then continued to dress. Vince's suits were modest and businesslike but perfectly tailored. Today's choice was pearl-striped with a Mason's pin on the lapel.

He continued to hum.

In hell we will meet.
In hell we will meet.

The garage of the Excaliber held a Four Seasons company car for Vince. A peacock blue 1959 Ford Galaxy, unostentatious and professional.

Vince swaggered toward it, got in, revved it to life and drove away.

When in Chicago, he regularly dined at the Villa Roma Ristorante, a popular nightspot in Norwood Park Township that enjoyed performances by some of America's most famous entertainers and patronage by Chicago's most infamous racketeers. He hoped that his best friend in Chicago, Mario "the sissy" Pacissi, would be working tonight. Mario was the general manager of the Villa Roma. He was also the son-in-law of Stefano "Mr. A" Anacondini, the boss of Chicago.

After a twenty-minute drive the neon blink of Villa Roma came into view. Vince pulled up to the valet parking, stepped out, threw his keys to an attendant and entered the ristorante.

Music from the old country, the kind of music his daddy had loved, was being performed by a strolling three-man combo just a few feet away from the host's podium near the foyer.

The familiar figure of Mario "the sissy" Pacissi was standing there, formally dressed, head down, examining reservations.

Vince walked up.

"Hey, fellow, got an extra seat anywhere?"

"Do you have a reser—?" A slim pigmy of a man, attractive in a Mickey Rooneyish sort of way, looked up, recognizing him, and smiled a toothy, flawless smile, then frowned.

"Mr. Bosco, Mr. Bosco. Good to see you. A moment, please."

Vince was taken aback. Mario had not even offered his hand. Something was up.

Vince watched as Mario nervously made a quick note and slipped it into the menu.

"This way, please, Mr. Bosco."

Mario's formality was especially bewildering to Vince considering that Mario was usually the life of the party, warm, ebullient. Vince warily followed Mario through the interior of the restaurant.

The Villa Roma was extravagant. Fully carpeted with box sitting-booths like Vegas, a huge stage and discreet lighting.

Mario seated him. Handing the menu to Vince, Mario added, "Your waiter will be with you promptly. Thank you, Mr. Bosco."

Vince shook his head, uncomprehending of Mario's behavior, then the note fell from the menu explaining everything.

SURVEILLANCE—WATCH OUT.

Strange, Vince thought, the Villa Roma was usually a safe place. Vince scanned the luxurious eight-hundred-seat showplace, testing himself. His talent for spotting surveillance, honed to perfection over the years, detected nothing.

He watched Mario whisper to a tuxedoed waiter, then return to the front. The waiter walked over to Vince.

"Mr. Bosco, Mr. Pacissi has asked me to ask you to meet him in the hallway at the left rear exit in exactly ten minutes, please. Would you like a drink while you wait?"

"Sure, I'll have a scotch on the rocks."

Minutes later the waiter served him. Vince downed his drink in a matter of gulps, stood and nonchalantly made his way left and rear.

Mario was in the slate-black corridor waiting for him.

"Christ, Mario! What the fuck's going on?" Vince was incredulous.

Mario embraced him and spewed into his ear, "You

wouldn't believe me if I told you, Vin."

Vince laughed at the absurdity of that suggestion, "Tell me, Mario, this has got to be good!"

Mario looked around, checking for eyes and ears in the darkness.

"Vin, the fucking feds think Mr. A. is sleepin' with Mr. K. from Boston."

Vince sighed. The joke was getting thin.

"C'mon, Mario, stop fuckin' around. Who the fuck is Mr. K.?"

The "sissy" put his lips to Vince's cheeks.

"John Kennedy."

Vince restrained himself from laughing hard.

"What the fuck? That *pezzonavante*! With what his brother did to us at that McClellan Committee wingding? Why would Mr. A. even speak to the prick?"

Mario answered, "Hey, *Paisan*, things aren't always what they seem. Rumor has it that Kennedy's concerned about the Cook County political vote. All I know is that the heat is boiling around here. Maybe you ought to chow down elsewhere, you think?"

Vince glared into Mario's eyes, "Listen, Mario, I got nothing to do with nothing. All I know is that jerk, Robert, put Charlie through a lot of shit at those McClellan committee hearings. So why should I do them any favors? As a matter of fact, if Johnny K. himself walked in I'd kiss the son of a bitch just to make him look bad!"

Mario shifted his stance, "Vince, Mr. A. gave strict orders to be cool. There's a giant scam going down somewhere and I don't know who's running it or what it is, but when Mr. A. talks, I listen."

"Well, when Charlie Nuccia talks, I listen and he don't like them fuckin' Kennedys one bit."

Mario gave up. He did not want to challenge the strong will of Vince Angeletta. "Okay, okay, you win. Go ahead and eat the best, on the house. We'll talk later. Oh, hey, have you seen Mona yet?" Mario had introduced Vince to Mona.

"All day, doing great. She's a good girl," Vince paused. "Awright, Mario. Don't make me worry about you. I get shook up when you look so rattled. If you ever need anything, anything, call me."

"Sure, Vince. Now go stuff yourself."

"Good idea, Sissy. Who knows what the Gods are up to anyway, huh?"

"Fuck, yea. Who even wants to know. That kinda knowledge is good for nothing but getting you killed, right?"

"Right!"

Vince's stomach rumbled at 8 p.m., then burped from post-fettucini indigestion. He was parked at the Sandhurst Center, viewing with amazement the construction that had been completed thus far; the major portions of three department stores and two rows of shops and walkways.

His mind drifted, wondering where tonight's $500,000 was coming from. Of course, with Stefano "Mr. A" Anacondini's family it was impossible to know. Anacondini was a high profile figure in the tradition of Capone. He was always jerking off with lots of Hollywood and national political people. That's what Vince liked about Charlie Nuccia. He was what he was. Not a hypocrite or bullshit artist, but a father to his men.

As Vince's mind continued to wander, a horn sounded twice nearby. His rendezvous was to take place as usual in the offices of a Four Seasons Insurance affiliate, Hazel Life and Casualty. George Hazel's office was 58 miles away.

The normal courier procedure was that Vince would wait no longer than fifteen minutes for a car to pull up at a prearranged location and blow its horn twice. Tonight's pre-arranged location had been the Sandhurst lot. If Vince had not heard the horn within fifteen minutes, he would assume that the pickup had been canceled. Vince piloted his own Four Seasons corporate plane, a Cessna 172/Skyhawk. It was parked at a private airstrip in Wheeling, Illinois. He would usually drive to it immediately after pickup but tonight he had planned to delay his departure allowing for extra playtime with Mona Spazek.

The Hazel Life and Casualty Company was located in an area of Chicago called Park Forest. It took an hour and a half for Vince to drive there from Sandhurst. Parking near the office entrance and with security foremost in his mind, he stepped out of his Ford Galaxy and walked, the earlier hard rain having diminished to barely a mist.

George Hazel greeted him at the door, "Mr. Bosco, so good to see you again. So happy always to see someone from the parent office. Yes, very glad to see you. Happy, yes, yes!"

Hazel didn't shut up until Vince was well inside the small building.

"Hazel, you get crazier every time I see you. Cool it, will you."

The ruffle-headed ex-school teacher, who now presumptuously called himself an insurance specialist, gurgled.

"Mr. Bosco, we got a call today. Urgent message for you to go immediately to the Fountainebleau in Miami. They said to bring the damage assessment from here with you but to cancel the one in Detroit day after tomorrow. It's an emergency, I think."

Vince knew it had to be imperative. Charlie Nuccia would never have authorized a critical communication with George Hazel otherwise. Hazel was a flake.

"Where's the juice, George?"

"Here, all nice and neat."

A sack about the size of a mail bag appeared from behind Hazel's desk. Vince opened it briefly, then closed it.

"Was there anything else, message-wise?"

"No, not really, Mr. Bosco."

"The caller must have signed off somehow, George."

"Oh, yes, yes! I knew I would remember it. You know, I'm not as goofy as everyone thinks I am. I'm really not!"

"For Christ's sake, Hazel, spit it out!"

George Hazel spit.

"The message, Mr. Bosco, was signed off ... Rosalie ... Rosalie ... Ann ... Sedoux ... Angeletta."

Chapter Three

July 21, 1960

Brigadier General Alexander T. Mancus was deputy commander of the Special Warfare Center at Ft. Bragg, North Carolina.

The Special Forces team leader and two team members that had been summoned by the Chief Pentagon Liaison Officer for Military Personnel/Detached Services from Operation White Star had arrived eight hours earlier. They were now showered, shaved and sitting, listening to General Mancus.

It was 1 a.m.

"Gentlemen ... for you, Operation White Star is finished. Your assignments with your field training teams in Laos are as of now officially over. You are being reassigned from 77th SFG Abn to what will be referred to as SFG Team Legerdemain. This reassignment will last until 1964, which for all three of you is within your current enlistment guidelines. Program Evaluations CIA, your control in Laos, is aware of your reassignment even though they are unaware of its nature. Instead of sheepdipping you men, what we've done is black page your records completely. Sheepdipping would have put you on record as having officially resigned from the military, then having gone undercover for the CIA. By black paging each of you, it's like you never existed. In fact, everything connected to you, from birth certificates to driver's licenses to Social Security numbers, has been sealed and since none of you have any family ties, your falling off the face of the earth will go relatively unnoticed. This assignment will, of course, count toward promotion and retirement but all unofficially."

"Now, the preliminary brief on Special Op Legerdemain is as follows: Legerdemain is an alpha crypto priority special operation. Alpha crypto priority meaning that it is an ultra top secret domestic national security concern. As SFG Team Legerdemain you three will be controlled by the CIA Directorate of Plans (DDP)-Western Hemisphere Division. Specifically by an individual code-named Thessalonian. He will be here at zero seven hundred hours this morning to conduct for you the first of what will surely be many planning and logistics briefings."

Captain Archer Marsh—Team Leader—31 years old, Specialist Second Class Anthony "Tony" Taylor—Demolitions Specialist—18 years old, and Sergeant Roland Holt—Radio Repairman—19 years old, were glued to their special operations room chairs.

"Intelligence reports," General Marcus continued, "indicate that there is an influential political office holder in this country who is a Communist agent. He is well known and his personal cover is spotless. A highly publicized sanction to convince Moscow that America is not to be toyed with may be in order. If so, you three as SFG Team Legerdemain will be responsible for this. Now, go and get some sleep and return here at zero seven hundred hours. Dismissed, gentlemen."

As they walked out of the operations room, Captain Marsh looked at his two teammates, gauging their reaction.

"Them there North Carolina nights, whattya think, men? My daddy used to say southern nights were as mellow as a wildfire. What with possums and snakes and bobcats. A little adjustment from Southeast Asia, no?"

Captain Archer Marsh was from Alabama. He looked like a cross between a Viking and a Confederate soldier. He had twenty-inch biceps and a bowlegged walk with a tattoo on each calf. One tattoo for the 77th SFG Abn and one for Lola, his first love. Blond-haired, blue-eyed Alabama boys back in 1946 weren't supposed to date black girls. Archer Marsh had. Lola was her name. At sixteen he had been ridiculed and spat upon by his family and friends, turning him into a bitter young man with a penchant for violence. Even after he had stopped seeing Lola, the nasty remarks continued. He killed his first man the night before his seventeenth birthday. A man who had kept asking him what it felt like to have those big black lips around his white cock. First, he had knocked him unconscious, then had driven him out of Mobile to Kalioke Swamp. There he had cut his throat, bashed his skull in with a bat and urinated on the corpse. What had amazed him was the enjoyment—the power of killing. He joined the army the next day and had been in fourteen years now, never once having spoken to his family again.

"Yep, Carolina ... smoke, anyone?" Captain Marsh did not smoke but habitually carried a pack when acquainting himself with new soldiers and new assignments.

Specialist Second Class Tony Taylor accepted the Captain's offer. Chesterfield was his favorite brand, especially when listening to music and drinking. He loved the song *Mack the Knife* by Bobby Darin, the number one seller in 1959. In fact, he looked like he could have been born on a dance floor with his All-American good looks and natural grace; curly brown hair and soft brown eyes, hardly more than a kid. Sometimes he was amazed that just two short years ago he had been hula hooping with about 30 million other high schoolers. His decision to join the army had been his father's, not his. His father's tubercular cough could be heard nonstop daily throughout the Taylor house, a house Tony and his father had lived in alone since his mother had deserted them when Tony was a baby. Shortly before he died, Tony's father had asked Tony to promise him that he would join the army. Tony didn't break his promise. Two days after his father's death he enlisted at the Long Beach, California Army Recruitment Office. He had been sold on a program of Special Forces by the recruiter and had attacked it with a vengeance. A year later he had been chosen for Operation White Star in Laos. He had become a demolitions expert.

Captain Marsh offered another Chesterfield to Sergeant Holt, which he declined. Marsh took a close second look at Holt. This soldier wasn't much of a talker, he concluded. On the flight from Laos, Holt had barely said five words. Marsh and Taylor had at least bitched some about the food on the transport plane but Holt had not. He was spooky.

Sergeant Roland Holt had been involved with White Star for a year and a half. The F++ teams there usually rotated on a six-month basis, but not radio repairman Holt. He was a nineteen-year-old legend within the 77th SFG Abn. For Roland Holt loved the art of communications. He had received several commendations for his expertise in speaking the Laotian language. When he wasn't working, though, he preferred silence and meditation. He wore his hair in a '57 style Apache cut and was a master practitioner of Tai Chi Chuan. Every early morning Sergeant Holt could be seen in his quarters doing his oriental exercises. He had dark features and reddish brown skin. Maybe he was an Apache, Marsh thought. He was definitely spooky.

"Captain Marsh, is it legal?" Tony Taylor dragged deep on his Chesterfield.

"Is what legal, Taylor?"

"Is conducting a domestic special op legal? I had always heard that the CIA was not authorized on home ground."

Marsh responded ... carefully.

"You're right, they're not, technically. Let me make it clear, boys. Both the CIA and Special Forces originated from the OSS. But where Special Forces operates within a military structure, the CIA does not. Its charter is based on a thing called the National Security Act of 1947. That act says they're not supposed to conduct business within our borders, but they do. They have to. There are foreign students going to U.S. colleges that have to be monitored, turned, trained and that's just one domestic area the CIA is involved with, or at least that's what I hear. So I guess in most folks' eyes their home ground activities are allowable exceptions."

Sergeant Holt said his first words of the night.

"We're talking domestic wetwork here, Captain. American political assassination. Is that an A-llowable exception?"

The Captain reacted quickly.

"Listen, Holt, let's get the ticks off your hide before we go any further. I'm not control for this Legerdemain thing, and don't know zip about it. What I am is a good soldier and I follow orders. If you've got questions—reservations—gripes—take'em upstairs. Got it, Holt?"

Sergeant Holt saluted a crisp, "Yes, sir," and walked away. Taylor saluted, too. "See you at seven hundred hours, sir."

Captain Marsh returned the salute.

"Get some rest, Taylor. I'm sure we're all going to need it."

⌖ ⌖ ⌖ ⌖

"Miami Tower—this is Cessna 631 Bravo—requesting landing instructions—over."

"Cessna 631 Bravo—this is Miami Tower—clear for landing at runway eight two—winds from southwest at 17 miles per hour—over."

Vince Angeletta was exhausted. Worry and lack of sleep was prompting him to lose more than just altitude. He was losing his concentration. Coming in over the everglades always gave him the willies. At most, three times a year was too much. Added to that, Vince had had to refuel at a Nashville FBO, prolonging an already long journey.

It was 4:30 a.m.

Suddenly a warning horn deranged the cockpit's calm.

Crap! The plane was too high for landing.

Vince was wide awake now. Unlit cigar clenched in his molars. Shirt unbuttoned, face taut, feeling worn and torn.

C-631 Bravo was beginning to drop.

In emergency situations like this, Vince depended on some deep-seated reserve for guidance. It had never failed him—yet.

He put the nose of the plane down, pushed full throttle, the ground approached rapidly. Vince held his breath. He pulled back on the yoke as the horn stopped.

He stabilized his course and continued on to runway eight two.

Twenty feet—ten feet—above ground—wheels contact—landing.

"Cessna 631 Bravo—this is Miami control—What is your destination? Over."

"Miami Control—this is Cessna 631 Bravo—destination Pandora Aviation. Over."

"Cessna 631 Bravo—taxi to Delta right then Charlie left. Welcome to Miami."

Vince chuckled. "Thanks a half a million!"

Thessalonian was punctual. At exactly 7 a.m. he walked into the Operations Room at Ft. Bragg with General Mancus.

Marsh, Taylor and Holt didn't know what to make of him at first. The man did not look like a government agent. He had on a pair of Frisco jeans with engineer boots and his colored T-shirt was covered by an expensive black leather jacket. Captain Marsh half expected to see, when Thessalonian took off his jacket, a pack of Lucky Strikes rolled up in the sleeve. There were none, but there were scars. Burn scars visible on his throat and arms. Thessalonian also had a dead-fish pair of gray eyes with small black microdots for pupils. His cheekbones were high, his lips and nose thin and dry. His hair was about as blonde as Marsh's would be in twenty years, which meant that to the captain Thessalonian looked about fifty years old. The man's voice was husky and hypnotic.

"Good morning, men. I hope your trip from Laos was not too uncomfortable."

He began pacing.

"Men, you will know me by the code name of Thessalonian. I will be your control for Special Op Legerdemain; however, in a strict military sense, Brigadier General Mancus here will be your commanding officer."

Captain Marsh perked at this information. If General Mancus was involved, it had to be the most serious of undertakings. Marsh knew that General Mancus had, in 1950, pioneered the concept of using enlistees fleeing from Soviet satellite states as Unconventional Warfare Units. For his conceptualizing Mancus had become, in effect, one of the founding fathers of U.S. Special Forces. He was a tall, slim man about sixty years old. His professorial demeanor and white strandy hair served him well as a father figure. General Mancus was known and respected throughout the program. From the tenth SFG in Germany to the Fourteenth SFOD in Hawaii. Marsh felt that Mancus's involvement with Legerdemain gave it instant credibility.

"As to team ranking," Thessalonian continued, "Captain Marsh will serve as Team Leader, then Holt as his second, then you, Taylor. As General Mancus has briefed you all thus far—there is a prominent politician in this country whom we know to be a member of and active agent for the Communist party. He masquerades behind a facade of old money and respectability when in reality he has been serving Moscow for years. As General Mancus mentioned, a highly visible sanction may be required as opposed to just an FBI arrest, imprisonment or a quiet kill. His identity will remain secret for the time being. There will be absolutely no margin for error in this operation. Accordingly, you men will receive in preparation for it the most extensive training of your careers. That training will begin in August."

Thessalonian's dead-fish eyes and microdot pupils stared demandingly at the three men before him.

"Cleanse your minds, men, and your spirits and enjoy the next few weeks of liberty. Remember this mission is an alpha crypto national security concern approved at the highest levels of our government. If any of you have any qualms about it, speak now or forever hold your peace."

Marsh looked to Holt. Taylor looked to Holt. Holt looked at Thessalonian. There was silence except for the faint steady hum of an air conditioner, unmercifully blowing hot air.

Chapter Four

July 22, 1960

Vince felt rested. For reasons unbeknownst to him, Calogera "Charlie" Nuccia, his underworld employer and mentor, had allowed him to sleep in after his arrival in Miami yesterday morning.

It was 8:30 a.m.

Vince stretched himself on the bed, feeling the silky rub of sheets against his crotch, missing Mona.

"Ralphie, what do you mean you have to leave tonight? There are no flights out this late," she had told him night before last.

"Baby, I'm driving, and look, take it easy. Something's come up. I'll see you in a few weeks. I love ya, kid."

"I love you, too, Ralphie. What about my new nightgown?"

"Save it, sweetcheeks."

Yes, Vince thought, Mona Spazek was beginning to melt his heart but she would never melt it as much as Rosalie had. God, what he would do to have Rosalie in his arms again, that sassy mouth on his ...

Then he remembered. Charlie's message in Chicago had been signed off Rosalie ... Rosalie Ann Sedoux Angeletta. Man, it must be important!

Nine years now as Charlie Nuccia's courier and never once had he been pulled off his route. Minor schedule changes weeks in advance, yes, but like this—no way! And to have invoked Vince's late wife's name was tantamount to a red alert. He was convinced Charlie would never have done that unless he needed Vince badly. Charlie knew how much Rosalie had meant to him.

But if a guy had to deal with a crisis, Vince mused, the Fontainebleau Hotel in Miami was a great place to deal from. Its U-shaped whiteness and colonnaded terraces were peaceful and magnificent. Nothing could spoil the Fontainebleau's oceanfront placidity, not even the countless intrigues going on within its walls. Vince stumbled to the window of his room and eyed the action below. Men in bathing trunks and Bermuda shorts taking in the early morning sun. Pink shirts everywhere. A few women in tube dresses and one-piece swimsuits. Vince enjoyed staying here. In Miami he was known as Tommy Nunez. He was even called Tommy Nunez by other members of the Nuccia family when they were in Miami. Vince was a stickler for using consistent aliases, and emergency or no emergency, he would continue to do so. He laid back across his bed, feeling a last enticing silk sheet rub, then reached for the phone.

"Give me the room of John Sincelli, please. This is Tommy Nunez calling."

After a moment, a throaty hello came on the line.

"Jake, how are ya, how are ya?"

"Hey, Tommy Nunez, not bad, you crazy cat, what's the scoop?"

"Hell, Jake, been gettin' kinda antsy, sitting around. Didn't the front desk tell you I got here yesterday?"

"Sure, Vin ... ah, Tommy. Yea, the man has just been in meetings, that's all. Hold on just a minute."

Vince could visualize Jake Sincelli asking his father, Johnny Sincelli, when Vince could come up.

"Okay, look, Tommy. We're in penthouse number 16B. Come on up."

"Okay, Jake, I'm outta here."

Vince hung up the phone and switched mental gears from sexual preoccupation to business. He had unfortunately left his clothes at Mona's in Chicago, so the only suit he had was the pearl-striped one that he had flown down in. He put it on, attempted to unwrinkle its wrinkles, combed his black wavy hair and split.

The Fontainebleau Hotel had 566 rooms and 30 penthouses. Top Man Charlie Nuccia had never, to Vince's knowledge, stayed in any penthouses anywhere. He came from the old school, preferring anonymity and low key. The fact that he was headquartered in a penthouse today meant something very, very big was happening.

Vince knocked twice, then three quick, on the door of No. 16B. Johnny Sincelli, Jake's father and Charlie Nuccia's consigliere, opened it and greeted him.

"Vincenzo, or excuse me, Mr. Nunez. *Come sta.*"

Vince replied in Italian as he stepped in.

"*Molte bene*, Mr. Johnny. *E lei*."

"*Bene, grazie*, Tommy. This way."

Vince waved to Jake, who was seated on the couch, as he and Johnny walked through the main den to a second door. Johnny and Jake Sincelli were like two peas in a pod with their country big bodies looking more like midwestern farmers than New Orleans racketeers, and facially similar with two almost Zapata, almost walrus mustaches which they enjoyed caressing endlessly. Johnny opened the second door for Vince.

"Go on in, Vinny, he's expecting you."

"Thanks, Johnny."

The "Top Man" of the New Orleans underworld, Calogera "Charlie" Nuccia, was sitting with his back to Vince in a chair by the oceanview sliding glass balcony window. With cigar in hand, he stood and turned to embrace Vince.

"Vincenzo, Vincenzo, good to see you."

"Don Nuccia, my respects."

After the traditional hug and peck Charlie motioned Vince to pull up a chair.

Charlie Nuccia was a short man who used his height, or lack of, with commanding effectiveness. He had curlets of oily dark hair snuggled atop a pock-marked, impassive face and stocky build, which made him appear, with his big brown eyes and thick menacing nose, at once teddy-bearish, outlawish, heavy. In 1960 at 54 years old he was the Sicilian-American Mafia overlord of Louisiana, Texas, Arkansas, Mississippi and Alabama. The press described him alternately as a doting grandfather type and a man as volatile as Sicily's Etna.

He offered Vince a fine Havana and waited till Vince had cut and lit it. He then shifted and tightened his rumpled bathrobe and began to speak in his unique crescent-city way.

"Vincenzo, my apologies fa having Johnny use Rosalie's name in the message. I had ta convince you it was important without saying so ta Hazel. You understand, Vincenzo?"

"Yea, sure, Charlie, I understand, no problem. What I'm worried about is why we're here, not how. What's up?"

Ever since Vince had gone to Charlie Nuccia for advice on dealing with Rosalie's death they had communicated informally, like father to an adopted son.

"What's up, Vin? Is the U.S. government ... " Charlie paused dramatically, then continued, "a few months back Anacondini's point man in Hollywood, Gaeteano Rossini, was approached by a CIA man about doing a job on Castro. Rossini contacted Mr. A. They then approached Marco in Tampa to see if Marco could arrange it. The name Marco Romano still carries a lot of weight in Cuba. Of course, Romano had to clear it through me. I don't know what ta make of it. The feds wanting us ta do a job? Sounds like a setup to me. Another government man is coming here today to talk to us about it. So, Vin, it's time fa you ta return the favor I did fa you. I need advice. I need ta put you, Jake and Johnny neckdeep in this with me so between the four of us we'll figure a way out."

Vince's silvery-brown eyes had opened wide. This was the first time Charlie Nuccia had ever asked for his input into major family business. He tried to figure out why.

Calogera "Charlie" Nuccia had been born to Sicilian parents somewhere along the Barbary Coast of North Africa in 1906. They had immigrated to America several months later and had settled on the west bank of New Orleans in the slum section of Algiers. He had only been in prison twice. Once in the Louisiana State Penitentiary at Angola in 1927 and once in the Federal penitentiary at Atlanta in 1930. In 1935, with sponsorship from a powerful New York Mafia family, Charlie Nuccia had consolidated his empire at the mouth of the Mississippi. His four brothers worked for him. Three of them as *capos*, the other, Guiseppe Nuccia, as underboss. Guiseppe was, however, in poor health and was expected to retire soon. Vince wondered if possibly he was being considered for that position.

"Charlie, I know what advice I would give you from the start."

"What's that, Vin?"

"Use this as a bartering chip to get them off of that deportation shit. Sure you'll let Romano whack Castro, but only if they ease up."

The U.S. government had been trying to deport Charlie Nuccia for years.

"Good, Vin, good. Thatssa something I've thought of, ta. But still, it feels wrong, very wrong. The layout, the balance.

Why us? True we've got old casino contacts in Cuba, but then so does the CIA. They probably have people sleeping with Castro. Why involve us? I keep asking myself that. You know how smart these spooks are. They're smart, Vince. Our game is limited. We're here. We're there. But these guys are all over the world. What they're doing is indebting themselves ta us and thatssa very stupid."

Vince thought for a second.

"Maybe, Charlie, maybe they know we lost a bundle in Cuba and figure they can just con us into taking Castro out. They just want us to know that we have their support ... and encouragement."

"That makes some sense. Anyway, we'll know shortly. Their man will be here ta see us this morning. Get this, Vin, they call him Thessalonian. Where do they get these *pazzo* names—cereal boxes?"

Vince laughed and puffed on his Havana.

"Ugh, ugh, Charlie. Thessalonian's a part of the Bible. I wonder what their reason is for calling him that. Those fuckin' guys always have reasons for using a certain name."

Charlie was slightly amused at this, as if playing marbles with children.

"Another thing, Vin. Marco and Mr. A. are both going to be here, too."

"What?" Vince was so astonished that he began to choke on his cigar.

"Geez, Vin, you okay?" Charlie solicitously patted his back.

"Charlie ... damn ... Mr. A. and Marco. Fuck, why don't we just throw in New York and we've got a commission meet."

"Yea, thatssa true."

Vince paused to clear his throat.

"You know, Charlie, rumor has it that Mr. A. is playing footsies with John Kennedy. At least that's what I heard from Mario, his son-in-law, when I was in Chicago the other day."

"Really! Good, Vin, because Mario's here with Stefano. Since you're close ta him, try ta get a line on what Stefano's doing. That pazzo bastard is liable ta be doing anything. He's gone nuts since he let his wife divorce him."

"Okay, Charlie. Exactly what time and where does this CIA meet happen?"

"At 11 a.m., right here, and I'm calling down ta get you another suit. You look like you've been in a wreck in that one." Charlie rose and walked to the phone.

Vince said after him, "Funny you should say that. I just about crashed coming in."

"Crashed! Goddamn, Vin! I thought we gave you the best flying lessons money could buy nine years ago."

"You did, Charlie. I was just dead tired the other night. By the way, the Sandhurst project is going great, and I got the ah ... damage assessment in my room. You want it now?"

"No, it can wait. Let's get you suited first."

Vince nodded. "After all, we've got an image to protect, right, Charlie?"

Charlie Nuccia looked up from the phone with a cryptic expression.

"No, Vin, a tradition ... we have a tradition ta protect: half reality ... half myth ... thatssa all there is ta it."

⌖ ⌖ ⌖ ⌖

ANNUIT COEPTIS—He (God) has smiled on our undertakings. The reverse motto on the great seal of the United States of America. The seal on the back of a case folder in front of a man called Thessalonian.

It was 10 a.m. In one hour he would be meeting with three powerful criminals. Powerful in a way unfamiliar to him. Street powerful—gang powerful—mob powerful.

Marco Romano from Tampa ... Thessalonian thought, that duplicitous, sly piece of shit. He probably thinks we're unaware of his having cut a deal with Castro to get out of Cuba alive after Batista fell. A special deal insuring his ass and his assets. He pipelines information to Castro constantly. And Stefano "Mr. A." Anacondini from Chicago ... he's already got a setup brewing to swing the Cook County political machine for JFK. Taking care of Castro will be, in his mind, just the right favor to guarantee the bureaucratic neutralization of Bobby Kennedy's crime crusade. Then there's Calogera "Charlie" Nuccia from New Orleans. Now he's a different breed—old school. He'd have to gain personally to get involved. Like I'll whack Castro and you drop deportation. Nuccia is the cleverest of the three. He might see through my charade.

Thessalonian had flown down from Ft. Bragg late yesterday afternoon after his initial briefing with Marsh, Holt, Taylor and Mancus; Team Legerdemain. He had checked into Room 294 at the Fontainebleau and had slept uneasily. At 6 a.m. he awoke and took a hot, therapeutic shower allowing the jets of hotel water to massage the irritation of his burn scars. Though inflamed, with each rinse he remembered ...

It was a mission two years ago to assist rebel groups in Indonesia. That assistance was in the form of a failed assassination attempt on Indonesian President Sukarno. His entire three-man team—not unlike Team Legerdemain—had been killed and he had been burned severely in an automobile explosion. The failed attempt, however, had not damaged Thessalonian's CIA career since all the team members had been rebels from the island of Sumatra. In fact, Thessalonian ended up turning the incident to his advantage by using it to illustrate to his superiors that only direct military action could unseat Sukarno. CIA B-26 bombers had begun bombing a week later.

Thessalonian was a methodical, precise man. His speech, his mannerisms and his clothes were always coordinated for specific results. Thessalonian adhered to the intelligence tradecraft rule that the best disguise was the least disguise and in doing so had become a master of physical deception. He had dressed like a motorbiker yesterday in Ft. Bragg so that Marsh, Taylor and Holt, all young men, would think of him subliminally as "cool." Today he would dress like a mortician so that Romano, Anacondini and Nuccia would think of him as "death." He chuckled at the irony. He enjoyed staging himself. His mother had been a prominent Broadway actress and had encouraged him after high school to study drama at Stephens College in Annandale-on-the-Hudson, New York. He spent years of half-ass effort there and had finally, upon graduation, come to the realization that actors were pansies—soldiers were real men. This simple awakening began to guide the course of his life. At the beginning of World War II, at thirty, he joined the Army. His college degree proved to be invaluable as he secured rank within the Office of Strategic Services and took on his first assignment with OSS detachment

101 in Burma, 1942. He was a natural clandestine operative, becoming "proficient" in areas of weaponry, demolitions, cryptology and especially the quick kill. He continued working in the Pacific theatre for the remainder of the war. His reputation as a thoroughly effective covert special operator had skyrocketed since then, making him the logical choice for Legerdemain.

Thessalonian, at fifty years old, was the best there was.

He began to darken his brownish-brown eyebrows and stuff cotton in his mouth. His high cheekbones and thin lips were altered slightly by this, as was the timber of his voice.

At 11 a.m. Thessalonian would be ready.

"Mario 'the Sissy' Paccissi, fancy meeting you here!" Vince Angeletta's sense of phone humor was deceiving. It concealed his tension.

"Hey, Ralph—or what is it in Miami?"

"Tommy Nunez, you numskull. How about breakfast?"

"Can't, Vince—sorry—Tommy ... Mr. A. is in a tizzy. He's been yelling at me like I'm a dog. I don't know what's got him this way but I sure wish he'd knock it off. I don't like being treated like shit."

"Yea, I'm with you, Mario. Hey, Mario, any idea what's happening here? I mean we were both in Chicago two days ago, now we're in Miami. I wonder what's up?" Vince asked as if he didn't know.

"No idea, Tommy. I guess it's some of that Mr. K. bullshit we had talked about avoiding. I do know it's not just a rumor anymore. Mr. A. talked a lot on the plane down here about trying to get Mr. K. elected. Something about coolin' Bobby out. Beyond that, I don't know," Mario answered sincerely.

"Yea. Look, let's get together before you go back to Chicago. I want to give you a present to give to Mona till I see her again."

"Sure, Vince ... ah, Tommy ... got to go. Mr. A.'s yelling for his robe. Talk to you later. Bye."

At 11 a.m. Thessalonian knocked on the door of Penthouse No. 16B. Johnny Sincelli opened it slowly. The man standing before him looked like death. He had on a blue-black, oversized three-piece suit with white shirt and mummy-colored tie. His dark eyebrows were thick and in stark contrast to his puffy cheeks and gray eyes. The man's entire face looked sallow. He extended his hand to Johnny's and shook it, his firm grip contradicting any hint of sickliness.

Johnny Sincelli asked the prearranged question.

"So you are from Old Havana, Senor? Are Calles Obispo and O'Reilly still the main thoroughfares for business?"

Thessalonian answered in kind.

"Yes, they are and there are still restaurants serving *Cangrejos moros*—Moorish crabs."

Without further exchange, Thessalonian entered. Jake Sincelli stepped up to search him. Once clear, Thessalonian reconnoitered the penthouse. The main couch seemed to have been moved off to the side to accommodate a large oval table. There were four chairs around it. Three of the chairs were occupied by Stefano Anacondini, Marco Romano and Charlie Nuccia. Standing behind them were other men, most of whom Thessalonian had been briefed on: Mario Paccissi, Johnny Sincelli, Luigi Bertucci and the man who had searched him, Jake Sincelli. There was only one man in the room that Thessalonian could not identify. A handsome man who hovered protectively behind Charlie Nuccia almost like a son. Thessalonian wondered who he was. Charlie Nuccia's marriage had produced only daughters, but his four brothers had had sons. Maybe he was a nephew.

Thessalonian sat in the fourth chair.

He began his presentation—his pitch—in a manufactured Ivy League style.

"I am most grateful for you gentlemen to have granted me an audience. I know you are all busy men with important agendas, so I'll try to be succinct."

Thessalonian paused, making eye contact with each man at the table.

Marco Romano, a wiry bespectacled man, at 60 years old refused to return Thessalonian's stare, and Stefano "Mr. A." Anacondini, at six feet four inches, a physical giant by Sicilian standards, had his eyes downcast. Only Charlie Nuccia met Thessalonian's gaze.

The phrase *"Gli occhi di un pugnale"* ran through Charlie Nuccia's mind as their eyes locked. This man Thessalonian has the eyes of a dagger, Charlie thought—I sense he is not what he appears to be.

Thessalonian continued.

"Bluntly put, gentlemen, I have come here to Miami to discuss the assassination of Fidel Castro."

Charlie Nuccia shot back. "Discuss or arrange? Discussion is a waste of time since we all know why you want him dead. Arrangement, however, Thessalonian, is a different thing. Please be succinct as you promised."

Thessalonian had expected skepticism but not hostility. "Very well, Mr. Nuccia. As a representative of the Central Intelligence Agency, I am authorized to discuss, or rather arrange, terms for Castro's disposal."

Stefano Anacondini broke in roughly. "What terms?"

Thessalonian became specific. "First ... when Castro dies we can guarantee that the new regime replacing him will be sympathetic to your business interests. Also everything lost after Batista will be returned to you. Second ... we can guarantee that the next administration in this country will curtail its systematic attack on organized crime. No more Kefauver Committees, no more McClellan Committees and no more disruptions like Appalachia 1957. Third ... on a personal basis, Mr. Nuccia, we will drop deportation action against you. Mr. Anacondini, we will put a stop to the unrelenting FBI surveillance you've been experiencing, and Mr. Romano ... we will end a revealing Internal Revenue Service audit that, if continued, will surely put you in Federal prison."

Stefano Anacondini was ecstatic with this proposal. In combination with the favor he was doing Kennedy by swinging the Chicago vote, killing Castro would make his position ideal.

Marco Romano had started worrying. He was still making money in Cuba that none of his Italian friends knew about and he didn't want to start sharing the profits now. He had thrown his hat in with Castro when he had been stuck in that Havana jail—for better or worse. This was definitely worse.

Charlie Nuccia was skeptical. The proposal did seem logical

and generous but something about this Thessalonian character was unreal. He had the eyes, the moves of a killer. He was not the mid-level Ivy League bureaucrat he was pretending to be. But then again, Charlie thought, my only role in this scenario would be to give Tampa the O.K. Marco could handle it with or without Stefano, that would be his business. Charlie's big brown eyes did not waver from Thessalonian's as he responded.

"Why us, Thessalonian, and what if we fail? What if we attempt it and fail? Castro, I hear, is surrounded by a small army of bodyguards. They taste his food, they start his cars. He's very well protected."

Thessalonian fidgeted slightly, then answered.

"Mr. Nuccia, it is just too explosive a political situation for us. If a CIA operative were to be caught attempting to kill Castro, Kruschev would not be happy. Besides ... our reach within Castro's personal entourage is limited. And as to if you fail ... the only concession that will be denied you is the first concession, since without Castro dead there will be no free Cuba to return your businesses to. If you agree, however, that over a period of the next year you will do everything in your collective power to kill Castro, then the other two concessions will be upheld on our end for that same period. No committees—no harassment—no deportations—no prison. If after a year Castro is still alive, then all deals are off. But at the worst you will get a year of breathing space to repair some of the damage that's been done to you recently."

Charlie Nuccia liked what he was hearing. With a simple O.K. to Tampa he could clear the deportation threat against him now, and even if Castro were still alive after a year's time, he would have had a year's reprieve to strengthen his house in New Orleans. He didn't trust this Thessalonian character but his proposition was sound.

Vince was standing rock silent behind Charlie. He was not allowed to speak, but if he had been, he would have approved. Charlie had nothing to lose and everything to gain. It was a sweet deal.

Charlie reproached Thessalonian again.

"I'm not trying ta be the devil's advocate here, but I'm curious. This business you bring ta us had ta have been approved not only by Eisenhower, but also by the next President.

Considering that six months through it he will take office. Are you people claiming ta have discussed this with all potential party contenders and that they've agreed ta these concessions?"

"It has been discussed by all and it has been agreed that Castro must go at any cost short of a world war," Thessalonian lied.

Charlie Nuccia nodded and reached behind for Vince. Vince bent down to listen. Charlie whispered in his ear and Vince walked away. Vince moved quietly through the second door past the den and retrieved a bucket of champagne on ice and an unopened box of Havana cigars. He walked back out to the oval table and set them down.

"Thessalonian," Charlie Nuccia said, "you must know before I give my approval of these arrangements that we Sicilians do not take kindly to promises being broken. If we are double-crossed or betrayed and do not receive all concessions you've guaranteed ... someone's head will roll. No one—and I mean no one—is immune from a bullet. Do we understand each other?"

These were the words Thessalonian had wanted to hear.

The activation of Special Op Legerdemain was dependent upon one happenstance: that of John Fitzgerald Kennedy being elected the next President of the United States.

The controllers of Legerdemain did not expect this to occur, but if it did, they had to be prepared. The controllers had already influenced the process considerably by securing Lyndon Johnson as Kennedy's vice presidential candidate. They could not risk any further involvement. They could not risk detection. Besides, Johnson would make an acceptable head of state should tragedy befall JFK.

All of this shuffling, however, would hopefully be avoided by a Nixon victory at the Republican National Convention on July 27, then a subsequent Nixon presidential victory in November. A John Kennedy presidential victory, though, would be disastrous for them. With that in mind, the lie—the sleight of hand of Legerdemain—had been mobilized.

The entire operation was divided into three contingencies. Contingency LED-1 had begun yesterday in Ft. Bragg. It was the only contingency involving direct action. Contingency LED-2 and 3 were designed to create false commitments between Kennedy, if he were by outside chance elected President, and two strong underground factions. Contingency LED-2, indebting Kennedy to the Sicilian-American Mafia today in Miami, and Contingency LED-3, indebting Kennedy to Cuban exile groups whom Thessalonian was scheduled to meet with tomorrow in Guatemala.

The psychological profile of JFK, in the form of a dossier analysis, had been studied microscopically by the controllers of Legerdemain. It predicted that Kenedy would never repay the favor Anacondini was doing for him with the Chicago vote, much less any other favors these Sicilians granted especially favors he had never even hinted at, like killing Castro. But failing to return Anacondini's favors would be minor compared wth double-crossing Charlie Nuccia.Thessalonian had pegged the "Top Man" of New Orleans correctly. Nuccia was old school—tit for tat, a deal is a deal—and would not hesitate to kill anyone—anyone who betrayed him! Also it was unlikely that JFK would authorize full air support for an invasion of Cuba by Cuban exiles. He would probably agree to provide a few planes for pre-invasion bombing as long as they were not piloted by Americans, but total reinforcement of the exiles was unlikely.

On the other hand, if, as expected, Nixon were to get elected, Nuccia, Romano and Anacondini would get their year's reprieve. And if they actually managed to kill Castro, they would even get a little more, but nothing like the concessions Thessalonian had just outlined. If the Mafia bosses protested too vehemently at that point about Nixon's treatment of them, SFG Team Legerdemain would simply kill them. The Cuban exiles were also in relatively good hands with Nixon. He would assist them in their invasion unconditionally.

So Contingency LED-1 was direct action, but Contingencies LED 2 and 3 were merely chains of events set in play. All Kennedy had to do if elected President was to follow his stated policies and act/react to events accordingly. Chances were that at the end of his first year in office he would have two powerful underground organizations, the Sicilian-American Mafia and the Cuban exiles, feeling betrayed by him.

Thessalonian did not doubt for a second that they would both want revenge, that they would both want Kennedy dead.

Thessalonian took the glass of champagne handed to him and proposed a toast, looking squarely at the Top Man of the New Orleans underworld as he did.

"To life's infinite complexities ... and death's absolute simplicity—*Salute*!"

Charlie Nuccia smiled at how appropriate it was that these words were being spoken by a man dressed like a mortician.

"*Salud*, Thessalonian ... *Salud*!"

Chapter Five

July 23, 1960

The knife pierced the S-shaped intestine then sliced upwards through the rena cava and the aorta. Blood spewed from the wound onto the handle of the knife, matching the red of her fingernail polish.

Today, July 23, 1960 at 10:50 a.m. Margareta Jimenez was being merciless.

Before her, tied and gagged to a rickety wooden chair, sat a man she had recruited into her father's Cuban Revolutionary Directorate. The dying man had pretended great loyalty to her father's cause. He had traveled with them here to Quezalenango, Guatemala, six months ago, where they had begun training along with other Cuban exile groups for the invasion of Cuba. Margareta had learned yesterday that he was a spy for Castro.

She twisted the knife from side to side, watching him grimace, hearing the rattle of his last expungement, his blood now squirting on her wrist and arm. It excited her. She jerked the knife from his chest cavity and looked down in wonderment.

Death and sex.

Sex and death.

She had met the man, whose name was Rigoberto, on a four-hour flight from Mexico City to Havana about a year ago. He was a sociologist. He said he had been living communally with the Indians of the Yucatan and was returning to Havana to complete his doctorate. By the time they had landed at Rancho Boyeras Airport they had become fast friends. An hour later, fast lovers.

She was tempted to cut the dead Rigoberto's cock off. He had stuck it inside of her many times, planting his traitorous seed within her womb. But instead she dropped the knife and ordered her father's men to take the *hijo de puta* away. Her father's men did as they were told.

Margareta Jimenez was strikingly attractive. She had dark

autumn-leaf brown hair, loosely curled, and a pair of slanted cafe au lait eyes. A charming, upturned nose completed Margareta's lovely face and petite build. Even in her maniacal rages, she retained her physical beauty.

She stooped and walked out of the open flaps of the U.S. Army tent. A hot, mid-morning sun was bearing down on the volcanic highlands of southwestern Guatemala. Margareta lifted her face and bathed in its rays.

She needed to fuck ... someone soon ... something. Thessalonian, she whispered to herself, your presence is required—now!

Thessalonian carefully touched the inside of his mouth. The cotton that had been stuffed in it as part of his mortician's disguise had dried it raw. Thessalonian had had to stay in character longer than expected in Miami because the unidentified Mafioso that had been hovering behind Charlie Nuccia had insisted on driving him to the airport.

"No need to worry," the mystery man had said, "about being seen with a criminal. I am a different person in every town. Very few people in Miami know who I really am."

Thessalonian had kept silent and in character on the drive. Rethinking his suspicions, he had concluded that the unknown man in the driver's seat beside him was probably in his late-thirties or early- to mid-forties—too old to be Charlie Nuccia's nephew. So who was he? Thessalonian had made a mental note to find out as soon as he returned to Ft. Bragg.

For now, though, at 3:30 p.m., high over Guatemala, only Juan and Margareta Jimenez occupied his thoughts.

The U.S. Army helicopter that had carried him from Guatemala City descended swiftly into the Quazalenango Camp. The wind whipped his fatigues wildly as he jumped from the chopper and ran. He steadied his sidearm, which was a military issue .45-caliber pistol, with one hand while his other hand pulled at the strap of his 7.62 x 39mm AK-47 assault rifle. Juan and Margareta were standing about twenty yards away. Juan waved as Thessalonian approached.

Juan Jimenez had been a Batista loyalist and respected member of Havana's merchant class. He had been employed as an assistant general manager for the Internacional Hotel, which had been one of the finest hotels in the West Indies. Juan had raised his daughter, Margareta, in the Varadaro beach area near the Internacional. In 1959, when Castro overthrew the Batista government, they had fled. Juan was determined to bring his daughter home if it was the last thing he ever did. He looked like an overweight Hitler with his stern features and small rectangular mustache. He was a proud man—a fanatic—which made Thessalonian's job that much easier, for fanatics were easily led and manipulated.

Thessalonian had begun his manipulation of the Cuban exiles six months earlier when he had moved them to Guatemala for military training. He had done this as part of another covert operation called "Pluto" prior to the mobilization of Legerdemain. The exiles' role, however, had not changed. They were still scheduled to invade Cuba in April of 1961.

"*Buenos dias*, my friend. I trust you are well?"

Juan Jimenez extended his short, fat hand. Thessalonian grabbed it quickly and released it. He then extended his own hand to Margareta's, lifting hers to his thin lips and kissing it.

She smiled, "Thessalonian, as always, your manners are impeccable."

Their eyes met for too long. Thessalonian's stare broke first as he turned to Juan.

"We must talk, Mr. Jimenez."

The three revolutionaries walked towards the same U.S. Army tent that Margareta had slaughtered Rigoberto in five hours ago.

Death and sex.

Sex and death.

She smiled to herself ... viciously.

Vince laid the roses at the base of the tombstone. It was 5:30 p.m. He was bleary-eyed, having just returned to New Orleans from Miami a couple of hours ago. He had spent a bundle in Miami on a diamond necklace for Mona and in some perverse way had had feelings of guilt about it. Standing by Rosalie's grave now comforted him.

Rosalie was buried in the "City of the Dead," a euphemism

for St. Thomas Cemetery off of Esplanade Avenue. Her grave marker read in Italian:

Alla bellissima
fanciulla col cuore
di una Francese e l'anima
di una Siciliana
t'amo eternamente
Rosalie Ann Sedoux Angeletta
1925-1954

Translated it meant:

To the most beautiful girl
with a Frenchwoman's heart
and the soul of a Sicilian
I love you—eternally
Rosalie Ann Sedoux Angeletta
1925-1954

Memories of their nine years together seeped through the late afternoon humidity. Rosalie did have the soul of a Sicilian, Vince reminisced. She understood vendetta and *omerta* and the world in which I lived. She would lovingly joke with me about being too soft, that I was not true Mafioso, then grin as if to say, I'm glad you are soft sometimes, my big puppy.

Vince was not by nature a killer, as evident of his having spared his father's murderer in Texas, but he had been forced to kill two men in self-defense in Huntsville Penitentiary, then another in 1945 on orders from Johnny Sincelli. The latter was a man who had raped the daughter of one of Charlie's legitimate real estate agents. That killing had earned Vince his formal membership into the Nuccia family.

It wasn't that Vince lacked balls, it was just that he felt it smart to avoid killing if possible. He preferred doing his work with his hands. He had been nicknamed "Angler" in Huntsville because of his effective hand to hand fighting technique. No matter what hold another man had on him, he seemed always able to angle his way free. Regardless, for the last nine years as the Nuccia family's main money courier—main *spalloni*—neither killing nor strong-arming had ever been necessary.

Vince's retrospection was interrupted abruptly by the sound of Jake Sincelli's voice.

"You're gettin' old, Vin, lettin' me sneak up on you like that. You're hangin' loose too much."

Vince turned and flashed a treacherous smile at his friend as Jake continued to chide him.

"Now you think you can clutch up on me, huh, Vin? Well, save it. If I can't be sarc with you, then who can? C'mon, buddy, Charlie needs you."

"What Charlie needs is some rest," Vince corrected Jake.

The two men walked out of the above ground cemetery. As Vince moved to get into the front seat of Jake's black 1958 Cadillac, Jake motioned otherwise.

"Back here."

The waning sun had made it difficult for Vince to see the figure of Charlie Nuccia sitting in the rear seat. Charlie had on the same pair of dark glasses he had worn all morning on the flight from Miami. The only addition to his wardrobe was a porkpie hat leaning down on his forehead.

Vince hopped in and the Cadillac slowly, smoothly pulled away from the cemetery curb. Charlie was all business.

"Vincenzo, what was your reading on this Thessalonian yesterday when you took him to the airport?"

"Ah, nothing, Charlie. He didn't say a word. I felt him eyeballing me some, you know, like he couldn't quite figure out who I was."

"Very few people know who you are, Vin, except fa the money people."

Charlie looked down at his manicured nails.

"For that reason, I've chosen you ta handle this Castro thing."

Vince tensed. "But, Charlie, I thought Marco was in charge?"

"I've changed my mind about our role. Technically Marco will still be in charge but you, Vincenzo, will be my representative fa the duration. You see, Vince, I suspect that Marco may not want Castro dead. I've been hearing rumors fa about a year now that money is still being made down there. So your job is twofold. Find out if Marco's double dealing us and make sure every real effort is being made to kill Castro."

"Okay, Charlie." Vince accepted his promotion, cautiously. "What do I do first?"

Charlie removed his shades. His big brown eyes bored into Vince's anxiety. "I told Marco that you would get with his man, Luigi Bertucci, in Tampa tomorrow. Luigi was the one with Marco at the meeting ... " Charlie squinted, "and listen, Vin, trust me ... trust me the way I trust you. I know this job is out of your range but I need you there. You're an unknown factor with most of these people and I want Castro dead!"

The tip of Charlie's manicured finger poked Vince's leg. "With him dead, the government will be in our pockets till doomsday. Don't let Marco fuck it up, intentionally or otherwise."

Charlie Nuccia sat erect on the Cadillac black leather seat, calmly returning his dark glasses to the bridge of his nose.

"*Prendi questa pietra dalla mia scarpa*, Vin. Take this stone named Castro out of my shoe, then fuck him with it—right up his ass!"

"It's official, Mr. Jimenez." Thessalonian paused. "Your people have the unconditional backing of the next White House occupants—whoever that turns out to be. We've met all the parties involved and their sentiment is one of full cooperation. Up to and including the beachhead air support you were so concerned about. That, amigo, is a guarantee."

Juan's black rectangular mustache spread along the curve of his smile. He and Margareta were seated side by side on an aluminum bench inside the army tent. Thessalonian laid his machine gun down and leaned against an oil drum. He rolled up his sleeves. He knew that Margareta loved to look at his scars.

"Thessalonian, our people thank you and I thank you."

Juan stood and again extended his short, fat hand to Thessalonian. Thessalonian exuberantly put both of his hands around Juan's.

The lie of Contingency Legerdemain 3 was secure.

FOUR MONTHS LATER
November 9, 1960
Scudder Avenue Compound
Hyannisport, Massachusetts, USA
Early Morning

Jesus, they're already here, and it's not even daylight. They must have slept even less than I.

How many are there? Fourteen, fifteen, sixteen Secret Service men, at least.

This must mean I've won ... Baughman would never have unleashed his men unless ... unless ... I've won!

Illinois, California, Michigan, Minnesota ... they must have pulled our way. I've got to stay calm ... this is like waking up on Christmas Day ... I've won!

But by what margin? Too narrow, I'm afraid. Nixon, I know, carried the farm states ... Iowa, North and South Dakota, Kansas, Nebraska ... probably the Mountain states, too. So what did I carry?

Enough to be called President Kennedy, the 35th President of these United States ...

... That's all in the hell that matters, isn't it? ... Mr. President?

Chapter Six

November 10, 1960

"Needless to say, I'm stunned."

It was 10:45 a.m., November 10, 1960. A faint scrambler blip could be heard on the Pentagon-CIA phone line. Major General Marion Armstrong III, Deputy Director for the Pentagon Office of Special Operations (OSO), continued, "What were the exact figures, Plato?"

"Kennedy, 303 electoral votes, Nixon, 219 electoral votes. The popular vote was tight—Kennedy, 34221463, Nixon, 34108582. How do you want to proceed with Contingency LED-1, Ratchet?"

"As planned. Continue training, but begin the audio visuals. We need to get Team LED mentally prepared. As far as Contingency LED-2, make sure Thessalonian well provokes New Orleans with the inevitability of RFK being appointed Attorney General. Dulles, CIA, and Hoover, FBI, will probably be appointed today."

"What about LED-3?"

"Thessalonian may want to double secure Guatemala in the near future, but as it stands they're set."

"Any idea on projected op completion date?" Plato Smith of the CIA's Directorate of Plans (DDP)-Western Hemisphere Division was obviously concerned.

"Patience, Plato, patience."

General Armstrong replaced the receiver and moved to his maple cabinet. The 030601 phone appeared seconds later. He lifted the receiver and waited anxiously for the gruff voice to answer. A minute later it did.

"0-3-0-6-0-1"

Armstrong replied, "030601, this is Intercept Eagle. Legerdemain Contingencies shift from Mobilization to Activation. Repeat ... Legerdemain Contingencies shift from Mobilization to Activation ... over."

The gruff voice responded, "Intercept Eagle. Received. Legerdemain Contingencies shift from Mobilization to Activation. Acknowledge ... clear."

Major General Armstrong hung up the special phone and returned to his desk. He seated himself and began reading his Daily Defense Intelligence Summary (Dinsum). His aide, Corporal Forrestol, knocked and entered with a steaming pot of coffee on a silver tray. General Armstrong thanked him, but waved him off before the Corporal could pour. The General did not like to be waited on. It was then, as he reached to pour his own cup, that General Armstrong realized his hand was shaking and his palms were sweating profusely. The burden of Legerdemain was breaking him!

Chapter Seven

November 11, 1960

Luigi Bertucci was sucking on his teeth. Vince felt like slamming his fist into them. He hated this rot gut motherfucker. The fact that Marco had someone like Luigi as his underboss said it all.

It was 9:30 a.m. and Vince had had to put up with Luigi's dumbfuckness for four months now. Vince had watched Luigi bungle three separate plots to kill Castro. When he had first met with Luigi in July at the behest of Charlie Nuccia he had felt differently. Luigi had exuded confidence then. There had not been the slightest hint that Marco Romano's Tampa family didn't want Castro dead as much as Chicago and New Orleans did. They had even obtained extensive blueprints of Castro's headquarters and considerable data on Castro's personal habits, all within 48 hours of the Fontainebleau meet.

The three failed assassination plots had been as simple as poisoning Castro's cigars, bombing his toilet, and bribing his mistress to kill him. But the cigars had never arrived, the wrong toilet had exploded and the mistress, after being approached, had immediately informed her lover. The entire thing had become a comedy of errors with Luigi Bertucci as its master comedian.

He even looked like a fat, funny man; an ugly Jackie Gleason, with a wart on the side of his nose the texture of snot. Unformed and often mistaken for snot, it was unfortunately his most outstanding facial feature. Combined with his bell-shaped belly, spindly legs and myopic eyes, he was grotesque.

Vince hated to be close to him as he was now, but persevered, swallowing his revulsion. They were crouched on a rooftop in Havana, positioned close to the La Cabana; an ex-fortress of Anglophobe Carlos III, now a prison. Thousands of 19th century Cuban patriots had died within the La Cabana's walls. Today Fidel Castro would be memorializing them. Tomorrow, if Vince Angeletta had his way, the Cuban people would be memorializing a dead Fidel.

Vince brought a pair of binoculars up to his furry eyebrows and squinted. He could see two men crouched, as he and Luigi were, on an adjacent rooftop. They were the Cuban assassins Vince had contracted weeks ago. The morning sun was steaming, but the harbor breeze was cool. Boat horns and traffic horns could be heard moaning lethargically. Vince had had enough of teeth sucking.

"Luigi, shut the fuck up! Has anybody ever told you that you are one vulgar cocksucker!"

Luigi flinched, anger in his bloated features. Vince stared him down, then continued to look through his binoculars at his paid assassins across the way.

Vince had hired the two men through an intermediary—a cutout Johnny Sincelli had arranged. Vince had not told Luigi of his plan. Vince now agreed with Charlie Nuccia's premise that Marco Romano, for reasons of profit, did not want Castro dead. Vince had, therefore, acted secretly in preparation for today's fourth assassination attempt. He had brought Luigi along as a throwaway. Luigi would take the fall for the assassination. Charlie wanted a clear message sent to Tampa that he knew about Marco's Cuban game and would not tolerate it. Luigi would have to die along with Castro and Vince was responsible. These were Charlie Nuccia's orders.

Vince crawled behind a corner pigeon drop a few feet away and pulled out a black exercise bag. He slowly lifted out of it a Mauser Model 98K, heavy barrel bolt-action rifle with a Zeiss scope. He pointed it at the sealed off empty entry road leading to the gates of the La Cabana, adjusting it. The fanfare of Castro's cheering parade could he heard approaching. The marching band's music was loud and nationalistic.

"What da fuck is that and what da fuck are you doing?" Luigi asked, as he pointed to the rifle, his myopic eyes twirling in different directions.

Vince glared at him, "Just keep your mouth shut and we'll be fine."

Luigi began to panic. Fine to this unknown Vince Angeletta was not fine to him. Marco Romano had given strict orders that not one pimple on Castro's ass was to be squeezed, much less popped—or else! Contemplating the "or else," Luigi pounced.

He slammed Vince's chest with his left elbow. Vince fell to

the cement, his binoculars shattering. Vince's rifle, too, fell from his grip, hitting the rooftop hard. The Angler rolled sideways as Luigi attempted a snap kick to his head. He palmed Luigi's foot and jerked down. The underboss lost his balance and toppled over on his face. Vince raised himself to his knees, letting the rifle lay, reaching behind to the small of his back under his windbreaker for his .22 Ruger pistol.

A chorus of Cuban patriotism broke out in the crowd a half mile up the street. Fidel Castro neared the cordoned-off road leading to the La Cabana.

Vince put the barrel of his .22 to the back of Luigi's head. The fat master comedian of errors had made his final one. Vince pulled the trigger twice, simultaneously with a cymbal and bass drum crash below. The bullets entered Luigi's hind brain where the pons, medulla oblongata and cerebellum lay. They were blown out. Vince quickly put the .22 back in his belt, raised himself slightly, and went over to where his rifle had fallen. He lifted it and peeked over the side. Without his binoculars it was difficult to see the movement of his two assassins on the adjacent roof.

Castro's parade had entered the road leading to the La Cabana. The bearded figure himself could be seen waving from the back of a military jeep, still triumphant from his New York trip in September.

Where are my shooters? Vince thought. Shit!

He peeked over the side again, scanning the opposite roof just in time to see the shapes of at least ten Cuban militia invade it. He heard shots. His hired guns were being taken!

Shit! Shit! Shit!

Vince's same deep-seated reserve that had saved him when his plane had stalled over the everglades in July again kicked in. He became perfectly calm. He raised the rifle to his shoulder and aimed the crosshairs of his Zeiss scope directly on the oily profile of Fidel Castro. He pulled the trigger. Nothing happened. The goddamned rifle had been damaged in the course of his struggle with Luigi.

Shit! Shit! Shit!

He had to move quickly now. Castro was entering the La Cabana. It was too late. Vince pitched the broken rifle in the bag and scurried down the outer stairwell, looking back at the dead body of Luigi Bertucci. Luigi's teeth-sucking days were over, Vince thought, taking to a fast walk down the Calle.

The boat horns, the car horns, the loud music overwhelming his senses as Luigi's brain dried on his hand.

Shit!

Lafitte's Westport Club was Charlie Nuccia's most lucrative gambling joint in Louisiana. He had named it after Jean Lafitte, the legendary Bayou Baratorie pirate prince. Lafitte's club was located on the west bank of New Orleans in the small community of Gretna. It appeared, at first glance, to be nothing more than a huge and deserted warehouse. In actuality, though, it housed one of the largest gambling operations in the South. It was a plush and seductive speakeasy, offering Black Jack, roulette, craps, slots and baccarat to men who gambled daily much more than they could afford to lose.

Thessalonian had gambled in coming here. It was 1 p.m. He was seated low in the rear office of Charlie Nuccia before a massive mahogany desk with the letters CN emblazoned on its front. Charlie, Jake and Johnny were in the office with him. Thessalonian was disguised exactly as he had been at the Fontainebleau—like a mortician. He was also pretending skittishness as the bearer of bad news, anxious about having his head chopped off.

"Mr. Nuccia, I am here to inform you of a most disquieting development." Seconds passed like hours as the Top Man stared through him. "John F. Kennedy, now President Kennedy, has reneged on our Cuban arrangement."

Charlie Nuccia's backbone tightened like a spring and his face became pale. He carefully loosened his amber tie and unbuttoned his gold cufflinks, issuing an order to Johnny's son, "Jake, call the Rotary Club, cancel the luncheon this afternoon."

Jake rose and in his lumbering gait walked to the phone in the bookshelf across the office. Jake's left hand was rubbing his mustache. Johnny Sincelli had pulled his chair closer to Charlie's desk to speak.

"If I may, Don Nuccia." He looked towards Charlie who nodded. "What form, Thessalonian, has Kennedy's betrayal taken?"

Thessalonian's darkened eyebrows raised at the calmness of Johnny's counselor-at-law voice. "Mr. Sincelli, he intends to appoint Robert F. Kennedy Attorney General of the United States. In doing this he has signaled Mr. Nuccia that all markers are canceled. Robert will be coming after your people with both barrels, just like he did with the McClellan Committee."

Legerdemain's brilliant lie was taking shape. Candidate Kennedy had never even been aware of, much less in consent of, any deal with Charlie Nuccia to assassinate Fidel Castro. And even if he had, he wouldn't have honored it, just as he was dishonoring Anacondini's vote-buying in Chicago with his choice of Robert as Attorney General. As predicted by the controllers of Legerdemain, JFK wanted nothing to do with the Sicilians.

"Has Stefano been informed, Thessalonian?" Charlie asked. Vince had told Charlie at the Fontainebleau that Mario had confirmed Stefano's vote-fixing for Kennedy in Chicago. Charlie now wondered what Stefano's reaction would be to this double-cross. Probably a lot of yelling—nothing more. After all, Stefano was not old school like he was. No one—repeat—no one was going to fuck Charlie Nuccia!

Thessalonian answered, "Yes."

Charlie stood up, breathing heavily. His normally impassive, pock-marked face flushed with hatred. "I had a feeling something like this might happen if the Kennedys got in the White House." He sighed. "You see, Thessalonian, I hate them fa two reasons." Charlie raised his pudgy forefinger. "One, Robert put me through hell at the McClellan Committee hearings, and two," his middle finger came up, "his blue-blooded hand has been the one pushing for my deportation. That's why I asked you the question about presidential contenders at the Fontainebleau. If Nixon had won, maybe our Cuban arrangement would have been honored. With Kennedy, though, I had serious doubts. But you—you, my CIA friend, guaranteed it." Charlie sat back down and yawned, his hatred subsiding. This had become just another business transaction for him. "So, Thessalonian, how are you going to compensate us?"

Jake Sincelli took his cue and stood directly behind the shoulder of the man dressed like a mortician. Jake's sport coat was open and his right hand was on his shoulder holster.

Charlie continued. "Considering that as we speak I have a man making his fourth attempt on Castro, a man who's like a son to me and a brother ta us all." He cupped his hand, pointing to include Johnny and Jake." ... He has spent four months on this. Today he may even die over it and now you tell me it has all been fa nothing."

Thessalonian's mind flashed to the mystery Mafioso who had driven him to the airport in Miami in July. A man Thessalonian had yet to identify. Putting that detail aside for later, Thessalonian went into his prescribed role, using every acting technique that Stephens College had taught him.

"But, but, Mr. Nuccia. I'm here, am I not? I'm showing you respect by facing you. I could have not told you and you would have kept trying to kill Castro for another eight months. At least, I'm being stand-up about this!"

"That'ssa not enough," Charlie coldly replied.

Thessalonian looked around and noticed Jake behind him, poised to strike. It was time for the clincher.

"Okay, Mr. Nuccia, I'll hand you the President. How's that for honoring my word?"

Charlie Nuccia was startled. He looked to his *consigliere*. Johnny's hand was frozen on his mustache. He was stunned, also. Jake was unaffected. He just kept staring at Thessalonian like so much meat for the grinder. A fleeting suspicion ran through Charlie's mind as he looked at the CIA man who had the eyes of a dagger. Could this have been a setup all along, he asked himself? Charlie stood once more, walking to the front of his desk. He extended his hand. "Thank you, Thessalonian. You are an honorable man. Contact us in six months. We'll decide then what's to be done. Jake, walk our friend to the door." He looked again at the CIA man, piercingly.

"Good-bye, Thessalonian."

Jake rudely escorted a truly surprised Thessalonian out.

Charlie Nuccia had baffled him!

Vince had been traveling for the last four months from South Florida to Cuba by light plane. A Piper Cub, similar to his Four Seasons Corporate Cessna 172/Skyhawk, but not as reliable. He was headed to the light plane now from Havana with a quick stop first. He had to get a message to Charlie in New Orleans. A message stating that not only was their fourth assassination attempt on Castro a failure, but that their two hired guns had been captured and/or killed and that Vince was on his way home. His only good news to Charlie would be that Luigi was dead.

The intermediary—the cutout with whom Johnny Sincelli had arranged to hire the two killers for this attempt—was the only man in Cuba Vince could trust to send this message. The cutout also needed to be advised that he was in grave danger of exposure if his two snipers were still alive and were broken by Castro's interrogators.

It was 5 p.m.

Vince's plane was waiting on a strip carved out of a sugar cane field in Pinar Del Rio, approximately 125 miles southwest of Havana. In between Havana and Pinar Del Rio slept the lazy, very small town of Fueges. This is where the intermediary—the cutout—Manuel Marinello lived.

Vince had miraculously maintained his composure on the drive. The escape jeep Marinello had arranged for him had been modified for speed and, as Jake would say in his fifties slang, was a screamer, a draggin' wagon. Regardless, it had still taken Vince hours to get this far. The road he had been forced to travel on was half gravel, half asphalt, barely negotiable.

He zoomed into Fueges and turned down a dirt side road leading to the Marinello properties. He skidded to a stop in front of the main house. Two of Manuel's workers, armed with knives, pistols and automatic weapons approached him. Vince, over the last four months, had spent time off and on here. Enough time to where Marinello's people knew he was a friend.

"Where's Manuel?" he asked the giant black man standing by.

"The back patio, senor. This way."

Vince's windbreaker was still blood-stained, but his hands were not. He had managed, shortly after leaving the rooftop near the La Cabana, to wash Luigi's blood off them.

Manuel Marinello was relaxing on his patio overlooking an undersized backyard fishing pond. Upon seeing Vince he stood quickly and ran to him, putting his hands on Vince's upper arms to steady him.

"Amigo, how did it go?" he asked, immediately noticing the blood stains on Vince's windbreaker.

"Total bust, Manuel! Total fucking bust! The militia captured your two shooters and I had a problem with Luigi—he broke my fucking rifle!" Vince allowed himself thirty seconds of stillness to regain his composure. "Manuel, I've got to send a message to New Orleans, urgent." Vince's arrogant nostrils were wide from breathing too fast, too hard, for too long.

Marinello, on the other hand, was as calm as his fishing pond.

"Vincza, *vamos*!"

He led Vince to the guest house where Vince had stayed several times over the last few months.

Manuel Marinello had been a silent casino partner of Charlie Nuccia's in Havana before Castro seized power in 1959. He was a rich landowner in a country where private wealth was now illegal, who had just barely evaded Castro's financial crackdown. Manuel's protection for the time being came from a still highly connected ministry official whom he paid. Marinello considered Vince a kindred spirit and liked him a lot. Both were dashing, middle-aged, playboy widowers, caught up in intrigue way beyond their experience.

In the back of the guest house was a short-wave radio. Manuel pulled a wicker chair beside the table it was sitting on and turned it to 29.7 megahertz. Vince was busy scribbling his message so Manuel would not have to waste words or time when contact with New Orleans was made.

The message read:

To Rosalie:

Florida marriage unsuccessful—divorce finalized—Cuban fling disastrous—leaving the woman—immediately.

Angler

Ten minutes later and nine minutes after Manuel had finished speaking Vince's message into the headset a reply came through. Manuel patiently, expertly, wrote it down. Finished, he lowered the earpiece from his right ear and read the return message slowly to Vince.

To Angler:

Entire affair over—Bible salesman visited us—admitted his employers have canceled our order—romance without religion—impossible—expect you soon.
Rosalie

Seconds after Manuel completed reading Charlie's message, gunfire erupted on the Marinello estate. Manuel, suddenly alert with fear, looked to Vince.

"Our two rooftop friends must have broken and revealed me. I am lost, Vincza."

He stood and moved quickly to a front closet in the guest house. In it sat a large metal trunk which held a vast supply of small arms and ammunition. Vince followed his lead and began to reach down for the weapons. Manuel held up his hand, signaling Vince away.

"No, Vincza, you must leave. This is not your fight."

"But, Manuel, I've gotta help!"

"No! Charlie cannot afford to lose you at a time like this—go! There are horses in the stable fifty yards back. Go, now!"

With that, Manuel locked the 9mm Baretta pistol in his hand and began to shoot his short-wave radio to bits. Vince put his arm up to his eyes and ears as the loud bangs echoed in the small guest house, shattering his senses. When the shooting stopped Vince lowered his arm and viewed the destruction of the radio, the table and the wicker chair Manuel had been sitting in. The stench of cordite overwhelmed him.

With no options remaining, Vince walked up and embraced the Cuban he had befriended four months ago. Manuel's deep brown Latino eyes spoke to him with the expectation of death. Vince turned away and ran out the rear entrance, the roar of automatic weapons fire crescendoing on his heels!

Chapter Eight

November 12, 1960

Brigadier General Alexander T. Mancus, the deputy commander of the Special Warfare Center at Ft. Bragg, North Carolina, tore the encoded mimeograph off the teletype. It was from Thessalonian in New Orleans, instructing the General to begin the audiovisual portion of Contingency LED-1 for SFG Team Legerdemain. It was time for Marsh, Taylor and Holt to be introduced to their target.

It was 11 a.m.

The extensive training that had been promised Team Legerdemain in July had begun in August with advanced mountain exercises at Fort Carson. In September Mancus had moved them on to Camp Lejeune for advanced amphibious maneuvers. In October, to Fort Hale for advanced winter warfare courses.

General Mancus, with memo in hand, stepped out of his deputy commandant's office and walked towards the same Ft. Bragg Operations Room in which Contingency LED-1 had begun four months ago. Marsh, Taylor and Holt awaited. He did not speak to them upon entering the room, only motioned for them to be seated while he dimmed the lights. He moved to the rear and seated himself next to a film projector. He flipped the projector switch to play.

Black and white pictures of an orgy in progress flashed upon the screen. A group of eight people were sexually intertwined in three separate couplings. There was a woman on a bed servicing two males with another woman on a mattress on the floor with her legs high up in the air, being penetrated by a third male. A fourth male was lying on his back on the carpet with two women sitting on top of him. One was straddling his waist, the other straddling his tongue. The camera focused on this man's face.

Suddenly the eyes of Taylor and Holt bulged. Their fists clenched and their mouths opened in shock. If it had been possible, the hair on their heads would have stood up straight, like Buckwheat's on TV's Little Rascals. Captain Marsh was, for his part, however, responding professionally, unemotionally.

General Mancus clicked the projector to a stop, freezing the frame, and walked up to the screen. His moves were assured and parental, his white strandy hair perfectly in place.

"Team, this film was taken years ago, but I'm sure you all recognize him." He paused, pointing to the face before them. That famous full set of teeth was only half visible under the woman's pubic hair and those famous eyes were closed in sensual concentration. "You should—considering that a few days ago this man became the 35th President of the United States—and also considering that he is the target/objective of Special Op Legerdemain."

A curious Captain Marsh turned his blond-haired, blue-eyed head to look at the expressions of his two teammates. Lawdy! Lawdy! he thought, in his Alabama twang. I bet the idealistic virtue of Sergeant Holt is taking a beating, and Taylor's naiveté ... Christ!

Specialist Tony Taylor bowed his head in embarrassment and disbelief, his hand running through his curly brown hair, unable to look at the film any longer, and Sergeant Holt felt the pain of an unraveling moral fiber; his country, his duty, his honor suddenly seeming as much a perversion of faith as the sexual perversions being played out on the screen before him. His dark features and reddish brown skin were pale and pitted with disgust.

Besides deriving sadistic pleasure out of his teammate's agony, Captain Marsh, too, was beginning to feel something. Not moral indignation or disillusionment, but the stirs of an erection.

The General continued, "This man, our newly elected head of state, is the second son of Joseph P. Kennedy. He had an older brother, Joseph, Jr., who was killed in 1944. He has two younger brothers, Robert Francis and Edward Moore. He was an average student at Harvard, where this film was shot, until his senior year when he wrote a masterful thesis entitled *Why England Slept*. He was a heroic navy man during the war, especially in 1943 when his PT boat was sunk and he led his crew to safety, overcoming grave injuries of his own to do so. In

1952, when he became the junior senator from Massachusetts, his ideology was moderate right. In 1953 he married Jacqueline Bouvier. In 1956 he wrote *Profiles in Courage*, winning him the Pulitzer Prize. Also in 1956, he came within a hair's length of winning the Democratic vice presidential nomination. After this loss his posture outwardly changed from moderate right to liberal." General Mancus paused. "His dark side, Team Legerdemain, has never been exposed, not the way it will be to you during the next week. He is a sexual deviant, a cohort of gangsters and, as you were told at your original briefing, a member of and active agent for the Communist party."

Sergeant Holt's devastation found it impossible to control itself any longer. He spoke up forcefully, questioning. "But, General Mancus, sir, why in God's name wasn't he exposed long before now? My God, why?"

General Mancus turned halfway around, faced the wall and stared at a black spot on it. It was time, he decided, for the central lie of Contingency LED-1 to be told. The room was stifling with intensity.

"Sergeant, you must understand that the tentacles of the Kennedys reach high. This film could easily be discredited with alibis and denials, claiming it to be a falsification or a simulation. We have no legal proof of our allegations—except through inadmissible circumstantial exhibits like this and sworn affidavits of hearsay by informers."

"But, sir, if there's not enough proof for a court of law, how could there be enough proof to justify his termination. For that matter, I'm unaware of any law that says a man can't make love to two women at the same time."

General Mancus was not enjoying this verbal jousting with the 19-year-old Sergeant Holt, or anything else concerning this distasteful deception. Of course, he silently pondered, this film could be discredited because the man underneath the women was not really JFK—but a young JFK look-alike. No matter, this was his mission! The General, ignoring Holt's last remark, employed every ounce of his professorial demeanor to return to the projector and flip the switch again to play.

The two women slid slowly off the JFK look-alike. They moved over with the third woman who had been on the mattress to assist their fourth friend with the two males on the bed. The third male, who also had been on the mattress, stood and walked over to the prone body of the JFK look-alike. The young man bent to his naked knees and kissed the look-alike. His right hand then reached down to the look-alike's genitals and began fondling them. He turned around on the carpet to where he could perform fellatio on the look-alike as well as enabling the look-alike to perform it on him. Both men were basking in one another's oral homosexual stimulation.

General Mancus froze the frame once more.

"Team, look at these men! LOOK ... TEAM!"

Taylor and Holt were slumped and defeated now, while Marsh's erection had become massive.

"This man has won the presidency of our great country. This SICK MAN! This perverted MAN! This Corrupt Man! This TRAITOR! Why or how is unimportant! We must stop him! We MUST! HE IS OUR MISSION! LOOK! LOOK!"

Seconds after the General unfroze the frame, saliva resembling sperm began to drip from both of the young men's mouths!

Preflight.

Pinar Del Rio to New Orleans, 640 statute miles, 552 nautical miles. Two ten-gallon tanks that'll burn five gallons an hour at cruise and a little more than three-quarters of a gallon on takeoff. Ten to twenty minutes to get to cruise altitude, which will be at 5,000 feet.

Vince's ass hurt like hell!

He had been horseback riding only once in his life before yesterday and today, and that had been with Charlie shortly after Rosalie's death. It had been a relaxing experience then, not comparable to these last twenty hours of grueling bareback. Twenty hours in which he had managed to traverse the remaining sixty miles from the Marinello Properties in Fuegas to the sugar cane field-landing strip in Pinar Del Rio.

It was 1 p.m.

There had been a series of explosions that had sent his horse running wild. It had been a miracle that he hadn't been thrown then or lost later, he thought, as he continued his preflight calculations. His windbreaker was torn to shreds, his arms and legs severely scratched and his ass was literally throbbing. Still, he was alive and on his way out of Cuba.

Even though less reliable than his Cessna 172/Skyhawk, the Piper Cub in front of him looked as good as gold. Besides, its nonturbo engine, capable of 50 horsepower on takeoff and 25 horsepower on cruise, was all that mattered to Vince now.

He made a quick check of wind direction and weather conditions, as well as a visual of the runway for obstructions. The wind was mild, blowing about ten knots from the southeast, and the Cuban sky on this November afternoon couldn't have been clearer. The sugar cane field-landing strip that had been cut precisely to accommodate his aircraft was unobstructed.

Cigar clenched tightly in his mouth, Vince moved carefully to the cockpit, slowly sitting down on the hard leather seat. A sudden sense of failure enveloped him. He paused to gather his thoughts. He had failed himself and, even more so, had failed Charlie Nuccia. He was determined to find a way, some way, somewhere, somehow to make it up to his Top Man. This he promised himself; *"questo te prometto."*

Vince ignited the engine and steered his Piper Cub down the brush runway, gathering speed and lift until he soared into and on his way out of Cuban air space. Part of his message sent yesterday to Charlie echoed in his mind: Cuban fling—disastrous!

⌖ ⌖ ⌖ ⌖

"How can Kennedy's proposed financial outlay for Special Forces be explained if everything we've just heard and seen is true? And why has he given us official permission to wear our Green Berets if he's the punk Commie that they say he is?" a still morally depleted Sergeant Holt rambled on, half to himself, half to his team leader, Captain Marsh.

Captain Marsh snickered, "Ha! He probably just wants to see all of our cute asses in them there tight-fitting uniforms with our cute green beanies!"

He raised his hand above his blonde head and pointed with his forefinger down to the center of his green beret, laughing.

It was 3 p.m.

SFG Team Legerdemain, Marsh, Taylor and Holt, were dining in a crowded and noisy Ft. Bragg officers' mess. They had left the operations room minutes ago. General Mancus had issued Taylor and Holt special passes to get into the OM.

Captain Marsh looked at the distressed faces of his team members and wished he were by himself. Taylor had been chain-smoking Chesterfields since viewing the orgy film, and the usually silent and stoic Sergeant Holt couldn't stop mumbling. Marsh had another reason for wanting to be alone besides distancing himself from these youngsters. He needed private time to sort this crazy, fucking dilly-dally called Legerdemain out. He considered this as he continued to stuff his face full of down-home southern eatin's, attempting to block out the verbal lamentations of Sergeant Holt.

"It doesn't make any fucking sense," Sergeant Holt expressed vehemently, talking to no one in particular. Captain Marsh stopped in mid-mash-potato-chew, astonished at having heard a profanity uttered from Holt's usually pure mouth.

"Thirty-five million dollars, that's how much he's going to ask from Congress for Special Forces. Why would a Commie agent do that, seriously?" The young sergeant now stared directly at Captain Marsh for an answer. Specialist Taylor was staying quiet, observant.

The Captain grinned and finished chewing his potatoes. His twenty-inch biceps were tensed and his Viking features stone-like. He set his metal fork down, determined to put an end to this incessant babble.

"Holt, are you or are you not a soldier in the United States Army?"

Sergeant Holt answered, maintaining his stare, "Yes, sir, I am."

"And are you not a member of the 77th Airborne Special Forces Group currently on reassignment to Special Forces Group Team Legerdemain, stationed at the Special Warfare Center in Ft. Bragg, North Carolina?"

"Yes, sir, I am."

Captain Marsh's fist shot across the table and grabbed Holt by the collar, pulling a handful of reddish brown skin through the chicken and black-eyed peas. Marsh, through gritted teeth, set the record straight—two inches from Holt's face.

"Then start acting like it, soldier! You are on an alpha crypto priority national security mission. I'll tell you one more time. Get them ticks off of your hide, boy! Now! And start acting right! Do you read me, Sergeant?"

In one deft Tai Chi Chuan maneuver, Sergeant Holt could have shoved the Captain's nose cartilage directly into his brain. He stared at Marsh, wondering if the blindly dedicated 31-year-old career army man knew how close to death he was. He obviously did not. He was still clenching Holt's throat.

"And for the duration, Sergeant," Marsh continued, "whether it's months or years, I don't want to hear any more crying. Understood?"

Sergeant Holt choked out a curt, "Yes, sir," still maintaining his stare.

The Captain released him, shoving him back on the bench, then stood abruptly, throwing his table napkin in the turnip greens. He walked out, unaware of Sergeant Holt's murderous glare following his bowlegged exit.

As he stormed out of the OM and began to walk the compound, Captain Marsh's situational analysis became clearer. He had worked for CIA Directorate of Plans (DDP)-Western Hemisphere Division before—back in '57. He knew their technique. He had been part of a team that had killed an alleged civilian heroin dealer during a military police arrest at Pope Air Base, North Carolina. The killing had been made to look like a justifiable shoot by military police. Marsh always suspected, though, that the dealer had actually been a foreign spy. That is where he had first become intimately familiar with those Carolina nights and the DDP.

This was, though, by all indications, a completely different scenario. Holt had a point. Kennedy did appear to be very supportive of Special Forces. Much too supportive for a Communist agent. In fact, the whole "Red scare" angle being fed Team Legerdemain was probably total bullshit. The sex and gangster angles, maybe not, but the Commie angle smelled phony. Marsh stopped cold with a realization.

Someone very powerful wanted Kennedy dead. Someone within the control apparatus of the CIA's Directorate of Plans and with control over the esteemed General Mancus, Deputy Commander of the Special Warfare Center here at Ft. Bragg.

A quiet idealist like Sergeant Holt couldn't conceive of such a power, and a kid as naive as Tony Taylor... Shit! He wouldn't know that kind of power from his ass or a mole hill!

But I do, Marsh concluded. I do ... all too well!

FIVE MONTHS LATER
April 1, 1961
Oval Office, White House
Washington, D.C., USA

Late Night I hope they understand that I'll not hinder the exiles ... will even encourage Dulles's people with their orchestration and provide planes for pre-invasion bombing, as long as they're not piloted by Americans ... but I'll not provide full beachhead air support ... I'll not do so unless I'm absolutely sure! Kruschev would love it ... justification for all of his anti-imperialistic rhetoric, as well as fertilizer for more.

I hope the exiles take back their Cuba at this Bahia de los Cochines and do away with that swine Castro ... I sincerely do. My prayers are with them ... but not my planes ... Will history say I was a coward? If they succeed, no ... if they fail, yes, Kennedy was a coward ... I wonder?

Chapter Nine

April 13, 1961

"Ratchet, we've finally got movement with our prompting the Attorney General to hasten the principle of Contingency LED-2's deportation. Thessalonian feels that that will be the breaking straw in New Orleans. Just in time for his six-month recontact."

"I take it Contingency LED-3 is double secure, Plato?"

"Yes. Thessalonian will be with those elements in Key West tomorrow. He's reassuring them of Kennedy's unconditional beachhead air support."

It was 12:15 p.m.

An uneaten lunch of sweet ham and tuna salad sat before Major General Marion Armstrong III, the Deputy Director for the Pentagon's Office of Special Operations (OSO). His aide, Corporal Forrestol, had delivered it to him thirty minutes earlier. The General hadn't touched it, his stomach sourly anticipating Plato Smith's call. Plato Smith of the CIA's Directorate of Plans (DDP) Western Hemisphere Division continued.

"You know, Ratchet, the elements of LED-3 are doomed. There could be serious repercussions for all of us, and not just cosmetic ones. Legerdemain must be successful before the restructuring goes too far ... you do agree?"

"It will be," the General said, calming the CIA man, "but as I told you before, you've got to be patient, understand?"

"Yes."

General Armstrong dropped the receiver back in its cradle, inhaled a resistant breath and stepped to his maple cabinet. He pulled the 030601 phone out and after a moment's hesitation, lifted its receiver. Quicker than usual the gruff voice answered, "030601."

"030601—this is Intercept Eagle—Legerdemain contingencies activation status LED-2 and 3 at final sequence awaiting elemental response ... repeat ... Legerdemain contingencies activation status LED-2 and 3 at final sequence awaiting elemental response ... over."

The gruff voice verified, "Intercept Eagle ... received ... Legerdemain contingencies activation status LED-2 and 3 at final sequence awaiting elemental response. Acknowledge. Clear."

As he was hanging up, General Armstrong turned a jittery, disturbed eye to the cold lunch on his desk.

"Fuck sweet ham," he said to himself. "It reminds me of pigs—Bahia de los Cochinos—the Bay of Pigs!"

The gruff voice on the other end of Zero Three Zero Six Zero One sat concentrating in front of his huge communications console, having just disconnected Intercept Eagle's tie-in.

It was 12:35 p.m.

Its hours were long, its work tedious and stressful. It was an MIT graduate with a master's degree in communications electronics. Its clearance by the FCC and NSC were as high as any issued to civilian personnel. Its religion, its love, its devotion was American national security. Its work sacred. Its name was Dodd—Mr. Clemer Dodd.

Legerdemain was just another mystery to him—Intercept Eagle just another voice. He had noticed, though, that call number Zero Three Zero Six Zero One had been designated a very special tie-in, even apart from other Top Secret incodes. As a matter of fact, he had never seen a tie-in given such significant priority and he had been years at his job as Senior Classified Communications Expert for the North American Division of the INTERINPETTO ARMAMENTS CORPORATION (IIPAC).

Half of Clemer Dodd's day was spent here behind MAMA-WEST-IIPAC, a massive communications relay. The other half spent analyzing classified U.S. publications such as the National Intelligence Daily and the Secretary's Morning Summary prepared by the State Department's Bureau of Intelligence and Research for the Secretary of State.

His access to U.S. presidential information was also profound and limitless. Every morning with coffee, Mr. Dodd received by special courier an FTPO report—For the President's Eyes Only—a report full of secret compartmented information meant solely for the President.

Clemer's salary had grown outrageously over the years, but with it had come increasing professional isolation. IIPAC had chosen the Isla de Providencia in the Caribbean as home for its MAMA-WEST communications complex. Located a hundred miles east of Nicaragua's coast and legally a province of Colombia, the Isla de Providencia was not too far nor too close to the United States for IIPAC purposes.

Clemer Dodd's arthritic hand scratched his bald spot as if coaxing a genie out of its lamp, then slid itself downward to the left corner of the steel console, switching on the Pretex Com/A channel.

He began transmitting.

"MAMA-WEST HYPHON to ZURICH ... re Legerdemain ... FM Intercept Eagle ... contingencies activation status LED-2 and 3 at final sequence awaiting elemental response."

There were 45 seconds of silence, then a crackle—a hum—a reply.

"030601, this is Zurich. Receipt of Pretex Com/A transmission confirmed."

Chapter Ten

April 14, 1961

Margareta Jiminez was dreaming of Cuba.

Floating in the azure skies of her dream, looking down at white sails dotted off Cuban coasts, Cuban tobacco crop being harvested by hundreds of black workers, farmhouses with ragged, poor, but happy Cuban kids, Veradaro Beach, the Internacional. She was naked in and out of her dreams when she began feeling something phallic between her legs. Her dream bubble burst into consciousness.

She felt the rough edges of Thessalonian's arm scars reach around for her breasts. She helped them to their destination. He was kissing her neck so she could feel his throat scars also. She turned horizontally, her slanted cafe au lait eyes looking into his freshly open grey eyes with raw, almost hostile, lust.

When she fucked Thessalonian it was like combat. His thin lips would set in an evil mold as he would bend and penetrate her petite body in ways and positions she had never experienced. She would allow him to climax in her or on her in any way he desired. With him Margareta was totally submissive. Sometimes she would talk nasty to him while he was fucking her, "Deeper, harder ... let me wrap my slut's cunt around your monster prick ... " This morning, however, only the base sounds of their conjugation could be heard echoing through their rented Key West, bungalow.

It was 6:00 a.m.

After Thessalonian had spent himself on the cheeks of her ass, she rolled over languidly and rubbed the line of his thin nose with her palm. Even Margareta's attempts at displaying affection came across as too masculine.

"The name Thessalonian—what's the symbolism?"

Thessalonian swept aside her hand and a sandy, blondish spitcurl from his 50-year-old forehead, turned to look at her and answered. His early morning voice was even huskier and more hypnotic than usual.

"A few years ago I read the Thessalonians chapter of the Bible. It made its mark on me. 'In flaming fire taking vengeance on them that know not God and obey not the gospel of our Lord, Jesus Christ. Who shall be punished with everlasting destruction from the presence of the Lord and the glory of his power ... and then shall the wicked be revealed, whom the Lord shall consume with the spirit of his mouth and shall destroy with the brightness of his coming ... that they all might be damned, who believed not the truth, but had pleasure in unrighteousness.' It was the violence of the passage that stirred me, its strength, surety, so I adopted it as a covert ops code name." Thessalonian paused, awaiting comment.

"What's your real name?" Margareta coyly asked, knowing that it was a dangerous question.

Thessalonian was astounded by her stupidity and forwardness. He grabbed her waist and jerked her roughly onto her stomach. He sat his naked frame atop her and spread her legs like a wishbone. She stammered,

"No, no, Thessalonian ... it was just a question, a dumb question ... easy now, easy."

Without preliminaries or lubrication he violated her rectum by jabbing it with his cock. His scarred arms abrasively pinned her body down.

"My real name, whore? Is that what you asked? My real name is Mister Grudge," she was clawing the bed sheets, "Fuck. Mr. Grudge Fuck. Any other brilliant questions?"

Margareta was in too much pain to answer.

The first thing Juan Jimenez saw when he walked into the bungalow was a pile of bloody sheets on the floor next to the couch. He could tell that the couch was the kind that doubled as a foldaway bed. The next thing he saw was Margareta stepping out of the bathroom. Her normally coffee-colored eyes were red and her left hand was on her stomach. Her autumn leaf-brown hair was matted and flat.

It was 9:00 a.m.

"Are you okay, Margareta?" her father asked with dire concern.

"Plato—Thessalonian. How are we on Contingency LED-2?"

"All set, Thessalonian. The attorney general's due to grab Nuccia and deport him today."

Thessalonian's wide smile could be seen through the filthy glass of the Key West phone booth.

"Where to?"

"Tequicigalpa, Honduras."

"Fantastic. I'll leave for there tonight. Are the bombers ready?"

"They'll go off on schedule, Thessalonian."

"Oh, and Plato ... any answer to my query on Charlie Nuccia's unidentified hitter?"

"Our sources say that he's Nuccia's top money courier, nicknamed "Angler." Nothing further yet. We are cross-referencing police files, though. Remember now, when you meet Nuccia this time you've got to pull him in on Legerdemain. There will probably be no second chance. He will never be as angry at the government as he will be when you see him in Honduras, deported. Also be sure and offer him entry back into the States and anything else we can feasibly deliver, understood?"

"Yes. No problem. That's it?"

"That's it."

"Talk to you after I've met with Nuccia."

"Good luck, Thessalonian."

Charlie Nuccia and Johnny Sincelli were enjoying their beignets at the Cafe du Monde across from Jackson Square in New Orleans. Three times a month for the last five months Charlie and Johnny had gone through this ritual.

It was 10:50 a.m. and in thirty minutes Charlie was scheduled to check in with the Immigration and Naturalization Service located at the Masonic Temple building on St. Charles Avenue. Reporting to the INS three times a month was a condition of the agreement Charlie had entered into with the government until his alien resident status was either granted or he was deported.

The check-ins usually went smoothly.

This sunny morning, however, as he drank his last sip of espresso, adjusted his porkpie hat on his head, and licked his fingers, his underworld mastermind was filled with foreboding. Without revealing it as such to Johnny, he politely wiped the crumbs from his mouth and followed his attorney to Jake's 1958 black Cadillac waiting across the street. They drove away.

It wasn't until Jake turned the car down St. Charles Avenue that Charlie expressed his apprehension.

"Johnny, we don't have anything to worry about, do we?"

Johnny stopped rubbing his mustache long enough to assure his boss of their legal perspective.

"Charlie, they don't have a legitimate leg to stand on. Rest easy. Five months of these check-ins and you still let your blood pressure rise. Rest easy, Don Nuccia."

Charlie turned his now exposed head of dark curlets and stared at his trusted *consigliere*. "Sure, Johnny, I'm okay ... sure."

Jake pulled up to the side entrance of the Masonic Temple building. Charlie got out. Jake and Johnny waited in the Cadillac.

The INS office within the Temple building was relatively bare of furnishings, with just two desks and four hard metal chairs. Charlie walked to the desk where his check-in sheet was normally laid. It wasn't there!

A suited official that Charlie had never seen before entered the office and approached him.

"Mr. Nuccia," he motioned with his arms, "please be seated."

"Who are you?" Charlie sputtered. "I'm here fa the INS check-in and that's all." Sparks of panic had begun to ignite within the Top Man.

"Mr. Nuccia, please ... please be seated."

Charlie sat down uncomfortably in the metal chair nearest the wall. As he did, four identically dressed men, all wearing fedoras, whom Charlie assumed were more immigration officers, stepped into the room.

Charlie Nuccia was trapped. He looked over to the exit door furtively as the suited man behind the desk continued talking.

"This is a letter from the U.S. Justice Department, Mr. Nuccia." The suited man held up a piece of paper. "It states that the U.S. Justice Department, after an extensive investigation, has discovered that you were born in Tequicigalpa, Honduras and are therefore a naturalized citizen of Honduras. These gentlemen here are responsible for deporting you immediately back to your city and country of birth."

Charlie stood, outraged.

"What the fuck are you talking about? I've never even fucking been ta Honduras!"

The four men surrounded the Top Man of the New Orleans underworld, subdued him, handcuffed him, and escorted him outside. They walked by Jake's Cadillac. Jake, in the front seat, looked to his father and swung his right hand to his shoulder holster.

"Say the word, Pops."

Johnny reached for Jake's hand and calmly patted it, saying simply, "No." He stepped out of the car yelling.

"EXCUSE ME! ... EXCUSE ME! GENTLEMEN! Mr. Nuccia is my client. My name is Johnny Sincelli, Attorney-at-Law. What in the world do you think you are doing?"

The suited man farthest back turned to answer Johnny.

"We're doing what Robert Kennedy as Attorney General of the United States and as head of the U.S. Department of Justice has instructed us to do. We're moving this sack of Italian shit back to Tequicigalpa, Honduras, and if you don't like it, you high-priced Mafia mouthpiece, sue us."

He handed Johnny a copy of the letter that had been shown to Charlie. Johnny read it.

"Wait just a minute! What are you talking about—born in Honduras? This is a travesty of justice. You can't do this. He has no money. He doesn't even have a goddamn toothbrush. You'll never get away with this!"

The suited immigration officer sat Charlie down in the back of a New Orleans police car and sat down beside him. The blue and white police car then pulled out of and away from the Masonic Temple/INS lot.

Johnny ran back to Jake's Cadillac, got in it and screeched out of the same lot, behind what now had become a row of police cars. The sirens and lights of each were flashing wildly.

"We've got to get Vince," Johnny told Jake and added as an afterthought, "They must have forged a phony birth certificate, Jake. I don't think Charlie's ever even been to Honduras. Step on it, son!"

"Pops, I can't get any closer."

Their black Cadillac was directly behind the last police car. The entire motorcade was doing at least seventy miles an hour.

As they neared Moissant Field the last two motorcade patrol cars stopped suddenly, almost sending Jake and Johnny into a tailspin. The two police cars then attempted backing and turning to form a roadblock. Johnny yelled.

"FLOOR IT, SON!"

Jake floored it, reacting out loud, "Let's Draaaggg!"

The big, black, powerful, 1958 Cadillac barely squeezed between the two blocking cars. Johnny caught a glimpse of the motorcade up ahead driving towards the corner of the airfield where a solitary immigration plane sat. Their Cadillac skidded to a stop about 100 feet from the plane. Johnny leaped out, running for Charlie. A half dozen uniforms tried to stop him. He cried, "I've got to see my client! I DEMAND TO SEE MY CLIENT!"

The farmer's build of Johnny Sincelli was not easy to contain.

The immigration officer who had read the deportation letter to Charlie stepped forward. He looked at the blank faces of his co-workers and became suddenly fearful of screwing the entire deportation up. He walked over to Johnny Sincelli.

"You have sixty seconds, Sincelli. Sixty seconds with your client!!"

Johnny broke free from the suits that were holding him, brushed his clothes and walked quickly to the plane stairs and Charlie.

Charlie asked him if they should speak in Italian. Johnny told him he didn't think that was necessary. He did advise whispering, though.

Charlie began whispering angry but concise orders.

"Johnny, get Vincenzo ready. I'll send word as ta my exact location—he's ta fly down immediately—tell Guiseppe ta handle things in my absence, ailing or no he's the only underboss I have. Tell my other brothers to follow Guiseppe."

The sounds of planes landing on and departing from Moissant Field in the background made it difficult for Charlie to continue whispering. He kept trying, however, his normally impassive but now strained face right next to Johnny's mustache.

"Last—tell your stepbrother Frank to tell Tony Bartello in Lake Charles to take Vince off the Four Seasons payroll. His name's not to appear anywhere, anymore ... got it?!"

Johnny nodded, confidently.

The main suited immigration officer now stepped in between Charlie Nuccia and Johnny Sincelli. Their minute was up.

Johnny took a last look at his shackled boss, waved goodbye to him and walked back to his son's Cadillac.

Watching the immigration plane with Charlie Nuccia aboard taxi down the runway brought tears to Johnny's eyes.

Someone was going to pay!

"This has got to be it ... C'mon ... C'mon!"

Vince was in search of that magical Baccarat nine.

It was 12:30 p.m. and he was finding it difficult to keep his mind on his game even though, at this time of day, there were few distractions at Lafitte's Westport Club.

Since his return from Cuba in November he had found it impossible to engross himself wholeheartedly in anything. Charlie had put him back on his courier's route in January only to remove him from it in February. It was as if his Top Man couldn't decide what to do with him. Charlie had assured Vince time and time again that he did not hold him responsible for the failed Cuban assassination plots, considering the subterfuge of Marco Romano's people, but still the failures haunted Vince. Five months later and he was determined, now more than ever, to figure a way to make it up to Charlie Nuccia. When Johnny had told Vince back in late November that Thessalonian had offered to help them whack President Kennedy as compensation for the government's double-cross, Vince argued that they should agree and that they should allow Vince to be the triggerman. He assured Charlie that his rifle wouldn't break this time. Charlie had been unresponsive, though, said he smelled a setup. Vince had tried to convince him otherwise but to no avail. Charlie was immovable even after learning that his ex-Havana casino partner and assassination intermediary, Manuel Marinello, had died as a result of capture and torture by Castro's secret police. Charlie's mistrust of Thessalonian was too deep, Johnny had said.

So Vince had taken to Baccarat and Scotch and the blues. His French Quarter apartment was a mess, as was his social life. Friendly phone calls from Mona and Mario in Chicago went unreturned.

As he looked up now, though, from his two-card deal and one-card draw into the dimly lit elegant recesses of the Westport and saw Johnny Sincelli running towards him, he knew instinctively that his luck had changed.

"Vin ... Vin!" The lawyer's big arms were flailing like a crazy man's through the noon hour emptiness of Lafitte's.

Vince stood and moved to the corner of the Baccarat pit. "What is it, Mr. Johnny?!"

By the time Johnny reached Vince, he was winded. "Vin ... they ... got ... Charlie! The INS! ... when he went to check in ... we've just come ... from the airport. They fucking kidnapped him!"

Vince stumbled up the steps out of the pit. "They got Charlie!? Goddamn!? C'mon, Johnny, let's go in the office." Vince opened the door and turned on the leather-bound desk lamp. He led Johnny behind Charlie's mahogany desk.

"Vince, Charlie gave me some orders for you," he caught his breath, "He's being deported to Tequicigalpa, Honduras. As soon as he sends word of his exact location, which he will probably do tonight, you're to fly there and meet him. Also you're to forget about your Four Seasons job as of today."

"Charlie said that?!" Vince retorted.

"Sure did, Vince ... said for me to call my stepbrother Frank in Lake Charles and for him to tell his cousin Tony Bartello to take you off the payroll." The attorney wiped his fevered brow with the edge of his hand. "Charlie needs you, Vince, someone's going to die behind this shit. I think you know that."

Vince's five-foot-eleven-inch frame, wire taut with excitement, moved to the phone in the bookcase across the office. He lifted the receiver.

"Betsy, get the New Orleans branch of Pandora Aviation

at Lakefront on the phone. Tell them I need the Cessna 182/Skylane—not the 172, the 182. Takeoff tomorrow at daylight."

Jake charged in just as Vince was hanging up.

"Vin, you should have seen my Caddy ... man, was she screamin'!"

"Come on in, Jake. Come on, sit down. Why don't you and your father tell me exactly what happened," Vince suggested with a smile.

A smile of renewed opportunity ... and second chances!

Thessalonian instantly felt another presence besides Margareta's in the Key West bungalow. He stepped through the front door on his tiptoes. Margareta was sitting at the kitchen table, her eyes still red, her hair still a mess. He drew out his .45-caliber pistol from beneath his black leather biker's jacket, half expecting to see a Cuban exile or two preparing to avenge Margareta's honor. All he saw was Juan Jimenez walk out of the kitchen with a glass of water. His black, rectangular mustache was not smiling as it had been when he had greeted Thessalonian in Guatemala.

It was 1:00 p.m.

Thessalonian quickly put the .45 back under his jacket.

"Mr. Jimenez, I wasn't expecting you until later today. When did you arrive?"

Juan set the water down in front of Margareta and forced himself to be polite to this CIA man who he knew had just abused his daughter. A man he needed desperately to help him retake his beloved Cuba. A man whom after the invasion he would kill!

"Southern Air Transport brought me in from New York a few hours ago from the United Nations Assembly meet I was at," Juan said. "Upon arriving I made radio contact with the Blager and the Barbara J and the five merchant ships with our other men. They have made much progress since leaving Puerto Cabezas, Nicaragua. They should be in position by dawn on the 17th."

Thessalonian's gray eyes squinted, detecting the coldness in Juan's response. He slowly walked over to the foldaway bed where he and Margareta had been earlier that morning and sat down on it, determined to dispel the atmospheric pressure between him and Juan.

"Mr. Jimenez, tomorrow six U.S. bombers, piloted by loyal patriots of your Cuban Revolutionary Directorate, will bomb three Cuban air bases. Two days after that your troops will land on the thirty-six milewide beachhead of Bahia de los Cochinos. At that point our President Kennedy, as promised, will supply you with unconditional beachhead air support from nearby aircraft carriers." He paused. "Now, Mr. Jimenez, the future of your Cuba will be decided with these acts." The logic being conveyed by Thessalonian was indisputable. "Therefore, it would not make any sense for a personal problem between me and your daughter to come between me and you. After all, she's a big girl and tough to boot. Just ask Rigoberto." He grinned sarcastically.

Juan Jimenez, maintaining his composure, nodded his concurrence and sat on the opposite end of the foldaway bed. He reached into his pants pocket and retrieved an invasion map. Margareta, too, pulled her kitchen table chair close to the couch. She couldn't imagine how Thessalonian had found out about Rigoberto unless one of his American paramilitary trainers, who had been at the Quazelenango camp, had kept an eye on her for him. Of course, she concluded, Thessalonian had his grudge-fucking eyes and ears everywhere.

Thessalonian began his briefing. "Okay, as you've just confirmed, your 1500 men aboard the Blager and the Barbara J will be in position at dawn on the 17th. There will be three landing craft for vehicles and four for personnel. We estimate around seventy two tons of supplies. The bulk of your men, however, will go ashore in small fiberglass boats. The two main landings will be at Giron—blue beach—here," he pointed to the map, "and Playa Larga—red beach—here. There will be a parachute drop near Covadonga. All the landing zones will be marked before time by American frogmen teams. It will probably take days for Castro to react to the landings. Since you and Margareta will be on the spearhead at Giron-blue beach, there is a possibility that you will encounter initial resistance of about a hundred Cuban militia. Then again there may be no Cuban troops in the vicinity. Twenty of my paramilitaries will be spread evenly at both points, but I won't be there, Mr. Jimenez."

"What?!"

Thessalonian stood abruptly and walked towards the door of the bungalow.

"I said, I won't be there. Tonight I'll be leaving. I must make sure our bombers and your pilots take off on schedule, tomorrow."

Juan Jimenez was visibly upset. His overweight squatness reeled towards Thessalonian.

"How will that look to my people? I ask you, how will that look, amigo?" he grunted the last word with contempt.

Thessalonian was quiet for a moment. He had pushed his luck enough tonight, taunting Jimenez about Margareta. Thessalonian needed now to make his sudden departure as easy as possible, maintaining enough stead with Juan so as to be able to influence the course of his revenge. A revenge Thessalonian would promote after Juan's upcoming Bay of Pigs invasion failed. A failure which Thessalonian would lay squarely on the shoulders of John F. Kennedy and Kennedy's refusal to provide full beachhead air support. Thessalonian walked up to Juan and embraced him.

"You, too, my friend, you, too, must take a back seat in the fighting. We must not lose you."

"Bah, Bah, Thessalonian," he wheezed as he pulled away from the scarred CIA man. "I'll be the first hombre on the beach, the first one, with my brave daughter right beside me."

Thessalonian dramatically lowered his head, intimating great respect for this Cuban fanatic and his daughter, when in reality he thought they were fools. Thessalonian's bowed head made him appear for a brief second to be praying. He looked back up.

"God speed, Juan." Then to Margareta, "God speed, my beautiful one." With that, he turned and walked out the door. Reminding himself as he walked into the pleasant Key West afternoon to give two orders to his paramilitaries.

One—do a natural battlefield kill of Margareta during the invasion.

Two—keep Juan's ass out of harm's way; bring him back alive.

He stopped and looked up at the beautiful Florida Key

skyscape, confident that Contingency LED-3 was moving along just fine.

Now to Honduras!

Chapter Eleven

April 15, 1961

"Remember when Mario first pushed us together at the Amno Antilly? I thought you were a car salesman. All I could think was, 'Oh God, not another car salesman!' "

The long distance operator interrupted the line. "Is this Chicago?"

Mona countered in an exasperated tone, "Operator, I am talking to New Orleans now. We made the connection about ten minutes ago ... could we have a little privacy, please?"

A brief delay. "Of course, thank you, Chicago."

It was 4:30 a.m.

Vince kidded her, "So how many car salesmen have you had, Mona?"

"Ralphhheee!" she protested from the Chicago end of their long distance connection.

Vince continued, "Listen, baby, I'm sorry I haven't been up to see you or call you in the last few months."

"Nine months, honey, and nine months off and on just ain't gonna cut it."

Vince appreciated Mona's honesty. In that way, more than any other, she was like Rosalie.

"Have you been faithful?" Vince asked, not really wanting to know.

Without hesitation Mona answered, "Of course I have, baby. Mario has kept me posted. He said you had been out of the country for a while, then tied up in New Orleans. Baby, are you married?"

Vince chuckled.

"No, Mona, it's just that the claims adjusting business has been hectic as hell. I've been traveling a lot."

"You know, honey, Ralphie," she said, the tone of her voice soft, "I even sleep with your diamond necklace on, and I've got a whole new collection of nightgowns for you. Please come see me and teach me some more Sicilian."

Vince was surprised.

"You pronounced that perfectly. You must have been practicing."

"I have been. When will I see you, Ralphie? I miss you something terrible."

Mona was melting Vince's heart. She continued, "Do you realize I haven't seen you since the Excaliber back in July of last year, honey? I'm begging you."

Her plea was irresistible. It was useless. Vince wanted her in his life as much as she wanted him.

"Okay, Mona, this is what I want you to do. I want you to quit your waitress job and go talk to Carmine at the Sandhurst Shopping Complex in Mt. Prospect. Tell him I referred you to him, and that I want him to give you a job there in the management office. I want you to learn everything there is to know about managing a shopping center. Then in six months, baby, I'll see to it that you're transferred to New Orleans. You'll move in with me and have a new career besides."

Her shock was evident by the silence on the phone line.

"Are you serious, Ralphie? My God, baby, you want me to come and live with you?"

Vince was tickled by her response.

"Mona, I told you, I love you. But if you stay with me, you have to have ways to occupy your time, because I'm going to be busy and away sometimes. You'll have to learn to accept some things about my work. Okay?"

Mona was overjoyed.

"You got it, Ralphie, you got me. I'll see this, what's his name, Carmine, today. Yes, I accept, I do. Is this like ... a proposal, baby?"

"Yea, I guess so. We'll see. Come live with me, do good with your new career and we'll see. Fair enough?"

Mona was gushing.

"Oh, baby, honey, Ralphie, I love you, I love you. Six months and I'll be there and I'll be the best shopping center manager New Orleans has ever seen ... I love you!"

Vince was smiling.

"Mia amore, I love you, too. I've got to go now. I've still got some traveling ahead of me but our commitment and our promise stands, no matter what. You have my word, baby. Okay?"

"I love you, Ralphie. Six months. I'll see you. Bye-bye."

"Bye, sweet cheeks."

Vince hung up the phone, raised his nude body out of his second-floor French Quarter apartment bed and walked to the window. His flat was located on Chartres Street, in the heart of the Vieux Carre. Surrounded by Iberville, Bienville, Conti, Toulouse, St. Peter, St. Ann and Dumaine Streets, its location provided Vince a clear streetlighted view of pedestrians and otherwise suspicious characters that might want to surprise him in the dark. As he stood now by the window in the shadow of his abode, naked, his black wavy hair tousled, he couldn't resist grinning.

His primary reason for calling Mona, besides the obvious of expressing his love, was to be stimulated sexually. Like a gladiator before entering the arena, requiring a last imaginary touch of female flesh. He could picture her in Chicago, rubbing her perfectly tapered legs as they talked, maybe even licking her lips in anticipation of nestling with his own. When she moved down in six months he was going to have to tell her his real name. It would be impossible to maintain this Ralphie Bosco charade being shacked up with her.

"Rosalie," he whispered to himself, his mind drifting, "I waited as long as I could. I hope you understand. It's been almost seven years." He made a vow to himself to bring fresh roses to her grave when he returned from Honduras.

Honduras!

Damn, he'd better get his ass in gear! His departure was scheduled for dawn. The plane he had requested, a Cessna 182/Skylane, larger than either his Four Seasons Corporate Cessna 172 or the Piper Cub he'd flown from Cuba five months ago, was fueled and waiting for him at Lakefront Airport. Johnny had received word from Tequicigalpa last night as to Charlie's exact location. Vince surmised that the flight today would be technically similar to the flight he had made from Cuba, so last night he had rewritten those flight specifications.

He quickly moved away from the window towards the bathroom. He lifted his shaving gear out of the old-fashioned canister on his dresser drawer enroute. Standing in front of the mirror, splashing shaving cream on his face, he began to hum childishly:

Laughing Mirror, laugh—at my ugliness
Laughing Mirror, laugh—laugh if you must
Pretty Angels love me
So laugh, Mirror, laugh
In hell we will meet
In hell we will meet!

Report to: Directorate of Plans (DDP) Western Hemisphere Division Central Intelligence Agency

TOP SECRET MEMORANDUM TELEX

THIS MORNING AT O-FIVE HUNDRED HOURS, APRIL 15, 1961, SIX U.S. B-26 BOMBER AIRCRAFT TOOK OFF FROM OPA LOCKA, FLORIDA PILOTED BY CUBAN NATIONALS / STOP / THE AIRCRAFT WERE EQUIPPED FOR BOMBING AND STRAFING RUNS / STOP / AT APPROXIMATELY SIX HUNDRED HOURS THE SIX AIRCRAFT BOMBED THE FOLLOWING TARGETS—1 FAR AIRBASE IN HAVANA—2 FAR AIRBASES IN SANTIAGO.

THEY RETURNED TO OPA LOCKA, FLORIDA AT EIGHT HUNDRED HOURS APRIL 15, 1961 / STOP / ESTIMATE HALF OF CASTRO'S FAR AIR FORCE DESTROYED.

It didn't take long after landing in Tequicigalpa, Honduras, for Thessalonian to discover Charlie Nuccia's exact location. The Mafia boss was staying at the Camino, undoubtedly Tequicigalpa's finest hotel.

Thessalonian decided to register at the same hotel. His cover here would be that of an affluent plantation owner. He had dressed the part, distinctly American-turned-Latin uppercrust adventurer. He wore a straw sun hat, white suit, and supported himself with an ivory-knobbed cane. His brownish-blonde eyebrows were darkened and his cheeks were cotton-stuffed, just as both had been at his last two meetings with Nuccia.

It was 2:00 p.m.

He had flown to Tequicigalpa from Key West last night aboard a U.S. military transport plane. Ironically, it had been the same plane that had transported Marsh, Taylor and Holt—SFG Team Legerdemain—from Laos nine months earlier. Thessalonian had rested on the overseas flight, aware that his next encounter with Nuccia would be critical to Legerdemain.

Thessalonian had been truly baffled by Nuccia back in November when Nuccia had refused to even discuss killing Kennedy. Especially after Thessalonian had led Nuccia to believe that JFK had reneged on their Cuban arrangement.

Charlie Nuccia had reacted prudently then, but by now, after having been deported ruthlessly to this illiterate land, Thessalonian predicted Nuccia's desire for revenge would be all consuming.

As Thessalonian sat on his Hotel Camino bed, wading through speculation after speculation, a knock sounded on the door. He had left a message at the hotel desk for Senor Nuccia—requesting that the esteemed Senor meet with him as soon as possible. The message referred to the desired meeting as a six-month re-contact. He assumed, therefore, that the gentle knocking now was a reply from Nuccia.

He had assumed wrong.

The instant Thessalonian released the latch, a huge Spanish Indian Mestizo rammed inside. He clutched Thessalonian's throat with his left hand and swung his right elbow up to Thessalonian's chin. With a resounding crack Thessalonian fell. The attack and blow had startled the CIA man but had not rendered him unconscious. He could feel his scarred arms being stretched and his white-suited body being dragged across the hotel floor to another room. When the dragging stopped, he could hear voices.

"This is the one for the Senor?"

"Si, this is the one."

Twenty seconds later Thessalonian heard the sound of what was probably the door to an adjoining room open and close. He heard footsteps coming toward him. His barely opened microdot pupils, however, distinguished nothing but a blur.

Charlie Nuccia was standing over the CIA man, looking down at him, wondering if his prior suspicions had been wrong; that this Thessalonian character was more than what he appeared to be—a killer, perhaps. Because now, lying on the floor, dressed like some ridiculous banana man, Thessalonian looked exactly like the picture of a simple Ivy League bureaucrat trying to play spy. If this were the case, then maybe ... just maybe ... they could do business, Charlie thought ... maybe.

As seconds became minutes and Thessalonian's vision became clearer, the first face he saw, half kneeling on the floor next to him, was Charlie Nuccia's.

"Ugh ... Mr. Nuccia." He tried to raise himself, feigning more grogginess than he actually felt, acting more vulnerable than he was.

"Thatssa okay, you're okay. My Indian friend here just got a little carried away. Really. Sorry, he didn't know who you were." Charlie paused, showing much more concern than he felt, with his hand on Thessalonian's shoulder, comforting him.

Thessalonian groaned and managed to sit up slightly.

"Mr. Nuccia, you said to contact you in six months. It's been about six months."

Charlie stood abruptly and walked to the door, motioning the Indian inside the room and the Honduran guarding outside, away. He walked back inside the room and looked at Thessalonian.

"How did you know so fast where I was?"

Thessalonian, still on the floor, held his middle-aged blonde head in his hands as if wrestling with a terrific headache. He quickly sucked the cotton wads further back into his mouth and answered.

"Remember, Mr. Nuccia, I work for the CIA. I simply called a contact of mine at the INS. They told me Tequicigalpa, so here I am."

"I take it you want ta know if I've reconsidered your compensation offer dealing with Kennedy?"

Thessalonian hesitated.

"Look, Mr. Nuccia, frankly I don't care what you do. All I want to know is that I'm released from my obligation to you and your people. I offered Kennedy to cover my ass. He fucked me and made me look bad in front of some real serious people—namely you, Romano, and Anacondini ... so, to hell with him. If you want him I can hand him to you. If not, then just release me from my commitment and you'll never see me again—ever!"

Even Thessalonian was amazed at how convincingly this lie had fallen off of his thin lips.

Charlie Nuccia knew that he would have to make a decision about Kennedy soon. There were so many considerations beyond vendetta, beyond Cuba, and Vince; he had to know if Vince was still willing to pull the trigger.

"Okay, listen carefully, my CIA friend. I want you ta go back ta your room and stay there. Send out fa food, don't make any attempt to leave. Within 24 hours you'll know my decision. But do not leave your room, *capisce*? If you do you're dead, *capisce*?"

Thessalonian offered Charlie a soft-willed smile as he stood. He wobbled dumbly, adding just the right touch of weakness to his performance.

"I understand, Mr. Nuccia. I'll be there, waiting."

Charlie Nuccia watched Thessalonian's back as he exited. The phrase *Gli oochi di un pugnale*—the eyes of a dagger—seemed misplaced now.

Thessalonian was scared, and the more cowed Thessalonian seemed, the more comfortable Charlie became with him.

Maybe they could do business after all. Maybe.

As Vince's 182/Skylane taxied to the rusty airshed at Tequicigalpa City Airport he yawned. It had been a long and tedious flight from New Orleans. There had been turbulence over the Gulf of Mexico and thunderstorms in Merida, in the Yucatan, where he had refueled.

It was 6:30 p.m.

A timeworn automobile moved swiftly towards Vince's plane. Vince identified it tentatively as a 1950 Pontiac Catalina. There was a huge Spanish Indian Mestizo driving it. He parked about thirty yards away and remained in the car.

Vince hurriedly gathered his gear into his new black exercise bag, locked the cockpit, and ran toward it.

After having heard the details of Charlie's deportation from Johnny and Jake yesterday, Vince had organized himself. He had bought some new clothes, including a new flight jacket, much sturdier than his old windbreaker, and a new black exercise bag. It contained amongst his toiletries four new weapons. A Colt .38 Special, an M-3 submachine gun, a Smith & Wesson .357, and a British-made Sten submachine gun. He had also done some private research yesterday on Honduras. He knew that the Mestizos comprised 90% of the population. Therefore, if Charlie had hired a batch of them like the driver of this Pontiac, then Vince's "Top Man" was safe. Money makes you king in a country like this and King Nuccia had arrived. He opened the car door.

"Senor Nuccia's driver?"

The gigantic Indian silently nodded. Vince got in.

The Hotel Camino in downtown Tequicigalpa was a pleasant surprise for Vince. Unlike the shanties and poor subsistence farms that they had passed on the incoming drive, the Hotel Camino looked civilized. It was not Miami's Fontainebleau, but it wasn't bad.

The Mestizo pulled the Pontiac up to the hotel's front entrance. A slight drizzle was falling as Vince grabbed his bag and followed the Indian upstairs. The lobby appeared nearly deserted.

Vince had a sense of deja vu stepping into Charlie's room. The "Top Man" of the New Orleans underworld was seated just as he had been at the Fontainebleau, with his back to Vince. The only difference being that now there were no oceanview sliding glass balcony windows for Charlie to gaze out of. In fact, there were no windows at all. Charlie stood, cigar in hand, just as he had nine months ago.

"Vincenzo, how was your flight?"

"Fine, Don Nuccia."

They hugged and pecked.

"Vince, come over here." Charlie guided Vince to the adjoining room where Thessalonian had lain, beaten, hours ago. He motioned Vince to sit on the edge of the bed as he pulled a straightback chair next to him. Vince's Mestizo driver had remained outside.

"Charlie, is that all you have … one guard?" Vince had expected more.

"No, Vince, there's another, but he's guarding another room."

"Another room?"

"Thatssa right, Vince," Charlie said as he chewed the end of his cigar, then calmly added, "Thessalonian's here."

"Thessalonian?! How the fuck did he find out where you were so quick, Charlie?" Vince was more than surprised.

"He is CIA, Vin ... said he had an INS connection. Vince, he's scared shitless. He just wants out." Charlie was noting Vince's reactions very carefully.

"What does he mean out?! He owes us ... big time." Vince did not want to lose his second chance at making things right with Charlie. He knew that there would not be a third.

"Vince, he claims that the Kennedy offer was just something he came up with ta cover his ass." Charlie's short, stocky build barely contained itself in the hotel chair.

"But, Charlie, what do you want to do?" Vince was selling now. "It's not just that Kennedy reneged on the Castro hit, but indirectly he almost caused a war between us and Romano, almost caused me to get my Sicilian ass shot off and was responsible for Manuel getting killed. Charlie, you should have seen the look in Manuel's eyes when I left him in Fuegas. It was fucking pathetic. Then Kennedy spits on us after he's elected and now his cocksucking brother has deported you. Ever since the McClellan committee hearings that son-of-a-bitch has been after you. So, Charlie, you may not feel a vendetta towards them but they sure as hell are acting like they have a vendetta against you."

Charlie seethed with rage listening to Vince's litany of Kennedy betrayals and dirty deals.

"Vin, months ago you tried ta convince me of this same thing, that Kennedy should be taught a lesson. That we should deal with him as personally as he seems ta want ta deal with us. Today, sitting in this hell with my wife, my daughters, and my brothers worried sick, I'm inclined ta agree with you."

Charlie Nuccia looked at the cigar in his hand, puffed, then popped the magical question to Vince.

"If you agree to handle it, Vince, I'll approve it. But it's not an order. It's strictly a request. What do you think?"

Vince smiled a big smile.

"Charlie ... Don Nuccia, I would be honored." All Vince really wanted was to never again disappoint this man who had saved his life after Rosalie's death. This man who had put wings on his soul and taught it to fly.

Charlie rose and began slapping the palm of his left hand with the back of his right. Smoke rings circled upward from the cigar now in his mouth.

"Okay, Vince, Thessalonian's going ta have ta be completely involved."

"You sound like you're beginning to trust him, Charlie."

"Let's just say I've seen the enemy and he ain't shit—nobody can pretend to be as scared as Thessalonian was this afternoon. The Indian slammed the piss out of him and dragged him in here. You should have seen it, Vin." Charlie kept slapping his hands.

"But ta answer your question—yes, I trust him ... enough ta hand us Kennedy. Let's bring him in."

Charlie called to the Mestizo and ordered him to retrieve the man from the other room. Vince took off his flight jacket and removed from the small of his back his new .22 Ruger pistol. He had discarded the old one after having shot Luigi with it in Cuba. Charlie watched Vince intently, knowing that Vince was fast becoming his most trusted *solidato* and that the historical task Vince was about to undertake was indeed awesome.

Thessalonian had speculated correctly. The final straw for Charlie Nuccia had been the insulting manner in which his deportation to Honduras had taken place. Until then Charlie had not been sufficiently riled to take action against the President of the United States.

Old school for Charlie Nuccia meant simply tradition. A tradition steeped half in reality, half in myth as he had cryptically indicated to Vince at the Fontainebleau. A tradition that held disrespect and dishonor as, by far, the most serious offenses possible against a member of the Unione Siciliano, La Cosa Nostra. He had always tried to conduct his business as a gentleman, as a man of honor like the legendary Don Vito Cascioferro, but when pushed, as he had been by the deportation, he could be wholly unmerciful.

Immediately upon entering Nuccia's room Thessalonian recognized the handsome Mafioso who had driven him to the airport in Miami after the Fontainebleau meet. The Mafioso Plato Smith had referred to as Angler, sitting on the edge of the bed.

He wished he knew Angler's real name and wondered if Plato Smith had cross-referenced those police files yet. Charlie Nuccia was standing next to a straightback chair with his hands folded, cigar burning between his fingers. His impassive face revealed nothing. Thessalonian, through the corners of his gray eyes, watched impatiently for the spics beside him to leave. The longer they were there, the harder it was to keep himself from killing them. Of course, he would never allow his character to lose control like that, but it was difficult.

Charlie dismissed the Mestizo guards imperiously, but did not offer Thessalonian a chair. Thessalonian knew the instant Nuccia began to speak that a decision had been reached.

"Thessalonian, when you came ta us—me, Marco and Anacondini—at the Fontainebleau last July, you made guarantees that you were unable ta keep. I warned you then that ta double-cross us would be a serious fuckup, that no one was immune from a bullet. Four months later we were betrayed by you and the new President. Then you offer us as compensation the new President's life. I wasn't sure at that time whether ta trust you or not so I let your counteroffer stand for five or six months. Now a decision has been made. I'm going to accept your offer, under certain conditions."

Thessalonian tried to calm his elation. Contingency LED-2 was working perfectly. Charlie turned to Vince.

"Vince—"

Without having had to discuss it with Charlie, Vince knew what was expected of him. He rose from the bed and walked directly in front of Thessalonian and stopped. As fast as fire and true to his nickname, Angler, Vince punched the CIA man solidly in the rib cage. Thessalonian could hear his bones crunching but was helpless to retaliate. He could not reveal himself as the killer he really was ... just yet. He fell to his knees in excruciating pain.

"That was fa your last failed guarantee. You're lucky it wasn't a bullet." Charlie puffed on his cigar. "There better not ever be another!"

Charlie wanted to test Thessalonian a final time before they proceeded. A killer would have blocked Vince's punch. A bureaucrat would have stood and taken it stupidly. Thessalonian had taken it stupidly. Charlie was convinced.

"Now, Thessalonian, what's your real name, home address and exact position within the CIA?"

Thessalonian was gasping, buying time. He wanted this "Angler" fuck to really think he had done some damage. Nuccia had called him Vince—Vince. He would remember that—Vince ... Angler.

He picked himself up from his knees slowly, tiring of the role he was having to play. Fuck being a bureaucrat! He could smash these hoods anytime he chose, like so many cockroaches! Thessalonian's thin lips set in an evil mold, just as they did when he was fucking Margareta. He answered Nuccia.

"My name is Barker—Miles Barker, and I'm on special attachment to the Mission and Programs staff—Directorate of Plans. Normally I work for the Office of Strategic Research under the Directorate of Intelligence. I live in Alexandria, Virginia—1414 Bluebonnet—Apartment 2093."

Charlie turned the butt of his cigar and used it as a pointer to emphasize his point to Thessalonian.

"You'd better be telling us the truth, Thessalonian."

Thessalonian nodded, straightening his legs to stand.

"If you want Kennedy, you'd better ease up on me. With me you got him, without me you don't. I'm no good to you if I'm beaten half dead."

Watching Thessalonian lift himself Vince had noticed the scars on his arms.

"Where did those come from?" Vince asked, pointing to them.

"Car accident when I was a kid."

"Where was that?" Vince questioned.

"Carbondale, Pennsylvania. Look ... what do you want? John Kennedy or my life story?" Thessalonian was trying to show just the right touch of indignation.

Charlie Nuccia stood and turned his back to both men, deep in thought.

"Okay, all right, Thessalonian," he said, paused, turning back, "this Office of Strategic Research—your normal job—what does it involve?"

"We structure scenarios, spy games, and contingencies all day long, Mr. Nuccia."

Charlie spoke, rapidly understanding.

"And let me guess, you have used their equipment and planned a scenario ta take Kennedy out—just in preparation for this meeting?"

Thessalonian realized again that he was going to have to be careful. Charlie Nuccia was not to be underestimated.

"Yes, I have, Mr. Nuccia."

"And I bet you've even come up with a clever code name to call it ... Operation so and so. Am I correct?"

"Yes."

Charlie and Vince looked at each other with the realization that Thessalonian, too, was not to be underestimated.

"And the name—what is it?" Nuccia asked the CIA man.

Thessalonian replied.

"It will be called Legerdemain, Mr. Nuccia, which means sleight of hand. L-E-G-E-R-D-E-M-A-I-N. Legerdemain!"

Chapter Twelve

April 17, 1961

Juan and Margareta Jimenez were sitting cross-legged in a small fiberglass boat. Also seated in the boat were two of Thessalonian's American paramilitaries and six Cuban Revolutionary Directorate members.

It was 5:00 a.m.

The Garcia Line Ship that Juan's exile invasion unit had launched from an hour ago was anchored a very short distance from the resort of Giron, Cuba, invasion code name "blue beach." Juan Jimenez was the operational commander of the blue beach exile invasion force.

As they approached the Giron beachhead, Juan and Margareta couldn't help but think about how it resembled the Varadaro Beach area of Havana; their home many years before Castro. The only difference being the markers, barely visible in the dim morning light, that had been set yesterday by U.S. frogmen. Juan was wishing that he had lost the weight he had intended to lose before this morning's battle. His stomach was bulging underneath his fatigues and he reeked with body odor. He turned adoringly to Margareta. To her father she looked like, in contrast to his sloppiness, the picture-perfect Latin warrior, cross-legged with her M-1 Garand rifle laid across her lap. He was determined to protect her at all costs.

Juan picked up and pointed a flashlight at his waterproof wristwatch. At any moment Kennedy's planes would be taking off from nearby U.S. aircraft carriers. Their attack should meet little resistance, he thought, considering the success of Thessalonian's pre-invasion bombing run two days ago. Thessalonian's planes had destroyed half of Castro's FAR Air Force.

Juan was still very angry with Thessalonian and had many questions about his behavior. For instance, why, after having launched the bombers, couldn't Thessalonian have returned to be with us? Why had he sexually abused my lovely daughter? His actions were unfathomable.

Juan's thoughts of revenge dissipated as the morning sun poured over the horizon. Thessalonian's two American paramilitaries were positioned at the bow and stern of the boat. The morning sun rising was their cue to turn the small horsepower boat motor off and begin rowing. They picked up oars and carefully guided the overloaded craft through the final 75 yards of treacherous Cuban surf.

Shooting could be heard along the invasion spearhead. Juan estimated that at least five of his unit seacraft had already landed with five more, including his, scheduled to break shore within the next minute.

Bullets hit the sand near their boat simultaneously with their beaching. Juan and Margareta dove for cover on opposite sides of the boat. Two of the six Cubans fell where they sat as a second shower of weapons fire hit them. Juan kept expecting to hear support planes overhead. Where were the *hijo de puta* planes? Where? Where?

Juan did not want to get separated from Margareta but when he tried to raise himself he felt a knee in the middle of his spine. Both of the American paramilitaries were beside him laying out a wide line of AKS machine-gun fire. It occurred to Juan then that Thessalonian must have given them strict orders to protect him.

The paramilitaries were yelling frantically at the four remaining Cubans about forming a flank, but to no avail. The Cubans had panicked!

Where are the planes? Where are Kennedy's planes?

Now Juan, too, was beginning to panic! Where is my daughter? Where is she?!

A large gloved hand shoved Juan's face in the sand. Friend or foe? Friend or foe? He couldn't breath and couldn't move. Someone had him pinned completely. Was it the paramilitaries? Weren't they there a minute ago?

As Juan struggled uselessly, the American paramilitary kneeling on his spine took aim quietly, precisely on Margareta Jimenez. She was twenty yards away, on her stomach, her M-1 Garand rifle down beside her. The paramilitary was acting in strict accordance with Thessalonian's orders; do a natural battlefield kill of Margareta during the invasion and keep Juan out of harm's way—bring him back alive!

The paramilitary's AKS machine gun proceeded to splatter Margareta from her skull to her pelvis down to the femur and tibia of her legs and tarsals of her feet. She exploded from the barrage, probably realizing with her last breath that death was nothing like sex.

The paramilitary shooter and his second, who had been providing cover, jerked the fat Latin Jimenez to his feet. Juan's face was covered with sand and he was hyperventilating. The trio ran down the beach in spurts, finally reaching another unmanned fiberglass boat. They fell into it, cranked the small motor and quickly fled the invasion beachhead.

Mission time, the paramilitary calculated, had been less than ten minutes. Right on schedule, their submarine would still be waiting.

Giron—blue beach—disappeared behind them along with the shredded remains of Margareta Jimenez as the wailing of a traumatized Juan Jimenez rose above the ocean torrent.

"Where were Kennedy's planes? WHERE WERE KENNEDY'S PLANES? KEENNEEDDDYYY!!!"

Chapter Thirteen

April 22, 1961

The idealistic mind of Sergeant Roland Holt had finally begun to consider the possibility that President John F. Kennedy was the punk underworld shill and communist General Mancus had accused him of being last November.

It was 7:00 p.m.

Holt had viewed with skepticism the Kennedy audiovisuals which had been shown SFG Team Legerdemain the week of November 12, 1960. In fact, after his dressing down by Captain Marsh in the Officers' Mess November 12, he had flatly refused to acknowledge their merit.

There had been three films shown Team Legerdemain that week. The orgy film, the gangster film and the communist film. The orgy film had initially deeply disturbed Holt but ultimately he had decided that it did not deserve so much as a second consideration. If the President wanted to have sex with a giraffe, let him, as long as it did not interfere with presidential duties. Besides, after reviewing the orgy film several times at Captain Marsh's insistence, it had begun to look staged and phony.

The gangster film was almost as inconsequential. It did nothing more than speculate on a link between Kennedy and Chicago Mafia boss, Stefano "Mr. A" Anacondini. It offered a series of bedroom shots of the six-foot-four-inch Anacondini having sex with a pretty dark-haired woman and then of Kennedy having sex with the same woman at a different time in a different place. There was also a copy of a telegram allegedly sent to this woman from Kennedy in July of 1960 inviting her to attend the Democratic Convention in Los Angeles. The woman's name, however, had been mysteriously scratched out. Again, Holt's conclusion was that if President Kennedy was an oversexed rabbit, so what?, as long as it did not interfere with chief executive responsibilities.

The premise of the Communist film was even more tenuous.

It contained the recorded interrogation of an alleged Russian defector claiming to have been Kennedy's KGB control agent from 1956 through 1957. This film, like the others, played unbearably on Holt's intelligence.

In truth, the entire audiovisual package was so intellectually patronizing that Sergeant Holt suspected General Mancus and Captain Marsh and Thessalonian of having assumed that he and Tony Taylor were too young or too stupid or too meek to doubt them. Yet for the last five months doubting his superiors had become a way of life for Roland Holt. Not openly, for he had learned his lesson about voicing his doubts from Captain Marsh that day in the Officers' Mess, but secretly, as his own counsel.

He kept trying to figure the equation. An equation consistently stumped when it came to the personality of General Alexander T. Mancus. The General was one of the most highly respected founding fathers of Special Forces, so what in the world would he be doing involved in something sinister? That question remained unanswered.

And now today! The General brings SFG Team Legerdemain into the Operations room and briefs them on the aborted Bay of Pigs invasion. Final tally: 1,214 Cuban exiles captured, several hundred killed and tons of supplies lost at sea or over reefs. Why? General Mancus explained. Because Kennedy as a Commie agent not only snitched the entire operation to Castro's people but also failed to provide beachhead air support, which he could have done easily. The carrier USS Essex had been nearby, as well as the destroyers Eaton and Murray. So where had Kennedy been? Since leaving the Operations room earlier this afternoon Sergeant Holt had begun rethinking his opinions.

Was General Mancus right? Was John F. Kennedy really America's Lucifer incarnate and he, as part of Team Legerdemain, an avenging angel? Was Captain Marsh right? Should he just follow orders like a good soldier regardless of why or what for?

This was his life, his dream—to be a part of Special Forces. He believed in America, he believed in the military, but to assassinate a President was to him—insanity.

He jumped from his bunk in his and Taylor's private Ft. Bragg barracks and tried to do some Tai Chi Chuan exercises. During the last five months of continued extensive training here at Ft. Bragg he had convinced himself that something was awry with this alpha crypto abomination called Legerdemain, but now he was not so sure.

He stopped in mid-Tai Chi Chuan motion, realizing his concentration was not there, and curled up on Taylor's bottom bunk. He had never been so perplexed or, as they say in Laotian, *Bpo:n ga:n*, in his nineteen-year life.

What in God's name was he going to do?

Captain Marsh was anxious about meeting the Chief Pentagon Liaison Officer for Military Personnel/Detached Services, Lt. Colonel Warren Bear, tonight, but hopeful that Lt. Colonel Bear could and would provide a missing piece to the puzzle of Legerdemain.

It was 9:00 p.m.

Not that Captain Marsh really gave a shit about killing Kennedy, but he had to know who was actually issuing the orders. General Mancus and Thessalonian, he figured, were just operatives but Lt. Colonel Bear—now he was a whole 'nother kettle of slop.

The Chief Pentagon Liaison Officer often worked out of the Pentagon Office of Special Operations—OSO—and Marsh reasoned that if the OSO was involved then Kennedy was as good as dead and Marsh's future was as good as secured; promotions, bonus, exorbitant pensions. Just the right stuff in the right amounts for an Alabama boy like Marsh who loved black pussy and hell raising.

Captain Marsh had received notification of tonight's meet with Lt. Colonel Bear from General Mancus after today's Bay of Pigs briefing. General Mancus had made it clear to Marsh that Colonel Bear was aware of the existence of Legerdemain but knew nothing of its substance and that he was not alpha crypto priority cleared for it, which meant his visit was strictly routine and that nothing sensitive should be discussed with him. That was fine with Marsh. He only wanted to ask Colonel Bear a single, simple question. From whom exactly had the orders originated directing him, Holt and Taylor off of "White Star" and out of Laos nine months ago.

If the Colonel confirmed that the OSO had issued the orders, then Marsh could rest assured that Legerdemain was not some high level outlaw operation. After months of analysis this had emerged as Captain Marsh's major concern.

In fact, this had become his only concern. His friction with Holt seemed to have ended with their confrontation in the Officers' Mess back in November and Taylor just kept close to Holt like the youngster he was. Both had even sat still, uncomplaining when Marsh insisted that they all view Kennedy's orgy film several extra times. Ha, what a kick!

Marsh walked out of his officers' quarters across the dark parade grounds of Ft. Bragg toward General Mancus's deputy commandant's office. He was dressed formally, his 77th SFG Abn Green Beret tilting correctly across his forehead, his neatly trimmed blonde hair tucked underneath it. He smoothly saluted Mancus's door sentry and entered the commandant's office. The General was standing by two men, next to a gray teletype machine. They all turned to him as he bolted to attention and saluted.

"Captain Marsh—reporting as ordered, sir."

"At ease, Captain," the General responded.

Captain Marsh spread his bow legs wide and clasped his hands behind his back. The men remained standing. General Mancus continued.

"Captain, I'd like you to meet Lt. Colonel Warren Bear, the Chief Pentagon Liaison Officer for Military Personnel/ Detached Services, and his aide Corporal Forrestol."

There was a round of handshakes as the General kept talking.

"Captain, me and the Colonel are going to make a quick tour of the base and get something to eat. Corporal Forrestol here would like to ask you a few routine survey questions." Then turning to the corporal, "He's all yours."

"Thank you, General," Corporal Forrestol replied.

Captain Marsh was surprised, having been prepared to ask a question himself of Lt. Colonel Bear, but General Mancus had slid the Colonel out of the Deputy Commandant's office so quickly that the Captain barely got a memorable glimpse of the man.

Captain Marsh looked at Corporal Forrestol. The corporal had the face of an Irishman. It was pointy and cheery and very white. He looked efficient as hell, Marsh thought, as the corporal offered him a seat and began to shuffle through a batch of papers in a brown manila file. After selecting a sheet of paper that Marsh could see had his name on it, the corporal spoke.

"Don't say a word, Captain Marsh, for the duration of this interview. Actually it will not be an interview at all." Marsh was becoming confused, like a bloodhound with a whiff of pepper up his nose. "It is true that I am temporarily assisting Lt. Colonel Bear with his survey but I am not his regular aide. What I am is permanent aide to General Marion Armstrong III, Deputy Director of the Pentagon's Office of Special Operations, and the message I'm delivering to you tonight has nothing to do with Colonel Bear."

Captain Marsh tensed. It appeared that he was going to get his question answered without ever having to ask it. The corporal continued.

"General Armstrong has sent me here to personally assure you of his full support for Special Op Legerdemain and to represent to you that Legerdemain is approved at the highest levels of our defense establishment. He does not want you to suffer a moment's anguish, or a moment's doubt, about Legerdemain. He says to be patient and disciplined and you will be well compensated."

All Marsh could think to do was smile like an idiot. Promotions, bonuses, and exorbitant pensions. Just the right stuff in the right amounts. Happy days to come, yes siree, happy, happy days. The corporal paused, nearing the end of his "interview." His posture straightened, his voice expanded.

"Just remember, sir, America is depending on you and SFG Team Legerdemain ... this nation's very survival is on your shoulders. Patience and discipline are the orders of the day."

Captain Marsh's idiotic smile refused to leave his Viking-like face as his mind sped like a missile.

Lola, my black baby doll, your ex-daddy's just hit the big time.

Happy, happy days!!

Yesssirrreee!

ONE MONTH LATER
May 19, 1961
Oval Office White House
Washington, D.C., USA
Mid-Afternoon

What a fiasco! The Bay of Pigs ... if Dulles and the CIA think that there aren't going to be changes ... they're in for a surprise.
First, there's going to be a board to investigate ... I'll call it the "Green Board" ... and, let's see, I'll put Dulles on it ... Admiral Burke ... Bobby to represent my interest ... General Taylor, the U.S. Army Chief of Staff, and some Pentagon people for technical input.
Why wasn't there more coordination? Why? To maintain deniability I had to distance myself—but someone should have realized how ridiculous it was to have 1500 men land on a beachhead thirty six miles wide.
Eisenhower and Nixon are looking at me like I am a fool ... a fool to have only gone half way.
They may be right ... but committing conventional forces is something that this President is just not prepared to do ... anywhere at anytime!

Chapter Fourteen

May 20, 1961

"Plato Smith is on the line, sir," Corporal Forrestol said.

Major General Marion Armstrong III, Deputy Director of the Pentagon's OSO, looked up from the letter he had received this morning requesting in firm language that he serve on a presidential committee to investigate what had gone wrong at the Bay of Pigs. The committee would be called the "Green Board."

It was 8 a.m.

He picked up the desk phone and said into it, "Plato, this is Ratchet. How are you over there?"

Plato Smith of the CIA's Directorate of Plans (DDP)-Western Hemisphere Division answered, "Fairly secure, Ratchet, but I'm sure Dulles and Bissel and their staffs are on their way out. How about you?"

"The OSO's going to be broken up, Plato. I'll be going to a new department called the Office of the Special Assistant for Counterinsurgency and Special Activities—SACSA—still as a deputy director. How is Contingency LED-3—Jimenez?"

"Thessalonian says he is primed and ready to go for Kennedy."

"Good ... listen, though. We have to change Jimenez's status from missing presumed captured to confirmed dead. Reason being, Kennedy wants me to serve in a technical capacity on this "Green Board". It's a committee investigating the Bay of Pigs, and I'm sure they are going to try and locate Jimenez to testify before it, which we can't allow for obvious reasons."

"That shouldn't be a problem, Ratchet. As a footnote Thessalonian says he's come up with the perfect shooter to represent Jimenez. A guy who supposedly can fall many ways."

"Fine, and I assume Contingency LED-2—Nuccia is all in order?"

"Yes, Thessalonian says that the Sicilians are hard to deal with and that he wants to beat the Mediterranean piss out of them, but they can be controlled and they're primed to go for Kennedy, too."

"And Mancus ... Contingency LED-1?"

"Mancus is fine. He knows which side of his toast is buttered. He told me that the audiovisuals worked well and that the three men of SFG Team Legerdemain will perform when need be."

"Good. Also, Plato, on Contingency LED-1. I saw fit about a month ago to send my aide, Corporal Forrestol, down to North Carolina with a personal message reassuring Team LED's team leader, Captain Marsh, that Legerdemain is a legitimate operation and for him to be patient—just as I've told you several times—I wanted to prevent any disillusion from setting in."

"Wasn't that risky, Ratchet?"

"Possibly, but look at it from their standpoint. They have a target/objective who has been a godsend to Special Forces. Hell, Kennedy is even planning to visit the Special Warfare Center later this year. I wanted to keep SFG Team Legerdemain from being swayed by all of Kennedy's stroking. These men—no let me rephrase that, this one man and two boys of Team LED, can't be expected to understand the intricacies of Kennedy's military policies."

"Absolutely correct, Ratchet. Smart move and I know what you mean about stroking. Before the Bay of Pigs last month Kennedy was stroking the CIA just the same, but his failure to commit US air and ground conventional forces during the invasion turned a lot of people around here against him, and his firing people left and right now only makes it worse for him. In fact, if there's ever a problem with Thessalonian, I could probably get a dozen operatives to replace him in a flash—nobody likes Kennedy around here now."

"You know, Plato," General Armstrong was talking man-to-man now, "what I don't understand is how a President can be so supportive of guerrilla warfare on one hand and so hesitant to commit conventional forces on the other. It's like he's part militaristic and part fluff."

"And a coward, too."

"You're right, Plato, and our controllers feel the same way. With their dossier analysis on him they were able to see the writing on the wall even before his nomination, thus the mobilization and activation of Legerdemain and getting Johnson as his VP. They know and we know that Kennedy will always balk at committing conventional forces—he'll never come through with the big guns—and that's bad business for all of us, very bad business. He's just too busy playing James Bond."

"Ironic, isn't it, Ratchet? That Kennedy's so in love with intelligence activities and Special Forces and that these will be the two principle instruments of Legerdemain that will take him. He should have stuck with reading James Bond novels instead of trying to live them."

"Definitely, Plato, most definitely."

General Armstrong, with a guffaw at Plato's last statement, hung up the Pentagon-CIA line, a sense of relief enveloping him, having discussed Legerdemain's deeper strategy with the CIA-DDP man. At this point General Armstrong's frayed military nerves could use all the relief they could get.

Feeling more confident than he had in some time, General Armstrong strode to his maple cabinet and pulled out the 030601 phone. He lifted its receiver and waited. Clemer Dodd's voice answered "030601." The General began.

"030601—this is Intercept Eagle—Legerdemain contingencies activation status LED 1 and 2 at trigger stage ... LED 3 at half-trigger stage. Repeat ... Legerdemain contingencies activation status LED 1 and 2 at trigger stage. LED 3 at half-trigger stage ... over."

Clemer's gruff voice repeated almost instantly, "Intercept Eagle ... received ... Legerdemain contingencies activation status LED 1 and 2 at trigger stage; LED 3 at half-trigger stage ... acknowledge ... clear."

The steel state-of-the-art communications console known as MAMA WEST-IIPAC felt smooth to Clemer Dodd's arthritic touch this morning.

It was 9:00 a.m.

It had been an exciting morning for the Inter Inpetto Armaments Corporation's (IIPAC) Senior Classified Communications Expert for the North American Division. Coded and non-coded transmissions had been signaling in from all over the world and the secret compartmented information in today's FTPO report (For the President's Eyes Only) was spectacular.

Both Eisenhower and Nixon had finally issued private opinions to Kennedy concerning the covert handling of the Bay of Pigs. They were to the point and laid blame where Clemer Dodd thought blame was due: on the intelligence community of the United States Government.

It had dawned on Clemer while reading the FTPO report that this very special tie-in on his console—030601—Legerdemain—and the worried voice transmitting—Intercept Eagle—may have been and may still be involved with all this Cuban activity.

"Ah—what I'll never know will never hurt me," Clemer concluded aloud, resigning himself to his beloved yet ineffectual place, figuring that there were worse fates than living here on the perpetually splendid Isla de Provedencia in the Caribbean, being paid a fortune for doing a patriot's work.

He ceased his ruminating and went back to work, his arthritic hand again reaching for the console, specifically its left corner Pretex Com/A channel.

He began his reply.

"MAMA WEST HYPHON to ZURICH ... re LEGERDEMAIN ... FM INTERCEPT EAGLE ... Contingencies Activation Status LED 1 and 2 at trigger stage ... LED 3 at half-trigger stage."

There were 25 seconds of silence—then a sputter—a buzz—a reply.

"MAMA WEST ... This is Zurich ... receipt of Pretex COM/A transmission ... Confirmed."

⌖ ⌖ ⌖ ⌖

The Inter Inpetto Armaments Corporation (IIPAC) maintained a retreat in Gastaad, Switzerland.

Today in the retreat sat a man who was also talking to himself, in clipped phrases, over a communiqué he had just received from Zurich.

It was 4:30 p.m. Central European Time.

"Trigger Stage—Legerdemain contingencies activation status LED 1 and 2 at trigger stage, LED 3 at half-trigger stage."

The man stood and began wandering through the palatial chalet.

"It's almost ready ... Legerdemain ... Sleight of hand ... a kind of shell game ... where the entire world will be guessing which shell it is under. It being the assassin or assassins who murdered the American President John F. Kennedy. It'll be just like the game little Horace used to play at Vanderbilt boarding school ... cheating the other boys out of their money. What a shyster little Horace was. He's dead now, killed over that Geneva stock swindle. Little Horace finally cheated the wrong person—a Sicilian Mafioso like Charlie Nuccia, I think. When it comes to peasant justice, those Sicilians certainly have a way about them."

The tumblers of the man's frigid heart were combining for the thousandth time, locking the motives of Legerdemain within.

"That dirty Eisenhower—if it weren't for him, none of this would have been necessary. His ceiling on American defense spending for these last eight years, and him being the foremost American military man of this century. Cockhumping incredible! Then he warns America about the military industrial complex in his farewell speech. Un-cockhumping-believable! And then Nixon ... all of our hopes and he sweats like a Sumo wrestler on TV debating Kennedy. And now Kennedy who advocates limited guerrilla wars and who's increased all branches of Special Forces ... but who will probably never make a commitment of full scale conventional forces. He petered out in Cuba. He'll peter out elsewhere ... and there must be, for us, an American conventional forces war soon. They're so close to it anyway in Southeast Asia. Christ, we've lost so much money in America during Eisenhower. So much cockhumping money!"

The man continued ambling through the IIPAC private chalet.

His name was Sosar Tomeen and he was the principle controller of Legerdemain.

"According to this FYDP—Five Year Defense Plan—Kennedy will open up the defense budget somewhat for conventional forces during his presidency, even though his Secretary of Defense, McNamara, is going to keep a tight centralized rein on weapons expenditures, but as far as recouping monies lost from the Eisenhower years—the only way to do that will be with a full scale conventional forces war and an increase in defense spending to 60/80 billion dollars a year. As indicated by our early 1960 dossier analysis/psychological profile of Kennedy, the chances of his allowing America to entangle itself fully in a conventional forces war like that are slim to none. He's in love with the guerrilla war concept and paramilitary intelligence operations but not full scale conventional Army and Marine commitment. So chances are, Sosar, he will never allow it."

George Whitten, a senior analyst attached to the Pentagon's Program Planning and Budgeting Systems Office (PPBS) for the American Department of Defense and covert associate of Sosar Tomeen, was speaking to Sosar now, seated across from him on an ornate mauve couch in the IIPAC retreat in Gastaad, Switzerland.

It was 6:30 p.m. Central European Time.

Whitten, in early 1960, had designed Operation Legerdemain at the behest of his long-time friend and secret employer, Sosar Tomeen.

The two had met in Germany in 1942. Whitten had been an American Office of Strategic Services (OSS) agent under deep cover in Essen. Sosar Tomeen had been a young accountant, American by birth, working in a local Krupp Armaments factory under the assumed name of Wilhelm Dollinger. The reasons for Sosar's subterfuge were complex.

Sosar Tomeen had been born in New York City in 1916 to affluent Danish-French parents. They had divorced in 1921, abandoning a 5-year-old Sosar to the Vanderbilt Boarding School in upstate New York. He lived there comfortably but orphan-like for the next twelve years.

The most significant person in Sosar's youth had been the headmaster at Vanderbilt named Rocknawell. Rocknawell, a failed accountant/entrepreneur, introduced the impressionable 10-year-old to the fascinating world of mathematics. He guided the formative years of Sosar's studies, continually feeding the boy's tender psyche with his own ruthless and cynical set of business ethics; unscrupulous ethics that the young Sosar Tomeen digested, refined and accepted as gospel.

At seventeen Sosar began his business career as a page for

the New York Stock Exchange, then moved to Berlin in 1937 as an accountant for the International Telephone and Telegraph Company. In 1940, when most Americans employed in Germany began to leave Berlin, Sosar illegally arranged to stay by buying false papers under the Dollinger name. He had done this so he could apply for a recently vacated chief accountant's post with the Krupp factory in Essen. To Sosar, the factory chief accountant's job was one of immense opportunity and well worth the sacrifice of having to live clandestinely. Besides, he was not patriotically loyal in any form or fashion to any country, including his native America, nor to any cause. He was merely a twenty-three-year-old realist, pragmatist and amoral merchant.

By 1942, however, more than two years after having secured the chief accountant's position at the Krupp facility, Tomeen began to see defeat on the horizon for the German people. So he decided then to contact the American OSS intelligence network he knew to be operating out of Essen at the time, reveal his born identity and offer his services as a spy. George Whitten had been the first OSS man he talked to. The tall and lanky Tomeen became not only Whitten's best spy but also Whitten's benefactor.

Sosar's skill at embezzling and arms black-marketing by then had refined themselves into an art. He would use Whitten's intelligence network to smuggle Krupp arms out of Germany under the guise of denting the Nazi War effort, when in reality huge sums of money were being made with each shipment. Money that was being deposited immediately into Sosar's secret Swiss bank accounts.

By 1944, Sosar Tomeen, at twenty eight years of age, had amassed a fortune. Sosar then informed Whitten, who too had been profiting for years, that he intended to go into the armaments business after the war. With Whitten's assistance and using bribery in all its forms, Sosar Tomeen began to buy a wide array of American military and intelligence contacts. His ventures, however, were not without personal risks.

In December of 1944 Sosar, as Wilhelm Dollinger, was discovered with his sticky fingers literally in the Krupp factory till. An older German accountant confronted him threateningly and Sosar did the only thing he could. He slapped the old man down with a stack of ledgers and attempted to strangle him. The old German fought like a bull and finally managed to push the tall but not physically strong Sosar off. A fierce struggle ensued, a struggle Sosar eventually won, but only after having two of his fingers cut off by the bulky old accountant.

Sosar escaped from Essen that night with the help of Whitten's network. After the fall of Berlin in 1945, Tomeen returned triumphantly to Germany and continued to direct his enormous financial bribing power toward select American military and intelligence commanders.

He named his company the Inter Inpetto Armaments Corporation (IIPAC); *Inpetto* meaning secretly, in the breast, and for the next eight years prospered.

Sosar maintained his international corporate headquarters in Zurich but had production factories in France, Brazil, and the United States as well as corporate marketing offices in over twenty countries. IIPAC even owned its own shipping line and a massive state-of-the-art communications complex affectionately termed MAMA. All told, IIPAC ranked among the ten largest armaments companies in the world, with America's conventional armed forces—the U.S. Army and Marines—its biggest customer.

It was understandable then when Dwight Eisenhower became President and put in place rigid conventional forces defense spending limits that IIPAC began losing money, and it was not alone.

Three other companies loosely engaged in a consortium with IIPAC—General Technologies, Inc., Brandtest and Set and BlairCorp—were sympathetic to Sosar's plight, especially considering that they, too, were financially as dependent as IIPAC on American conventional forces defense spending. So on these grounds of mutual interest and dilemma, top executives of the four companies met in early 1960.

Their original plan was to see to it that the easily manipulated Richard Nixon became President of the United States in November's general election. To hedge their bets, though, and to ensure their having a friend in the White House for the next four years, the consortium had decided to secure Lyndon Baines Johnson, an openly hawkish military supporter, as John Kennedy's vice-presidential running mate. This plan B went into action in 1960 at the Democratic National Convention in Los Angeles. They offered Kennedy, through a string of holding corporations, a huge financial political contribution if, and only if, he selected Lyndon Johnson as his running mate. Of course, the consortium still had their hopes pinned primarily on Richard Nixon, but by spreading their giant financial eggs into two baskets, they were wisely allowing for the unallowable.

Sosar Tomeen, himself, however, took several more drastic precautions.

He had commissioned his old friend and advisor, George Whitten, who by this time had secured cover employment as a senior analyst at the Pentagon, to:

1) Prepare a dossier analysis/psychological profile on John Fitzgerald Kennedy, and

2) Construct methods of either discrediting the man out of office, blackmailing the man, or as a last resort assassinating the man.

Whitten, after preparing alternate plans for discreditation and blackmail, as ordered, began constructing a multi-tiered, multi-contingency assassination plot dubbed Operation Legerdemain. The operation would cleverly utilize various elements of IIPAC's bribed military and intelligence network, which by 1960 had deeply entrenched itself into America's defense establishment.

Sosar's consortium counterparts at General Technologies, Inc., Brandtest and Set and BlairCorp, were purposely kept uninvolved and unaware of the JFK dossier analysis and Operation Legerdemain, not because Sosar feared their disapproval but rather because Sosar Tomeen deeply distrusted multiparty conspiracies.

Therefore, the control of Legerdemain rested solely with Tomeen and Whitten.

Tomeen, the principle.

Whitten, the architect.

George Whitten was 61 years old and a Texan by birth, a man of average height but unusual presence. He had closely-cropped gray hair now, just as he had had when Sosar first met him in Essen, accentuated by a broad face as seemingly open as the west Texas plains it had been raised on. Whitten's speech, however, did not contain so much as a buckshot of Texas drawl.

"Which means, Sosar," Whitten continued, "that as we suspected from the beginning—Kennedy must go and Johnson must come. By all indications Kennedy's military policies, even though not as meek as what his dossier analysis predicted they would be, are still unacceptable to us."

George Whitten shifted on the plush couch, put down the FYDP report and picked up another file marked in big letters GILPATRIC. He continued talking.

"Soon after his inauguration JFK commissioned a mixed panel, named it the Gilpatric Committee and ordered it to comprehensively investigate the American military posture in Southeast Asia. This committee had quite a few Pentagon researchers on it, as well as Army, Navy and Air Force experts. They issued a report to the President on May 6, of which I have a copy here."

Whitten put his reading glasses on, wetted his thumb, and sifted through the file.

"The committee recommended forty options ranging from No Action to sending in conventional U.S. forces."

Sosar interrupted him. "Were any of our people on the committee?"

George became a little flustered, "No, Sosar, it happened too fast. It was put together too fast."

"All right, go on, George."

"Anyway, Kennedy's decision was not totally unresponsive. He ordered an increase in the U.S. Military Advisory Group by four hundred Green Berets and authorized pay for a thirty-thousand-man increase in the South Vietnamese Army. Here I'm quoting—'expanding present operations in the field of intelligence, unconventional warfare and political psychological activities.'"

"So, he's still playing guerrilla warrior with no conventional forces backup," Sosar said, as his three-fingered right hand reached for a bottle of whiskey and two glasses that sat on the coffee table.

"That's right, Sosar, and there's no indication he will change." Sosar handed Whitten a glass of whiskey and propped his long legs on the table, crossing them, spreading one of his long arms out on the couch.

Sosar Tomeen's 6'3" frame looked relaxed, but George Whitten knew better. He could sense that the brilliant, 45-year-old mind of Sosar was blitzkrieging itself at full speed.

Sosar was not a physically attractive man, but like Whitten possessed an unusual presence and very disciplined manner. Sosar could silence a board meeting and strike fear into the hearts of his minions simply by raising his three-fingered right hand. He wore his otter-brown sideburns long with a Van Dyke beard in an attempt to hide a set of owlishly fat cheeks. Without the sideburns and beard his face looked incongruous and almost misshapen. His voice had the silky multilingual tone of a worldly, educated man; a voice without vulgarity except for the occasional use of the word "cockhumping."

"George, Kennedy's reaction to the Gilpatric report was more aggressive than anticipated, wasn't it?"

"Yes," Whitten replied.

"So there still is the possibility that Kennedy could come through for us?"

"Yes. But as I said, Sosar, the chances are slim."

Sosar, as usual in strategy discussions of this nature, threw a fast curve to Whitten.

"What about Johnson, George? Why haven't we done a detailed dossier on him as we did with Kennedy? How can we be so sure he'll actually commit conventional forces any quicker than Kennedy, besides his reputation, of course?"

The older George Whitten became more than flustered now. "Because, Sosar, Lyndon Baines Johnson is from Texas, my home state. Accordingly I've made it my business to stay familiar with his policies over the years. From a philosophical standpoint, I have no doubt that Johnson will favor sending in grunts—regular troops—into Southeast Asia to kick ass. From a practical standpoint, he acts openly as a legislative agent for several defense-related Texas contractors, but if you want, I can still do an analysis on him for you."

Sosar looked down into his whiskey.

"Yes, George, I think you should. But take your time."

"Take my time, Sosar?" George Whitten asked, baffled, feeling that time was the only thing Legerdemain lacked.

Sosar stood abruptly and began walking carefully, thoughtfully, near the couch.

"Yes, take your time, George. Let me explain. You've known me for twenty years now. You know that I'm only interested in results—the bottom line. Right now that line is the necessary economic resuscitation of IIPAC. If Kennedy alive can provide that, then fine, but if he can't, then we'll do what we have to do. Keep in mind, George, that Legerdemain was conceived by us as an absolute last resort. If we are forced to go through with it, it will have enormous historical ramifications and if by any chance our hand is revealed, we're doomed." Sosar rubbed his three-fingered right hand on his left cheek. "Legerdemain's design is brilliant, but it is, at best, a tremendously risky undertaking."

George Whitten countered.

"Undertaking, Sosar, is the correct word. It is an undertaking that has already been undertook. After you vetoed my discreditation and blackmail scenarios you said that this is what you wanted, to cancel it now would mean that I would have to tell Armstrong to tell Smith to tell Thessalonian to take everyone involved in all contingencies out. Domino time. Kill everybody. There will be panic."

"No, no ... don't misunderstand me. My decision is not to cancel, at least not as yet, but to delay to see what Kennedy is going to do when pushed by the escalating events in Southeast Asia. I want you to tell General Armstrong to put the operation on a holding pattern. Tell him to use his new SACSA position to try and convince Kennedy to go all the way in Southeast Asia—get him to commit conventional forces. All the while we'll keep circling, preparing for the kill, fueling the fires of revenge in Contingency LED-2 and 3 with the Sicilians and the Cubans and keeping Contingency LED-1 with SFG Team Legerdemain in harness, prepared for a second's notification of action, but we will not move until I am absolutely sure it is the most prudent thing and the only thing left for us to do."

The OSS-trained, covert Texas mind of George Whitten was already analyzing and calculating what to tell General Armstrong. Of course, Armstrong didn't know Whitten personally, even though they both worked in the Pentagon, but he did know Whitten's voice by the code name of INFIX and that when it spoke to him it was speaking for Sosar Tomeen, Chairman of the Board of the Inter Inpetto Armaments Corporation.

Sosar concluded, "Only with patience, perfection, and a deft hand, my old friend, will we achieve success with this for IIPAC—and we will achieve it without Legerdemain if possible, with it if necessary," he paused, "and that, my brother-in-arms, is a cockhumping guarantee!"

Chapter Fifteen

May 20, 1961

"Vincenzo Angeletta, no middle name, nicknamed Angler ... so that's that Sicilian prick's name."

Thessalonian was standing in a misty morning fog talking on an outdoor pay phone with his CIA-DDP superior Plato Smith, minutes away from the Shreveport, Louisiana Municipal Airport.

It was 11:45 a.m.

Thessalonian had arranged yesterday for Charlie Nuccia to fly from Tequicigalpa to Shreveport on a Dominican Republic Air Force jet. Nuccia would be landing in Shreveport within the hour equipped with a Thessalonian-supplied forged entry visa and an explicit set of Legerdemain instructions.

The Sicilian prick, finally fully identified by Plato Smith as Vince "Angler" Angeletta, had left Tequicigalpa a week before with his own set of Legerdemain instructions.

When Thessalonian had last talked to Plato a few weeks back he had been so frustrated with the arrogance of these dagos that he had been tempted to kill the lot of them and just take Kennedy out himself. Especially this fucking Angeletta. He was pushy and constantly asking questions about Thessalonian's past. This "Angler" had even ordered Thessalonian to stay cooped up in his Hotel Camino suite with Nuccia's Mestizo guard sleeping on a cot in the room. The situation calmed, though, as the finishing touches of the Sicilian version of Legerdemain, Contingency LED-2, were structured.

The final draft depended heavily on Vince Angeletta. His initial task would be to follow the President to as many domestic public presidential appearances as possible; to watch how JFK moved and walked and gestured. Thessalonian, of course, would provide Angeletta with the President's Secret Service itinerary.

Nuccia, for his part, was to act normally and to not contact

Thessalonian again unless it was an absolute emergency. Thessalonian had given Nuccia a list of his intelligence operatives in New Orleans to contact if need be, but all were almost wholly disconnected from Thessalonian himself. These operatives included an ex-FBI man turned private investigator and the president of the New Orleans International Trade Association. Thessalonian had also listed the name of a homosexual pilot that had on occasion piloted for Charlie Nuccia.

Thessalonian did not intend to personally meet with Nuccia this morning but did want to make sure the Mafia boss landed safely. Then it was off again to the Florida Keys and Juan Jimenez.

Plato Smith's voice on the phone interrupted his planning.

"Two other things: Legerdemain is, as of now, officially in a holding pattern operational stage and Jimenez's official status has been changed from missing presumed captured to confirmed dead, so keep the Cuban under close raps, okay? And look—any more on that shooter you have for Jimenez? The one you said was perfect, and could fall many ways?"

"Right. It'll take me a few months to work on him. I just got his file from the Office of Naval Intelligence."

"The ONI? Thessalonian, who is this guy?"

"His name is ... " Thessalonian reached his scarred forearm into his shirt pocket for a half-empty matchbook that he'd scribbled on. "Oswald, Lee Harvey ... got it, Plato? Oswald, Lee Harvey."

"The Sandhurst Shopping Complex."

"Yea, let me speak to Carmine."

"Please hold."

"This is Carmine."

"Hey, Carmine ... Ralphie. Did she contact you?"

"Hey, Ralphie ... the fuckin' comedian. Are you in Chitown?"

"No, this is long distance, Carmy. Well, did she contact you?"

"Who?"

"Mona Spazek, about working there at the Sandhurst. She was supposed to have given you my name."

"Oh, yeah, the looker. Yeah, we hired her about a month ago. Said she was moving to New Orleans in six months. Yeah, she's pretty nice, Ralph. Real class. Knows Mario, too."

"Yep, that's her. Look, Carmine, tell her I called, said hello, and that I'm still traveling, okay?"

"Yeah, okay, Ralph. Hey, Ralph, I heard you wasn't working for the Four Seasons anymore. Must have sumpin' to do with Charlie's problems. Huh, Ralph?"

"Can't talk, Carmy, got to go. Look, take care of my girl. But keep your stinkin', fuckin' hands off of her, awright?"

"Don't worry, Ralphie. I'll take real good care of her, real good."

"Yea, awright, penis brain. Talk to you later."

Busting chops was something Vince Angeletta usually refrained from doing but he always enjoyed joking rough with Carmine, even more so now after a week of Legerdemain.

It was 12:00 p.m.

After leaving Tequicigalpa a week ago, Vince had flown the Cessna 182 back to New Orleans and Pandora Aviation. While in New Orleans, he had spoken briefly with Johnny and Jake about how Charlie's brother Giuseppe was handling things and then had informed them to expect Charlie back in the country within a week and a half. They were surprised but pleased, accepting this as just another of Don Nuccia's miracles.

From New Orleans, Vince had flown to Washington, D.C. via commercial airline. Thessalonian had taught him how to disguise himself with a minimum of effort and had supplied him with several fake I.D.s. There was even a Secret Service special agent's badge included. Vince was confident and trusting of Thessalonian now. He had intentionally made it as uncomfortable as possible for the CIA man these last weeks in Honduras. His bullying and verbal abuse never provoking so much as a peep out of the government man. So by all appearances Charlie had pegged it right; Thessalonian was too scared to fuck with them.

Washington, D.C. was a place Vince had never been before. A rush of excitement and satisfaction coursed through him as he flagged a cab from the Washington National Airport Terminal, thinking that not only had he been given a second opportunity to make things right for his "Top Man" but his girl, Mona Spazek, was where she was supposed to be, doing what he had told her to do.

His life was beginning to make sense again in its own, unique, Sicilian way!

FIVE MONTHS LATER
October 15, 1961
Special Warfare Center
Ft. Bragg, North Carolina, USA
Early Morning

Should I have ordered more than 400 Green Berets to the Military Advisory Group in Southeast Asia last May? I don't know ... the Gilpatric Committee wasn't much help investigating CIA incompetency at the Bay of Pigs ... making the CIA appear nearly blameless ... what cod oil that was!

I believe I will order increases in Special Forces in both Vietnam and Laos. I'm also tempted to commit U.S. conventional troops ... maybe in the panhandle of Laos to block the Ho Chi Minh Trail ... but ... I ... can't bring myself to authorize it ... not yet anyway ... probably never.

Special Forces, yes ... conventional troops, no ... even with SACSA advising it. I'm just too uncomfortable with the idea.

So this is the famous Special Warfare Center ... home of the Green Berets. I want to make sure these men know how much I believe in them ... and trust them. I want them to remember the day their President visited them ... for the rest of their lives.

Chapter Sixteen

October 15, 1961

Plato Smith of the CIA's Directorate of Plans (DDP)-Western Hemisphere Division was hissing over the Pentagon-CIA line.

"Ratchet, we've been on a holding pattern for five months now. Don't the controllers understand that with Legerdemain I am running an unauthorized covert operation through the DDP and that I can't keep on with it indefinitely? How much longer do they reasonably expect this to continue?"

It was 7:00 a.m.

Major General Marion Armstrong III, now deputy director for the Special Assistant for Counterinsurgency and Special Activities (SACSA), didn't answer immediately.

"Plato, I suppose you'll continue until you're told to stop. I'm tired of having to tell you to be patient. Hell, I'm as anxious as you to finish it, but it's not our call. At least you weren't told to do everything possible to try and convince Kennedy to commit Army and Marine regular troops like I was. I'm having to deal with the man from my new SACSA office much closer than I ever anticipated. First the Green Board and now this and you know where he's at today?"

"Visiting the Special Warfare Center?"

"That's right. And Mancus, as deputy commander of the place, will have to be with him all the way. He'd better be on his toes. And I sure as hell hope this visit doesn't confuse our three-man team of Legerdemain."

"No, Ratchet, I don't think it will affect them adversely. Mancus probably has their heads turned around so much by now that they are immune to the President's charms. Besides, Mancus will probably order them in barracks during the actual visit."

"What's Thessalonian's status today, Plato?"

"He's been working on the Jimenez Contingency LED-3 shooters program for months now—and as far as Nuccia's shooter, Thessalonian hasn't had to expend much effort on him, considering that the shooter is just following JFK around, acclimating himself to the man."

"Okay, Plato—let me get back to work. I'm drafting another letter to Kennedy from SACSA advising him to commit conventional forces to the panhandle of Laos. Maybe if I can convince him to put in regular troops Legerdemain can be aborted."

"And not a moment too soon, Ratchet!"

General Armstrong's irritation at Plato Smith's momentary loss of composure was evident as he slammed the desk phone down and walked briskly towards his maple cabinet, now sitting catercornered in his new Pentagon SACSA office.

He pulled the 030601 phone out and lifted its receiver. Nearly two minutes passed before Clemer Dodd answered.

"030601."

"030601—this is Intercept Eagle—Legerdemain Contingencies status at holding pattern stage and impatient ... repeat ... Legerdemain contingencies status at holding pattern stage and impatient ... over."

Clemer's gruff voice hesitated, then answered, "Intercept Eagle ... received ... Legerdemain Contingencies status at holding pattern stage ... and impatient ... acknowledge ... clear."

⌖ ⌖ ⌖ ⌖

"I don't understand why I'm being held prisoner! Is it that you think I don't notice your men all around?"

A stern and now grossly overweight Juan Jimenez shifted his stance, his head and jaw dropping down to his chest as if the exertion of saying another word would collapse him.

It was 8:30 a.m.

His tone changed. "Thessalonian, where is she ... where is my Margareta? I know she'll be back here soon, she'd better be. We must dine at the Internacional tonight. Care to join us?"

Thessalonian shook his blonde head indicating "no" to the powerful but now mentally unstable Cuban. His scarred arm rested on Jimenez's shoulder.

Over the last five months the Cuban Revolutionary Directorate leader, as a man, had crumbled before Thessalonian's eyes. At best, Juan Jimenez was only semi-aware of his reality which complicated Thessalonian's orchestration of Contingency LED-3 considerably. The Cuban exile community would not cooperate with Thessalonian without Jimenez's backing and without them to counterpoint Oswald's every move, the illusion of Contingency LED-3 would not work. And triangulation was mandatory.

Only with the presence of a Mafia triggerman and a triggerman linked sympathetically to Cuba or the Cuban exiles and a Special Forces team of triggermen could Kennedy's death by sniper be reasonably assured and all worst case scenarios be covered.

And this Oswald, Lee Harvey, was beginning to appear like the one participant of the triangulation and the three contingencies who could feasibly take the fall for the entire shoot, placating what will surely be an outraged American public.

Lee Harvey Oswald's background covered all bases. He had been born in New Orleans on October 18, 1939, and his uncle was one of Charlie Nuccia's men. He had been a marine who had held a sensitive post in Atsugi, Japan, where he had been sheep-dipped by the Office of Naval Intelligence (ONI), taught Russian, given a publicly questionable discharge, then ordered as part of a joint DIA-CIA operation to defect to the USSR. He had done so over two years ago.

The only aspect of Oswald's background left undeveloped was his connection to Cuba directly. Using Oswald's defection, though, as proof of his Marxist leanings, would reinforce the notion of his having pro-Castro sympathies. Therefore, Thessalonian planned to pull Oswald out of Russia very soon, bring him back to the States, and construct a solid Cuban connection into his character.

When the actual Kennedy shoot took place, Thessalonian would make sure Oswald was captured and do his best to see to it that Nuccia's triggerman and SFG Team Legerdemain escaped from the scene. They could be disposed of later after the fact, Thessalonian had concluded.

Also built into the Oswald character by this time would be a "madman" element. Using his staged questionable discharge from the marines as a starting point, Thessalonian would order Oswald periodically to appear neurotic, schizophrenic, and psychotic. The magic of all this character hyperactivity combined with a murky past—part Mafia, part military, part Cuban, would give investigators more than enough leads to follow. Too many leads, in fact—too much data—too confusing. They would end up scratching their asses, Thessalonian smirked, asking themselves who really was Lee Harvey Oswald? Lone, mad assassin or part of a conspiracy? Mafia hit man? Government agent? Castro sympathizer? Cuban exile sympathizer? Substantial evidence would lend credence to each possibility with the simplest conclusion probably ending up being the historical one—Lee Oswald was a lone, mad assassin.

Of course, Oswald would have to be killed in jail shortly after capture, probably by a right-wing nut or patriot; maybe someone Nuccia could supply. But then, Nuccia thought that Legerdemain was solely his and Vince Angeletta's. Oh well, Thessalonian decided, that could also be arranged later. For now, Thessalonian had to build a Cuban element into the Oswald character and that would require the Cuban exile communities assistance. Juan Jimenez had to vouch for him, even though Jimenez seemed at this point incapable of vouching for anything. He was despondent over the loss of his daughter, his country, his home, a shattered man if Thessalonian had ever seen one.

They were in a secluded spot near Key Largo, Florida, accessible only by boat. Mangroves and exotic greenery preened themselves in the early morning sun as Thessalonian removed his hand from Jimenez's shoulder.

"Juan, she's not coming back—not now, not ever, not to the Internacional or Veradaro beach—not anywhere."

It was like Thessalonian had taken a needle and popped the Cuban's protective bubble. Jimenez crouched to the floor, sobbing uncontrollably. Thessalonian kept punching psychologically in his husky and hypnotic voice.

"Juan, Kennedy killed her—John Fitzgerald Kennedy—the President of the United States. Remember? He withheld air support on the invasion beachhead. She was cut to pieces by Castro's militia—Juan, Juan! You must snap out of it! Kennedy must be killed. He must be made to pay for Margareta. You must contact your people in New Orleans today. Now! Order them to work with me to provide anything I need. You must, Juan!"

The Cuban Revolutionary Directorate leader put his short, fat hand on Thessalonian's knee and leaned on it, still crying.

"Yes, I must ... I must avenge my brave Margareta. I will!"

Thessalonian affectionately patted Jimenez's head like a baby's.

"There, there, Juan. I promise you Kennedy is dead. I promise you ... " He continued to rub his scarred limb through Juan's hair, soothing the Cuban, thinking to himself, "And you, too, my crazy Cuban fanatic. You too, will die when the time is right ... I promise!"

Laughing Mirror, laugh,
hum, hum, hum,
swallow me sweet.

The face in the mirror was definitely not Vince Angeletta's, but really it was. It was just that Vince had become a master of subtle disguise over the last five months. Thessalonian had taught him well in Honduras; so well that Vince hardly recognized himself now. He had applied light beige makeup to his character lines—lessening their prominence—and to the sides of his nose. He had trimmed his thick, furry eyebrows.

It was 9:00 a.m.

He left the mirror and walked to the cheap motel room dresser, reaching for his briefcase. He unlocked its two combination snaps and pulled out the Secret Service identification wallet Thessalonian had supplied him with.

Holding the hard-to-obtain official badge and card in his hand brought to mind, forcefully, exactly where he was and what he was engaged in.

Vince had stalked President Kennedy for five months now, to various domestic public appearances. He had even been one of the 2,500 people present at the Quonset Point, Rhode Island Air Station when the President unofficially landed there in late September to begin a family vacation in Newport.

Vince was in Fayetteville, North Carolina today near Ft. Bragg to perform a test of Kennedy's security—to see how easy or how hard it would be to penetrate it, using his Secret Service identification. He was aware of the risk he was taking and that neither Thessalonian nor Charlie would have approved. But, Vince figured, it was he who had to know exactly how quick Kennedy's men were. Even so, the Mafioso did not intend to push his luck.

Vince put the Secret Service wallet down, reached for a cigar and began to dress. He wished he had been able to carry his black bag loaded with his new weapons out of New Orleans to Washington five months ago, but Thessalonian had strictly advised against it. Vince still insisted, however, on carrying his new .22 Ruger pistol that he had bought to replace the old one used in Cuba on Luigi. He carefully stuffed it into the small of his back. He then slicked his black wavy hair into place, looking like an Italian Dick Clark, put on a black government-like suit, tie and shoes, grabbed his Secret Service identification, briefcase and suitcase, and left the room.

The car Vince had rented was a 1960 Dodge Polara, the same make and model the Secret Service used according to Thessalonian. He intended to park outside the Ft. Bragg perimeter, then see if he could gain entrance inside the military installation by flashing his Secret Service wallet and bamboozling a military sentry.

It was a clear, cloudless North Carolina morning as Vince pulled into the Ft. Bragg outer parking lot. According to the Thessalonian-supplied presidential itinerary, Kennedy had arrived at 4:00 a.m. and would begin his official tour of the compound at 10:00 a.m. Part of the Commandant's barracks had been made available to the President for a nap and freshening up. Vince was early. He immediately spotted four Secret Service men at the front entrance huddled together with four military policemen. The four MPs wore Green Berets on their heads and MP arm bands. The four agents were dressed like Vince.

Vince didn't stop his car. Instead he circled the lot and drove back out of it as inconspicuously as possible. He knew he had to find another entrance where no Secret Service men were present, before the presidential tour began.

His fingers had wrapped themselves tightly around the Secret Service wallet as he began to murmur repeatedly in a determined Sicilian undertone, "Fuck ... Fuck!"

"Can you see him?"

Specialist Second Class Tony Taylor, with Chesterfield cigarette in hand, and Sergeant Roland Holt had their faces solidly pressed up against the glass window of their private Ft. Bragg barracks, searching for Kennedy.

It was 9:40 a.m.

Sergeant Holt turned his dark, reddish-brown features to Taylor. "What in God's name are you so excited about? Don't you understand that he's the target/objective of SFG Team Legerdemain—our team? Sometimes I don't understand you, Taylor."

"Well, sir, he's also the President of the United States, and I've never seen a real President before."

"But," Holt said, grabbing Taylor by the arm and forcing the All-American, good-looking kid to face him, "if everything we've been told and shown is true, he is also a Communist agent, an associate of gangsters and a sexual deviant. He forewarned Castro about the Bay of Pigs operation and God knows what else, so he's not really our President."

Taylor's soft brown eyes drifted and Holt noticed the lack of conviction in his own voice.

Taylor responded, "Sir, for months now I've watched how you've acted around Captain Marsh and General Mancus. I've seen the doubt in your face. Do you really believe what they've been telling us is true? Is it even within the realm of possibility, considering what we've learned about Kennedy during the last ten months of his presidency, that he could be that corrupt? And if he was, why have they waited this long to take him out?"

Sergeant Holt turned away from his team member and walked over to Taylor's bottom bunk. He sat down and rested his head in his hands.

"*He:t Hay: Ngo:na,*" he thought in Laotian—I am sure of nothing and unsure of everything.

Since April, Roland Holt had tried with all his mental might to convince himself that Legerdemain was legitimate. Even though he was less inclined to believe General Mancus a traitor than the President of the United States, nothing had broken his suspicion. Something underneath his '57-style Apache haircut inside his brain was rebelling against the premise that John

F. Kennedy was an evil man, and Kennedy being here today—Christ! How much more moral support did they expect the man to demonstrate?

Tony Taylor walked over to him. "Roland, I've kept quiet through this, satisfied just to wait and watch and see. But I can't stop believing what I believe. My father used to tell me that man's sense of right and wrong was just like the tuberculosis he had inside of him. It's something that's in you from the day you're born and that's that. You may try to change it, make compromises, convince yourself that you're really right when you're wrong and vice versa, but in the end, when the chips are down, that sense will tell you what to do."

Holt looked up at Taylor, astonished at hearing what sounded like the echoes of his own conscience.

"And what does your sense of right and wrong tell you now, Tony?"

Taylor answered, "That my commander-in-chief, Sergeant, is that man." He pointed out the window. "Walking around our base today—the President of the United States, and that no one can break the chain of command leading to him."

Taylor sat on his bunk next to the sergeant. "This is the way I've figured it. In other countries throughout history, when powerful elements have wanted to overthrow their leader, it's almost always been done in collusion with factions of the military." Taylor paused, enjoying the articulation of the words he had held in for so long. "And I suspect that that is what's happening here. A coup d'etat."

Holt was mesmerized by Taylor's performance. The youngster had obviously given a great deal of thought to this but had been afraid to speak up before now.

"It just doesn't play, Sergeant. If they really had the slightest bit of evidence against Kennedy, he would have been exposed long before he was elected President. I say that they have never had any evidence against the man and that everything shoved down our throats was fabricated and that the whole suggestion that a highly visible sanction to convince Moscow that America is not to be toyed with is utter, unadulterated cow shit, as Captain Marsh would say. And speaking of Captain Marsh, I think he knows much more than he pretends to. I suspect he's figured the whole thing out himself, but for reasons unknown to us he's going along with it, acting like a good little brainwashed soldier." Tony Taylor rose and completed his oration in a voice and manner far more mature than a teenager's. "But, Sergeant Holt, I'm not going to go along with it. I intend to get to Kennedy today and warn him of the entire operation, and I want you to be with me."

Taylor reached, habitually, for another Chesterfield and offered one to Holt. Holt, a non-smoker, slowly lifted a cigarette out of Taylor's pack. He was terrified beyond words at what the demolitions expert had just proposed. He wasn't even aware of putting the cigarette in his mouth and lighting it, still mesmerized by Taylor's confidence; a kind of confidence that exudes only from a man having reached a well-thought-out decision.

Holt inhaled the strong tobacco, coughed, then spoke.

"Did I hear you correctly, Taylor?"

"Yes, you did, sir."

Taylor's purposefulness was contagious, so much so that it spread instantly to Sergeant Holt, locking and loading within Holt its same sure sense of righteousness. He and Taylor should have talked a long time ago, Holt thought, as he inhaled again on the Chesterfield, this time without coughing.

"I'm with you, Taylor. All the way!"

Vince wondered if the light beige makeup on his face had smeared.

It was 10:00 a.m.

Thorny briar bushes that populated the forest surrounding the eastern sector of Ft. Bragg had torn his suit around his knees but had yet to scratch his skin. Vince was grateful for that, remembering the pain of the severe cuts he had experienced on his arms and legs riding bareback through the Cuban jungle last year.

The eastern sector gate of Ft. Bragg, according to the informative presidential itinerary Thessalonian had given him, was a supply and equipment entrance normally manned by only two MPs. Vince doubted any Secret Service men would be posted there considering the mile distance between it and the main Kennedy visitation area.

As he neared the edge of the forest line he felt for his concealed .22 pistol, worried that he might have to use it if his makeup had in fact caked or smudged. Putting his fingers on his cheeks, though, he concluded that it had not and that it would be safe to proceed. There was about ten yards of open ground between the edge of the treeline and the base fence. He quickly ran across it toward the fence, yelling to the Green Beret MP forty yards away, "Sentry, sentry!"

The MP at the forefront of the eastern sector entrance walked forward a few steps, bringing his M-14 to ready position across his chest.

"Secret Service, sentry. Get over here," Vince yelled again as he pulled out his Secret Service badge and flashed it high over his head. The North Carolina morning sun reflected off of it.

The sentry responded quickly now, running down the outside of the fence, his M-14 still at ready position. The rugged-looking sentry displayed no emotion as he ran up to Vince, which meant Vince's makeup was still intact.

"Here's my identification," Vince said, holding the Secret Service identification up to the soldier.

The MP made a perfunctory check.

"Yes, sir, what can I do for you?"

"Have you seen any trespassers? One of our men says he caught a glimpse of a few people walking through the forest off the western side of the compound. Probably just kids, but thought we'd check on this side, too, just to make sure."

"No, sir, no action here whatsoever. Supply road's closed due to the President's visit, haven't seen a thing."

The MP looked to be intelligent so Vince stayed alert, continuing to act like he knew exactly what he was doing.

"Okay, son, just checking. Lancer is damn tight about his security." Lancer was the Secret Service code name for Kennedy.

"Yes, sir."

Vince began walking towards the eastern sector entrance gate as if it were the most natural thing in the world for him to do. After all, he was Secret Service and today Ft. Bragg was theirs. The soldier did not question Vince further as the well-disguised Mafioso calmly stepped on base. Vince was amazed at the power of the Secret Service identification Thessalonian had given him.

He registered his bearings and decided the best place to go would be the Commandant's barracks where Kennedy would be beginning his tour ... right about now!

"If General Mancus or Captain Marsh sees us out of barracks, there's going to be trouble. Their orders were crystal clear." Sergeant Holt was speaking softly to Specialist Tony Taylor, both men now seated on Taylor's bottom bunk. It was 10:15 a.m.

"Then we should split up," Taylor suggested.

"Maybe, but wait ... let's think this thing through, Tony." Holt paused, closing his eyes for a second's concentration. "Okay, exactly who is with Kennedy today?" He pointed at and began counting off his fingers, answering his own question. "Press, Secret Service, the brass of Ft. Bragg, which will include General Mancus and at least a unit of MPs. Captain Marsh is probably holed up in his barracks just like us."

"Right," Taylor confirmed, then went on, "Sergeant, if I may, let me tell you the way I was going to do it alone, which is the same way I think both of us should do it now."

Taylor spread the palms of his hands on his military pantlegs.

"We walk right through the President's entourage to the President, even if he's in the middle of his speech, and we tell him before God and country, if necessary, that there is a plot on his life. If we are out in the open, General Mancus will be unable to do anything to us. He'll be forced to just stand and hear us out."

The true moral fiber of Sergeant Holt that had been disintegrating for the last year now took hold.

"We can't do that, Tony. We just can't. If the press gets a hold of this, the American people will literally piss on themselves. They'll lose faith in the military, no telling what repercussion it might have, and I know neither of us wants that. I don't think the entire armed forces should be made to pay for the actions of a corrupt few, do you?"

Taylor looked at his shoes. "No."

Holt closed his dark eyes again in concentration. This was a technique he had learned from studying Tai Chi Chuan. It was effective now. He opened his eyes.

"How about this: we write two copies of the same message, both demanding an urgent private meeting with the President concerning an alpha crypto matter of national security. We take separate routes leaving here; you take the route around the western side of the parade ground; I'll take the route on the eastern side." He paused. "But what do we do about his Secret Service men? They probably won't let us near him."

"Why can't we give the message to one of them?" Taylor offered.

"No, Tony, at this point we have no way of knowing how deep Legerdemain goes—we don't know who we can trust." Holt snapped his fingers. "I got it. We need two MP armbands. That way we can wait till Kennedy is moving from point to point and get directly next to him without much of a fuss, then just calmly hand him the message. We'll stay separated, but if one of us sees the other giving him the message, then we know he's got it. We stay close to him till he's finished with the tour."

"Mancus will surely spot us before then."

"That's true, but think about it. Mancus is probably very nervous today, afraid of revealing any sign of improper or unusual conduct. So even if he does notice us, he'll be in no position to find out what we're up to."

"That's it then, Sergeant?"

"Except for Captain Marsh. Are you sure he's in barracks today?"

Specialist Taylor confirmed again, "Yes, sir, he told me specifically that he's confined to barracks, just like us."

"All right then, you need to get in full dress while I go round up a few MP armbands."

"Roland," Taylor said, grabbing the sergeant's arm as they both stood up beside the bunk, "be careful."

"I will," Sergeant Holt replied, feeling better about himself than he had since July of 1960.

"Let's go!"

⌖ ⌖ ⌖ ⌖

Whenever Captain Marsh tensed the calf muscle of his right bowleg, the legs of Lola tattooed there would spread. They were spreading now.

It was 10:20 a.m.

Since his interview with Corporal Forrestol last April Captain Marsh had felt like a new man. His face was always flushed these days, similar to the shade of tan he used to bring to Lola's black face when fucking her; the flush of satisfaction, of dreams on the brink of fulfillment.

Not that there wasn't a certain degree of strain, too, with this new man. There was, but that could be dealt with. He was dealing with it this morning by doing five sets of fifty military pushups.

He hated being confined to barracks, especially knowing that his ticket to prosperity was marching within yards of him, like entitled royalty. King Kennedy. BFD—Big Fucking Deal!

The professional in him, though, was genuinely curious about Kennedy, feeling that if he could actually see the man, it would be easier to kill him when the time came. Marsh did not want some gnaw in the back of his brain telling him subconsciously: "Archer Marsh, the man you're killing is larger than life—a legend—a God—impervious to the likes of you."

That sort of mental doubt could affect a man's shooting—a twitch here, a reflex jerk there, and before you know it, a miss. No, Captain Archer Marsh didn't want that. He needed to sneak a look at the target/objective of Legerdemain, and that was that.

He stopped doing his pushups, stood up and ran a towel through his blonde hair and on his Viking-like face. The tattoo of Lola on his calf had returned to normal. He began to dress, speaking aloud, "King Kennedy ... entitle this!"

Vince was reading signs as he walked quickly down the Ft. Bragg sidewalk: *Officers Mess - OM*, *Quartermaster- Hospital*, then finally *Commandant's Barracks-HQ* with an arrow.

It was 10:25 a.m.

He had taken his Secret Service identification and hung it from the breast pocket of his black suit. No military personnel had stopped to question him.

As he rounded the corner following the arrow leading to the Commandant's barracks, he froze. A hundred yards away, in the far eastern corner of what looked to be a parade ground, stood a large group of people. Vince knew it was the President's entourage. He started edging himself backwards, very slowly, content for now just to watch how the group was moving.

He felt a bump and turned just in time to hear a young female civilian, nicely-dressed, say, "Excuse me." Vince flashed a winning smile, noticing the woman's skullcap hairdo. It vaguely reminded him of Mona's, "Sure, no problem," he said.

Their eyes met as hers traveled down to Vince's breast pocket, looking at his Secret Service badge pinned there.

"Are you one of Baughman's men?" she asked.

Vince stuttered slightly. "Yes, ma'am," he answered unsurely.

Her eyes lifted again to his, then she turned and walked away, moving gracefully across the parade ground towards the presidential party. Vince knew his cover was blown. There was no telling who this young woman was or who she knew. He had to get out, now! Besides, he had established what he'd needed to. Thessalonian's Secret Service identification was fantastic and the key ingrèdient to breaching Kennedy's security.

Vince turned and backtracked quickly down the Ft. Bragg sidewalk, feeling suddenly like a man—a Sicilian—very much out of place!

They were in full dress, MP armbands and all, as they stepped out of their Ft. Bragg barracks.

It was 10:30 a.m.

Specialist Second Class Taylor began walking around the outer western rim of the parade ground. He could see in the opposite far eastern end Kennedy's entourage. Sergeant Holt, walking around the eastern rim, would get to the President first, Taylor deduced. He was glad he had opened up to Roland. One of them would surely get their message to Kennedy.

He looked to his right, in the direction of Captain Marsh's

barracks. Nothing. Captain Marsh was probably—hopefully—following his confinement orders.

Taylor walked quickly past the Captain's barracks.

⌖ ⌖ ⌖ ⌖

It was 10:35 a.m. Captain Marsh was aghast at what he had just seen walk past his barracks.

He could've sworn it was Taylor, in full dress with an MP's armband.

What in the peter-eating cowfuck was he doing? Captain Marsh thought Taylor and Holt had both been given strict orders to stay in barracks today.

Marsh hurried his dressing and walked out of his door toward the parade ground and Taylor, tucking his shirttail in and slipping a pair of big aviator sunshades on as he did. Something was wrong. Damned wrong!

⌖ ⌖ ⌖ ⌖

Taylor had to navigate through four white frame, two-story, general barracks buildings to get to where he was going. It was 10:40 a.m.

He was halfway through them when he felt a large hand grab his shoulder and jerk him around. The sight of Captain Marsh, with that confederate sneer and big aviator sunshades on his face, made his knees buckle. Taylor was too stunned to grab his .45 caliber sidearm, too surprised to pull his knife, too scared to even swing a decent right hook. He just stood there.

"Taylor. What in the Godmammy hell are you doing?" Taylor was dumbfounded. "Well, what in the name of syphilis, boy, are you fucking doing?"

Finally, Taylor, from sheer, near-paralyzing fright, attempted to make a move. He tried to pull and shove his knee into Captain Marsh's groin, which in Taylor's mind seemed the easiest way to disable him. What he would have done from there, had he overcome Marsh, he did not know. It never mattered anyway. Tony Taylor wasn't the only one acting on pure impulse. Marsh blocked Taylor's dance-like kick and shoved the palm of his right hand into Taylor's chest cavity.

Marsh was not a martial arts expert like Sergeant Holt but he had excelled in hand-to-hand combat training throughout his military career. He liked the way his twenty-inch biceps propelled his body and as with the first man he had killed in Kalioke Swamp, Alabama, the enjoyment, the power was everything.

Taylor doubled with pain, but still managed to connect a full counter kick into Marsh's stomach. Though hurt, Archer Marsh, like an enraged viper, just kept biting and punching and biting and punching until his poison was let. He wrestled Taylor to the ground and pinned him there. Taylor's all-American face was bleeding—badly. And Marsh figured the boy to be only half conscious.

"You, son of a bitch, you traitor!" Taylor screamed at the top of his lungs. "You TRAITOR!" he screamed again.

The Captain put his hand over Taylor's mouth. Taylor's eyes were bulging now, like the rest of his body; beaten stupid.

"Legerdemain, Legerdemain," he mumphed and mumphed through Marsh's hand.

At hearing this, Captain Archer Marsh rolled Taylor over before he could scream anymore, put his knee in the middle of Taylor's back, grabbed Taylor's eye socket from behind and jerked Taylor's head up.

The last semiconscious thoughts Taylor had were of Roland Holt and John F. Kennedy and their brains spilling out their ears; their neck, spinal columns and cervical plexi snapping like Alabama chickens!

⌖ ⌖ ⌖ ⌖

Sergeant Roland Holt's dark eyes had Kennedy's entourage in view as he walked quickly around the eastern rim of the parade ground, not too quick though to cause alarm.

It was 10:50 a.m.

He had decided to post himself about ten yards behind the group of people crowded around the President, which he had correctly guessed contained members of the press, Secret Service and Ft. Bragg brass, including Brigadier General Alexander T. Mancus. Holt could hear the voices of the Army tour guides in their lecturing monotones. The sergeant saw no sign of Taylor.

"Where could he be?" Holt thought to himself, as nervous as a Laotian cat.

Within eighty seconds the group began moving. Sergeant Holt stayed ten yards behind them. No one even glanced in his direction. Every eye and ear was directed towards the center of the crowd, which is where Holt assumed President Kennedy was. They moved only a short distance away where a team of Green Berets appeared to be preparing for a special weapons demonstration. Holt remained still, at attention, hands clasped behind his back, feeling the paper with the message to the President on it in the palm of his left hand.

Suddenly he felt a human presence behind him and heard a voice whispering in an easily recognizable Alabama twang.

"Sergeant, don't do anything dumb. I've got a gun on you and would as soon kill you right now as look at your spooky fucking ass." Sergeant Holt was as taut as a tight rope.

Marsh kept whispering menacingly, "And I'd get away with it, too. Do you remember when we were first briefed, Mancus told us that you, me, and Taylor had been blackpaged. Remember? Good. Then you know I can shoot you as an unauthorized person and get away with it. And as far as this country's concerned, you never existed. So I want you to turn around and walk away slowly, like it was just a normal Sunday stroll. Now, you dogfuck!"

Sergeant Holt's mind was zooming.

If he screamed a warning to the President now, not only would Marsh shoot him but the entire U.S. Armed Forces would be brought to bear for his words. And he still loved his country and Special Forces, and like he had told Taylor, it would be a tragic mistake for the entire American military to pay for the actions of a corrupt few. He decided to stall.

"But, Captain, there are a lot of soldiers on base who have seen us together. They know I belong here. Your explanation might be very hard for some of them to swallow."

"You've got thirty seconds, Holt, to move, or I'll shoot you where you stand!"

Sergeant Holt was confident that he could take the Captain in a one-on-one, hand-to-hand fight. So he reasoned that if he followed him now, he could disarm him and still act to warn the President.

Holt, in a robot-like motion, put the written message to the President in his pocket, went to an at-ease position, turned, and began walking away—back down the eastern rim of the parade ground. Captain Marsh was beside him and slightly behind him.

Loud arms fire began booming near the President's crowd. Holt assumed it was the weapons demonstration he had seen his fellow Green Berets preparing.

Holt saw out the corner of his eye that Marsh had jerked with surprise at the noise. He and the captain neared a set of bleachers used by civilians to view Special Forces parachute jumps. They came up on the bleachers exactly as another volley of demonstration rounds exploded.

Holt moved simultaneously with the blasts. He grabbed Marsh's heavily muscled left arm and kicked with a left side snap directly into Marsh's ribs. This was the second hard blow the Captain's stomach area had taken in less than fifteen minutes. He bent over double but did not lose the 9mm pistol in his hand. Moving as fast as a cracking bullwhip, Holt lunged for Marsh's right wrist, the gun, and twisted it downward, then brought his knee down on the right elbow, attempting to break it. Marsh's 9mm pistol discharged just as a third weapons demonstration volley rang out from across the parade ground. The pistol fell from Marsh's partially disabled grip, clacking across the steel bleacher supports. Holt knew he had the captain now.

The sergeant moved closer to Marsh. He had accomplished what he had set out to do, which was to disarm the captain, but was temporarily at a loss as to what to do next with the career army man. Holt knew in his heart he couldn't kill him, seeing as how he did not know for sure Marsh's role in the Legerdemain deception, so he hesitated.

Captain Marsh, though disarmed and partially disabled, threw every bit of his right arm and still-functioning upper body at Holt. The sergeant was unprepared for the onslaught. The captain held Holt's neck in a one-arm bear hug and squeezed his windpipe three times in rapid succession, then expertly maneuvered around and dropped his throbbing left arm underneath the sergeant's chin. With devastating effectiveness Marsh pulled up, then pushed over with his right forearm, tearing Holt's trapezius muscle, then cracking his neck.

The sergeant slumped in Marsh's arms. Half out of his mind from pain, the injured Captain Marsh, barely able to stand, had an uncontrollable urge to find a stick and bash Holt's skull in then to unzip his pants and urinate on the young punk—goody two-shoes—who had caused him so much grief these last sixteen months.

Instead he lifted the dead sergeant and leaned him on his shoulder, like a drunk comrade, and made his way with difficulty back to his barracks; his exhausted mind swearing he could hear the spooky voice of Roland Holt taunting him.

"Archer Marsh, the man you will be killing, John F. Kennedy, is larger than life—a legend, a God—impervious to the likes of you. The likes of white Alabama trash like you!"

Chapter Seventeen

October 16, 1961

Not even sleeping pills had helped Brigadier General Alexander T. Mancus recover from the events of yesterday, last night, and the wee hours of the morning.

It was 6:00 a.m.

John F. Kennedy had concluded his tour of Ft. Bragg's Special Warfare Center by mid-afternoon yesterday and the General had immediately, upon the President's departure, gone to see Captain Marsh.

The Captain had walked up to the presidential crowd and to General Mancus around 11:30 a.m., during the final segment of the special weapons demonstration. Marsh looked bruised and stooped and was dressed irregularly, with a Military Police band around his arm and a pair of large aviator sunshades over his eyes. He had informed the General very quickly that there had been a crisis, that it had been contained, but that he needed to see him the minute the President left. Then Marsh froze for thirty seconds, staring at John Kennedy who was laughing and enjoying himself with members of the press.

General Mancus elbowed Marsh gently, trying to snap the captain out of his trance then motioned for Marsh to leave; the General hoping against hope that none of Kennedy's Secret Service men had paid much attention to the disheveled MP.

The odor that bombarded General Mancus's senses upon entering Marsh's barracks told him all he needed to know. It was the smell of decomposing death.

Marsh led the General to a corner closet and opened it swiftly. There lay the bodies of Specialist Second Class Anthony "Tony" Taylor and Sergeant Roland Holt. Both of their necks appeared to have been broken.

Even the death-seasoned General Mancus was aghast. He turned to Marsh, his face as white as bone, and asked dully, "Why?"

The Captain half gargled, half stuttered a reply.

"They didn't buy it, sir. They were trying to get to the President. Here ... I found this in Holt's pocket. I couldn't find one on Taylor but you can bet your bazookas he was going to deliver the same message." He handed the slip of paper to the General.

It read:

"Mr. President, there is a matter of urgent alpha crypto—national security importance—that we must talk to you about before you leave the base today. Please tell no one. We will let you know who we are. Two of your loyal Green Berets."

General Mancus hadn't vomited since he was thirteen years old and sick with pneumonia but he felt like vomiting now. A putrid bile had begun to rise in his intestines, the likes of which he had never felt before in his life. He, however, maintained his composure enough to help Marsh dispose of the bodies. They stripped them and wrapped them in blankets, covered them with a tarpaulin in the back of the General's jeep and drove them off the base. They then carried the bodies into a dense part of the North Carolina forest and buried them deep in the forest floor.

They had finished about 3:00 a.m. and the sleeping pills General Mancus had taken then hadn't even begun to kick in three hours later.

Legerdemain was becoming more than just a distasteful deception to the General and he was finding it increasingly difficult to rationalize it as just his mission. His mind flashed back to the first time he had met a representative of the Inter Inpetto Armaments Corporation. It had been in Berlin in 1945.

Mancus, then a Colonel and Commander of a tank division, had been lured by another U.S. tank division Colonel-Commander to a meeting with one of Tomeen's staff. At the meeting the IIPAC rep was blatant with his offer of bribery, which the honest Colonel Mancus had rejected, but for reasons he himself did not fully understand Mancus accepted and pocketed the rep's business card which had printed on it a U.S. and Swiss contact number. For years he kept the yellowing card and in 1950 had been forced to use it.

In January of that year a tragic case of hit and run had left his son paralyzed. The financially strapped U.S. Army at the time was only willing to cover the bare medical costs, leaving the payment for his son's experimental medication and therapy at the feet of the recently promoted General Mancus.

He contacted IIPAC, which within weeks began subsidizing his son's medical treatment and which, oddly enough, asked for nothing immediate in return. These huge sums kept being deposited in concealed shell accounts with not so much as a peep out of IIPAC. Even throughout the crest of the Korean War, IIPAC asked nothing from General Mancus.

Then in mid-1956 the hierarchy of IIPAC made its first request. They explained to General Mancus that President Eisenhower's defense spending policies were unacceptable. They asked the General to investigate any feasible alternatives by which to influence the man.

"The purchase of a General," Mancus said, sighing with regret. "My life ceased being mine then, that morning in 1956, a morning not dissimilar to today."

As he stood, his sixty-year-old shoulders slouched, his white strandy hair unkempt, at the window of his Ft. Bragg deputy commandant's office, he allowed himself for the first time to feel, wholly, his anguish over the killing of Taylor and Holt.

Then he thought of his son, who after receiving the best medical treatment money could buy for more than a decade, was still only half a man.

"But at least he's alive," General Mancus resolved.

It was time to contact Thessalonian.

SEVEN MONTHS LATER
May 9, 1962
Second Floor Sitting Room
The White House
Washington, D.C.
Late Night.

Not even the splendor of my trip to France last June could compare with the thrill of looking at the John Glenn Space Capsule at Cape Canaveral with Mr. Glenn in February. I couldn't believe my eyes ... to think that a man could actually live through a boost like that ... then to become a tiny speck dissolving in the sky. I wish I could launch Southeast Asia into outer space the same way ... after pulling out all the Americans, of course ... the supply units, the helicopter units, the Air Force mule teams and Ranch Hand and Jungle Jim units and all the Special Forces advisors. We're up to almost 12,000 troops now ... the Military Assistance Command Vietnam (MAVC) and even the Maxwell Taylor-Walt Rostow report of last November recommended sending in regular Army troops. It seems they don't understand how determined I am to keep a strict limit on our involvement there ...

In fact, the more consideration I give to Southeast Asia and the more I see of President Diem, the more I am convinced that we should not be there at all, except maybe for a CIA tribal level involvement with the Civilian Irregular Defense Groups.

I feel myself repulsed, yet cornered ...

I wonder what Honey Fitzgerald would have done ... ha ... I can hear him now ..."Do just te opposite of what te expect, Johnny Boy, just te opposite!"

Chapter Eighteen

May 10, 1962

"Has Thessalonian been monitoring General Mancus like he said he would?"

Major General Marion Armstrong III, deputy director for the Special Assistant for Counterinsurgency and Special Activities (SACSA), was determined to not mince words with Plato Smith.

It was 1:00 p.m.

Plato Smith, of the CIA's Directorate of Plans (DDP)-Western Hemisphere Division, could feel the grip of General Armstrong around his vocal cords. He answered patiently, regretting that he had impulsively pressured the General for Legerdemain's conclusion back in October. So much had happened since then.

"Yes, Ratchet. Thessalonian put Mancus under surveillance after the Holt-Taylor incident and has communicated with him regularly since. According to Thessalonian, General Mancus, even though shocked by the deaths of Holt and Taylor, is relieved now just to be dealing with Captain Marsh on Legerdemain. He feels safer, subsequently Thessalonian feels safer and I feel safer. So Contingency LED-1 is still well intact."

"What about Contingency LED-2 and Charlie Nuccia's man?" General Armstrong asked dryly.

"Solid as they come. He's still stalking. Thessalonian says the guy has lots of balls; followed Kennedy onto Bragg and Cape Canaveral."

"Okay, but tell Thessalonian to keep this guy in check. No more risks. And the Jimenez-Cuban Contingency LED-3; how's Thessalonian doing with the shooter's program there?"

"Excellent, Ratchet. Jimenez vouched for him in the Cuban exile community in New Orleans. He's currently developing the shooter through them and some of his other Orleans operatives. Thessalonian insisted that the guy he's got is perfect. Absolutely perfect."

"Good. Anything else?" General Armstrong was obviously not in a bullshitting mood.

"No, but Ratchet, I'm holding tough. No one's looking at me crosswise, so don't worry, I'm here for the duration."

General Armstrong quickly rebuffed. "Keep it that way, Plato. I don't want to ever hear again about your precious and precarious DDP position like I did in October. Legerdemain is on until we are told differently, which means that as is we are all at risk including, if not especially, me. Understand?"

"Yes, Ratchet."

The General laid the desk phone down into its holder and moved across his SACSA office to his maple cabinet, lifting out of it the 030601 receiver. General Armstrong did not have to wait long for the gruff voice of Clemer Dodd to answer.

"030601—this is Intercept Eagle—Legerdemain contingencies status still at modified holding pattern stage ... and stable ... repeat ... Legerdemain contingencies status still at modified holding pattern stage and stable ... over."

Clemer Dodd repeated, "Intercept Eagle ... received ... Legerdemain contingencies status still at modified holding pattern stage and stable ... acknowledged," then added, "and, Intercept Eagle, I have a priority supplement from INFIX ... any further breaches of security require immediate zero action ... repeat, require immediate zero action. Do you acknowledge, Eagle?"

"Acknowledge," said General Armstrong, his voice barely audible, "Clear."

"Clear," answered Clemer Dodd.

The 030601 line went dead.

Sosar Tomeen was seated alone in his gilded-cage-like office atop the Inter Inpetto Armaments Corporation building on the Zollikerstrasse in Zurich, Switzerland.

It was 8:00 a.m. Central European Time.

Yesterday Sosar had ordered George Whitten as INFIX to send a supplemental message to General Armstrong concerning any further Legerdemain security breaches.

"Immediate Zero Action," he had told Whitten to tell Armstrong, "Immediate Zero Action."

George Whitten had argued passionately against this but Sosar was convinced that IZA would have to be implemented if there were any more problems like the Holt-Taylor incident last October.

Immediate Zero Action was the equivalent of an operational self-destruct. Within 48 hours of its implementation Thessalonian would have to kill all parties involved in all contingencies with the exception of General Armstrong and Plato Smith. All the Mafiosos, all the Cubans, Captain Marsh and General Mancus would be terminated—Legerdemain would cease to exist—John F. Kennedy would live.

Sosar Tomeen, however, did not want to implement an immediate Zero Action. Especially considering that for the last year, since having placed Legerdemain at holding pattern stage, Kennedy had showed no further inclination to commit conventional forces to Southeast Asia. In fact, Sosar was becoming impatient with Kennedy and had been tempted numerous times to put Legerdemain back at trigger stage. Still, though, he was hoping that Kennedy would eventually see the light—IIPAC's light—and move decisively.

But in the interim Sosar was determined to shield himself, thus the Immediate Zero Action order.

The Holt-Taylor incident at Ft. Bragg in October had taken him completely by surprise, forcing him to realize just how much of a juggling act Legerdemain really was. And prison, Sosar had decided, was a place he did not want to go to. It would remind him too much of his lonely childhood spent at the Vanderbilt Boarding School.

He brought his three-fingered right hand to his lips, whispering through them, "Little Horatio, where are you when I need you?"

His mind drifted, wistfully appealing to the ghost of his childhood friend, "Help Thessalonian with this, Horatio—for he will have to be a master shyster and master scammer to pull this off. Just like you used to be, only better."

Chapter Nineteen

May 11, 1962

She was straddling Vince, rocking back and forth, in the throes of ecstasy.

"Oh, baby, Vince."

It was 7:00 a.m.

Her manicured pink nails scratched Vince's chest as she tensed, climaxed, then tightened her vaginal muscles around Vince's erection, coaxing the concurrent release of his sauce into her. She then lowered her mouth to his, planting there a luscious kiss of heartfelt sentiment. Vince returned the gesture.

Mona Spazek had been living in Vince's French Quarter apartment on Chartres Street since late October. He had revealed his true identity to her on the first night of her arrival.

"Mona, baby, my name's not Ralphie Bosco." He had paused, not wanting to scare her. "It's Vincenzo Angeletta. Most people call me Vince or 'Angler.'"

Upon hearing this she had stared into Vince's silvery-brown blue eyes for at least thirty seconds, then had simply asked, "Why?"

He explained to her that he wasn't really an insurance claims adjuster but that he worked for a group of men who were gamblers mostly and that his real job was to carry money around the country for them. She asked if his work was dangerous or illegal. He told her it was both but that he was good at it and that she had nothing to worry about.

"Vince 'Angler' Angeletta," she mimicked, "well, nice to meet you, sir."

She extended her lovely hand, smiled her best, most alluring Jayne Mansfield smile, then proceeded to make love to her mystery man, who had always treated her with respect and tenderness.

Since October Vince had followed Kennedy to six more domestic public appearances, the last of which had been in February to Cape Canaveral. There again he had penetrated both the security of Cape Canaveral and the President's security by flashing his Thessalonian-supplied Secret Service identification. After that, however, he had decided to lay low for a bit and return to New Orleans from Washington to spend some well-deserved romantic time with Mona.

These last three months had been happy ones for Vince. Not since Rosalie had he been so fulfilled, so tame. He would spend his afternoons and early evenings with Charlie at Lafitte's Westport Club, playing baccarat, pinochle, and poker, then pick Mona up at the Southport Shopping Center where he had arranged for her to work as a manager. They would dine out, usually at the Steak Pit on Bourbon Street which Charlie's brother Giuseppe owned, or have Italian po-boys at Castriconie's.

It had been an easy three months. Until yesterday.

Yesterday Vince had been contacted by Daniel Carthage. Carthage was the homosexual pilot and one of the three CIA operatives that worked for Thessalonian in New Orleans. Vince also remembered Carthage as having piloted Charlie a few times back in 1959. He had approached Vince on the corner of Dumaine and Chartres Streets.

"Angler?" Carthage had asked.

"Yea, who wants to know?" Vince had answered belligerently, guarded, not quite able to place the face.

"The name's Dan Carthage and I believe we have a mutual friend?" Vince didn't speak until the name registered.

"Carthage—oh, yea, the pilot, right. We're talking about the bible man."

"Yes. I have a message for you. Ten tomorrow night in Kenner near Moisant, the Look-See Bar. You know it?"

"Yea, the strip joint."

With that Carthage had walked away. Vince had been impressed by the pilot's professionalism. Thessalonian obviously had some capable people working for him.

Vince rolled over and put his romantic Sicilian lips on the pinkish brown aureoles of Mona's breasts, wondering silently if Thessalonian would have the final stage of Legerdemain ready for him tonight. He felt totally prepared to do what had to be done with JFK, fulfilling the promise to his Don Nuccia that he had made to himself after the Cuban disaster in November 1960.

"Questo te prometto, Don Nuccia," Vince thought as he sucked and lapped Mona's breasts like a baby ... innocently ... sexually ... milking from them ... the nectar of assassination.

Charlie Nuccia and his most important *solidato*, Vince Angeletta, were sitting in the rear office of Lafitte's Westport Club.

It was 12:30 p.m.

Charlie's leather-bound lamp shone brightly atop his mahogany desk, accentuating the letters CN emblazoned on the desk front. His thick, menacing nose curled downward as he puffed on his ever-present cigar, talking while he did.

"Vincenzo, that fucking Robert Kennedy has really been applying the heat on me ever since I came back from Honduras. We need ta get this dog's head chopped off so its tail will quit wagging, soon! When you see Thessalonian tonight press him ta get this thing finished." He exhaled a mouthful of smoke "Shit, it's been a year since either one of us has talked ta Thessalonian personally. For all we know it might be another year before we get ta again. Do you understand, Vin?" Charlie asked slyly, intoning that Vince should intimidate Thessalonian when he met with him.

"I understand."

Charlie kept on. "He does stay in touch through his operatives. Carthage the queen pilot, Bannerwell the PI, and Cross, the trade union guy, but never personally."

"Yea, Charlie. Carthage was the one that told me about the meet tonight," Vince added.

Charlie leaned forward, folding his short stocky arms atop the desk.

"Vin, how confident are you about doing it?"

Vince looked down at his hands then back up at the man who was more than a father to him.

"Charlie, I can take JFK. All I need to know now is where. I've followed him, watched him. The man's a sitting duck. But I'm like you, I'm ready to finish it."

Charlie leaned back, caressing the cigar with his lips, smiling.

"Good, Vincenzo. But stay on your toes with Thessalonian. Even though I felt he was being straight when he acted like a scared buffoon in Honduras, it may have been just that, an act. Be careful, Vin. Let's not get too comfortable or too confident."

Vince ran a hand through his black wavy hair and nodded at Charlie's suggestion. Charlie continued.

"That'ssa why they are called Central Intelligence, Vin, they are intelligent."

Vince smiled confidently. "But they're not Sicilian, Charlie, they're not Sicilian."

Charlie Nuccia grinned sardonically, with conceit.

Thessalonian's throat scars rippled and the cotton wads in his mouth shrank as he swallowed another huge gulp of Jax beer, his high cheekbones and artificially darkened eyebrows flinching from the aftertaste of the harsh New Orleans brew. He then methodically scanned the interior of the Look-See Strip Bar in Kenner, Louisiana.

It was 9:45 p.m.

His operative, Carthage, had selected this place for him to meet Angeletta mainly because of its close proximity to Moisant-New Orleans International Airport, allowing for Thessalonian to fly in and fly out quickly. The Look-See Bar was also one of the few bars in the New Orleans area that was not at least partially owned by the Nuccia family. Only the jukeboxes were Nuccia's, owned by his Fleur di Fleur Novelties Company.

Knowing that Nuccia's influence was limited in this establishment comforted Thessalonian little, however, as the CIA man was not looking forward to seeing Vince "Angler" Angeletta again. He remembered painfully how Angeletta had punched him at that first meeting in Honduras last year and how the prick had made him stay with that stinking Mestizo guard at the Hotel Camino while they put together the initial stages of the Sicilian version of Legerdemain.

It would be difficult to stay in character tonight, Thessalonian thought. He would just as soon cut the arrogant Sicilian's throat as have to deal with him.

When Plato Smith, his CIA superior, had first approached him with Legerdemain in early 1960 he had made it very clear to Thessalonian that he could refuse the assignment. Plato explained that Legerdemain would be a parallel covert operation mobilized by certain powerful factions in the defense department only if John F. Kennedy were to win the Democratic nomination for President, activated only if JFK actually won the presidency.

Thessalonian, being a talented high stepper through the CIA's bureaucratic mine field, had accepted, supremely confident that Legerdemain was a smart, once-in-a-lifetime career opportunity for him.

But he sure as fuck hated dealing with these Sicilians. He would love to kill every one of them; those cocky dago punks.

He was swallowing another huge gulp of Jax beer, attempting to squelch his murderous tendencies, when Vince Angeletta walked through the entrance of the Look-See Bar. Thessalonian had to admit that the finely dressed Mafioso carried himself well; like a Sicilian Adonis.

Vince sat down next to him without saying a word. A stripper appeared on the corner stage and began gyrating to the opening chords of *Sugar Man*, playing on the Nuccia-owned jukebox.

Thessalonian, too, began his performance. "Good to see you, Mr. Angeletta." He offered his hand. Vince just stared at him, unaccepting.

"Let's get to it, Barker," Vince said briskly.

Thessalonian was immediately taken aback by Vince's use of the name Barker. Miles Barker had been the name Thessalonian had given Nuccia and Angeletta in Honduras as his real name. It was not his real name, but the fact that this Sicilian jerk had used it so casually still made him nervous.

Thessalonian gave himself a moment, trying desperately to stay in character. Man, he thought quickly, would he enjoy killing this gangster son of a bitch!

"Okay, Vince. It's time for the next stage of Legerdemain. You've followed JFK, studied him and explored the effectiveness of the Secret Service ID I gave you. Now it's time for you to pick a spot."

Thessalonian reached into his black leather jacket pocket,

which in combination with his suit pants made him look like a geek trying to be cool, and pulled out a sheet of paper. He unfolded it.

"Here's a list of cities that will probably be put on the presidential itinerary before the end of '63. You need to travel to each of these cities and in each, plan a parade."

"What?" Vince asked, even-toned but uncomprehending.

"A parade. What you'll do is figure a route in each city that will provide you with the most opportunities for a successful shoot. Then diagram that route using the main airport in each city as a starting point. In most cases the presidential destination on these types of visits will be either city hall or some historical landmark or monument that that particular area is famous for. It'll be up to you to research each municipal area and choose what would be the most likely presidential destination."

"Fuck, Thessalonian," Vince interrupted, "there could be several likely destinations in each place. How am I supposed to know where he is going to end up?"

"Vince, it's like this: we're not trying to predict his moves, we are trying to premeditate them. I have a connection with the people who schedule the President's trips and what I'm going to do is use the information you give me to influence his route when we decide to hit. By my estimates it will take you at least until December to finish casing the cities on this list."

Vince grabbed the list forcefully from the CIA man and read it aloud.

"St. Louis, Detroit, Cincinnati, Dallas, Atlanta, Miami, Memphis, Kansas City, Denver, Minneapolis, Little Rock; all midwest, south, and south-central. Why?"

"Because they'll be the easiest for you to scout. It would make no sense to try to diagram places like New York or Los Angeles. They're just too big."

Vince was becoming so intent, scheming with Thessalonian, that he had almost forgotten Charlie's orders to put the squeeze on the man sitting next to him; the man who owed the Nuccia family so much.

"Seven months is too long, Thessalonian. Look, Charlie's already pissed that it's taken this long. He's not going to stand for another seven months."

Thessalonian, almost losing touch with his mild-meek-weak, play-acting disposition, retorted, "He's going to have to be patient, Vince. Tell him this sort of job is a waiting game. It's a hell of a lot different than putting a bullet in the back of somebody's head at point-blank range, then dumping them in the swamp. If we blow this, the fallout will destroy him and his entire family. I know what I'm doing but we can't move until you and JFK are perfectly in place. The same place at the exact same second. If we move prematurely, we are just asking for catastrophe."

The wind blowing the sails of Vince's intimidation calmed upon hearing Thessalonian's common sense. He was, after all, the expert programmer here. Vince folded the list of cities into his suit pocket.

"Yea, awright, Barker, but just don't forget who's in charge here. You owe us, not the other way around. You dance when we say dance, not the other way around. We're the band leaders here and you're just the arranger. And don't ever fucking forget it. Got it?"

Thessalonian's dead-fish gray eyes were about to bulge out of their sockets with rage.

"Sure, Vince." Thessalonian stood up, anxious to leave before he completely lost his cool. "I just want my debt clear with you people and that's that. Can I go now?"

Vince looked at the CIA man—bully to coward.. "For now, Barker, for now!"

Thessalonian stepped on board the last daily Pan Am flight from Moisant Field-New Orleans to the Los Angeles International Airport.

It was 11:15 p.m.

He was feeling good about having controlled his temper with Angeletta. Legerdemain had come too far for mistakes now. Besides, just maintaining this modified holding pattern stage—modified due to the Holt-Taylor incident—was difficult enough without further complications.

Getting Angeletta to traipse around the country drawing diagrams of prospective presidential parade routes was the only activity he had been able to think of to keep the Sicilians occupied. It was not easy bullshitting professional bullshitters. Then again, Thessalonian thought, the diagrams may actually be of some use when we go to full trigger stage.

The two other loose ends that demanded his immediate attention now were Lee Harvey Oswald—shooter for Contingency LED-3—and the right-wing-nut patriot to take Oswald out after the ex-Marine took the fall for Kennedy's assassination.

Thessalonian had ordered Oswald to be back from Russia by June 2, and intended to send the ex-marine/ONI operative for a brief stay in Dallas. That is, until Thessalonian's operatives had secured a place for Oswald within both the pro- and anti-Castro elements of the Cuban Exile Community. The exile formation of the Oswald character under the umbrella of Contingency Legerdemain-3 was Thessalonian's opportunity to show off to his superiors his own tactical and strategic skills. An opportunity he intended to take full advantage of.

The other loose end—arranging for the right-wing-nut patriot to take Oswald out after the Kennedy shoot—was what Thessalonian intended to tie up in Los Angeles. Thinking this aspect through these last months had led Thessalonian to varied conclusions. If indeed he were to recruit a man like this into play, the risks would increase substantially. Right-wing-nut patriots could not be controlled; they were undisciplined, they were wild cards.

So the next best thing, Thessalonian had figured, would be to get a man, a shooter he could control to kill Oswald afterwards then have the man act like and be sold as a right-wing-nut patriot. The man would have to have plenty of incentive to keep his mouth shut.

Again Thessalonian's mind kept coming back to the Sicilians. They had armies of men and associates on tap for this sort of suicide mission, but Charlie Nuccia and Vince Angeletta could never find out. Those two were operating under the assumption that they were alone in Legerdemain and that Thessalonian was paying off a debt to them by coordinating the presidential hit.

So Thessalonian had decided to turn to Los Angeles in his approach to Chicago.

The original approach in setting up Contingency LED-2

and the Sicilians with the Castro assassination in 1960 had been made through Anacondini's Hollywood point man, Gaetano Rossini. Rossini, even though a high-ranking member of Stefano "Mr. A" Anacondini's Chicago family, lived in Hollywood and collected for Anacondini there.

The original contact back in 1960 had been made by Thessalonian's man, Cross, the president of the New Orleans Trade Union, posing as a CIA agent, which in truth he was. Cross had then set up the initial meet for Thessalonian at the Fontainebleau in Miami. This time, however, Thessalonian would personally approach Rossini, who would then approach his boss, Anacondini, about a meet in Los Angeles to arrange for Oswald's shooter. He would convince Anacondini then that it was in the Mafioso's best interest to keep their arrangement quiet, away from the powerful New Orleans boss, Charlie Nuccia, and that he, Anacondini, would be scoring big, big brownie points with the new President's administration if he handled this for them.

Thessalonian knew that even though Anacondini was not old school Sicilian Mafia like Charlie Nuccia, he was probably irate enough with Kennedy to arrange for a man to handle the secondary shooting of Kennedy's shooter. After all, Stefano Anacondini had received nothing from Kennedy for having swung the Cook County political vote for him in the 1960 presidential election.

"Yes," Thessalonian thought as the big Pan Am jet soared into the south Louisiana night, "Stefano Anacondini is ripe for the taking."

It wasn't until after he completed his mental machinations that he noticed, seated next to him in the first-class section of the aircraft, a woman who resembled the great and so very late female Cuban freedom fighter, Margareta Jimenez.

"Espanol?" he queried of the beautiful girl.

She turned to him with a hard, transparently lustful gaze.

"Si, Senor. I am from Guatemala."

The CIA covert specialist smiled.

"Funny ... I used to know a girl from Guatemala. She's passed on now, but you look a lot like her."

"Oh?" she replied.

"No, not really—you are infinitisimo more attractive."

His scarred forearm reached for her hand and he kissed it.

She looked down at his scarred arm, then looked up into his passionless gray eyes, and said, "And I, senor, like men with scars."

Chapter Twenty

May 13, 1962

"The Beverly Hills Supper Club is not any more of a money maker than my Villa Roma Ristorante in Norwood, you bluster fucks!" Anacondini growled.

Gaetano Rossini and Mario "the Sissy" Pacissi exchanged covert glances with practiced patience at their boss's insults. Both men were fully cognizant of how hard it had been for "Mr. A." to let his wife divorce him back in 1958 and how much a thing like that could damage irreparably the ego of a man like Stefano. Even so, Mr. A. was, at times like this, unbearable.

It was 9:00 a.m.

Gaetano Rossini, Mr. A.'s slick Hollywood point man, had just informed the six foot four inch Anacondini of the CIA having contacted him yesterday in Los Angeles, requesting that he, Rossini, set up a meet for them with his Chicago Mafia boss.

"A very private meet is-a what they said, Mr. A., with just one of their men at the Beverly Hills Supper Club at 11:00 p.m. tomorrow night," Rossini had told him.

At the mention of the Beverly Hills Supper Club, one of the few Hollywood nightspots that Anacondini through Rossini did not own, Mr. A. reacted violently.

"That fucking BH doesn't have near the lights and seating we have at the Villa Roma ... and gross (belch) receipts (belch) ... they can't even come close to us ... those dipdong shits!"

It was apparent to both Rossini and Mario that Anacondini was on a morning drunk. Mario, looking this morning very unnerved in his Mickey Rooneyish way, stepped out of Mr. A's office to get his employer a cup of espresso. He was embarrassed to see his father-in-law in this condition, especially after Rossini had made special arrangements last night to fly to Chicago from California on this critical business.

Anacondini's office was located in the rear of the Ammo Antilly Lounge in Cicero, Illinois, not far from where Capone used to be headquartered. In fact, Anacondini in his early years had worked closely with the Orange Street Gang who used to run errands for the Capone organization. He had graduated from there to chauffeuring one of Capone's lieutenants. That lieutenant later rose in the ranks after Capone's demise to being one of the top bosses in the Chicago Mafia. Anacondini became his trusted underboss and heir to his throne, which he inherited when his boss was killed in 1952. Rumor had it that Anacondini had arranged for his boss's shotgun slaying, easing the path for his own ascension to Top Boss of the Chicago Mafia in 1953.

Stefano "Mr. A." Anacondini had always been a brutal, tactless man, blustering about in a city whose historical development read like a chronology of gangsterism. After his rise to prominence, however, his personality became even more despicable. His wife asked him for a divorce in 1959 for that very reason.

It wasn't enough that Anacondini was bedding a half-dozen famous Hollywood actresses, but he insisted upon flaunting it, too. His wife, an old line Sicilian matron, refused to be continually disrespected in this manner, and using her connections in Sicily, forced Stefano into a divorce. Of course, divorce was a sin in the Catholic Church, but then again so was adultery.

Anacondini was devastated by this, making him even more reckless with his high profile shenanigans. It was then that he began publicly associating with national politicos and influencing effectively, for a chosen few of them, the Cook County political machine in their favor.

He had done this for John F. Kennedy in what had turned out to be an unrequited gesture. He had tried again to earn JFK's favors by helping Romano and Nuccia with the Castro hit, only to be let down again by Kennedy's betrayal after being elected President.

"Jesus," he had thought to himself one night, wallowing in drunken self-pity, "me and Jack even fuck a few of the same Hollywood broads!"

So it was somewhat understandable that his bitter disappointment over these successive personal and professional failures had driven him to the bottle. It was because of this that Mario "the Sissy" Pacissi, his loyal son-in-law, fretted over him incessantly.

"What did you say, Gaetano?" Mr. A. said, asking his Hollywood lieutenant to repeat himself, sobering slightly after downing a few sips of espresso.

Gaetano Rossini was to the outer fringe of Hollywood's business and social community a "strategist"; at least that's what read on his business card. To the inner fringe, however, he was "the man with the connections in Hollywood." If you ran a theatrical or movie union and needed help, you would go see Rossini. If you wanted a couple hundred complimentary show tickets for a Las Vegas outing, you would go see Rossini. If you wanted to entertain prospective movie investors, you would get Rossini to supply the girls; girls that Rossini would get to suck off as well as sucker the naive wannabe moguls.

He was indeed the man with the Chicago Mafia connections in Hollywood, a part he looked and acted perfectly; stylistically dapper and moderately ostentatious in physical appearance with even-tempered mannerisms, he was alternately able to impress and intimidate Hollywood executives as well as movie starlets. He was six feet tall and wore his thick mass of black hair greased back. He spoke in broken English which only added to his already considerable exotic charm.

He had climbed the underworld ladder in Chicago with Anacondini through the Orange Street Gang. Knowing Stefano's background well and what the man used to be made it that much harder for Rossini to accept the new Anacondini.

His tolerance and patience fading, he answered his Chicago boss.

"Stefano, they want a private meet. It's to be a very private meet, just one of their men and us."

"What the fuck ... about Castro again?" Stefano nursed his cup of espresso.

"No, I don't think so. No Marco Romano, no Charlie Nuccia, nobody!"

"Where and when is this, again, 'eteano?"

"At the Beverly Hills Supper Club at 11:00 p.m. tomorrow night."

Mario could tell by the change in Stefano's face that Rossini had finally gotten through. Stefano's broken nose, too small and too hooked for a tall man, breathed heavily and his darkly under-circled black eyes unlidded themselves. He turned to Mario.

"Well, Mario, get a fucking move on it. Get us packed, get a plane, you heard what our Hollywood playboy said, the bastard CIA needs us again, only this time it's just us, no Tampa, no New Orleans. Move it, will you, Mario—we mustn't keep Uncle fucking Sam waiting."

Chapter Twenty-One

May 14, 1962

Anacondini's low estimation of the Beverly Hills Supper Club was justified. The lighting was insufficient and the seating was not nearly as comfortable or plentiful as his Villa Roma showplace in Chicago.

None of this mattered, however, to Thessalonian.

It was 11:00 p.m.

A big band was on stage at the Beverly Hills Supper Club, performing expertly a swing rendition of "The Chattanooga Choo Choo." Thessalonian stood by the bar, watching as the tall Chicago boss, Anacondini, bent and entered the premises. The slick-backed head of Gaetano Rossini followed Mr. A. inside and the very small figure of Mario "the Sissy" Pacissi trailed Rossini. To Thessalonian they looked like three Sicilian stooges.

He continued to wait in the shadows of the bar while they were seated. Thessalonian was sure that the three men felt uncomfortable being here.

The Beverly Hills Supper Club was not an Anacondini-Rossini owned establishment. It was owned by an independent Jewish show business combine outside Sicilian-Mafia influence. It was one of the few operating in Hollywood that could make that claim.

Thessalonian enjoyed immensely the obvious discomfort of the three Mafiosos, then squelching his hostilities and falling into character, began to walk to their table. For some inexplicable reason he hesitated, his precise mental faculties zooming.

Gaetano Rossini had not been at the Fontainebleau meet in July of 1960, so it would pass for him to see Thessalonian's face, but Pacissi had been in the Miami penthouse, standing next to Bertucci, Sincelli and Vince "Angler" Angeletta.

Thessalonian turned and walked back to the bar, slowly. He was fairly certain that Anacondini and Rossini, being the opportunists they were, would keep their mouths shut about this meeting, but he didn't know enough about Pacissi to make that assumption. And if word ever leaked back to Angeletta and Nuccia that he, Thessalonian, had cut a side deal with Anacondini to shoot a shooter the boys in New Orleans did not even know existed, then all the months of building up trust with Nuccia and Angeletta would be lost and Contingency Legerdemain-2 would fold.

That would be a mistake and as Thessalonian had concluded on his flight to Los Angeles, Legerdemain had come too far for mistakes now.

Back by the bar he signaled a waitress to him. He jotted quickly on a napkin: Just Rossini, get rid of the third man—tell him to wait in the parking lot. He pointed the waitress towards Anacondini and gave her a twenty dollar bill. Minutes later Mario "the Sissy" Pacissi stood and exited the supper club. Thessalonian waited to make sure that the short Sicilian was gone before re-approaching Anacondini's table.

"Mr. Anacondini?" Thessalonian inquired as he took his final steps toward the table.

Stefano's black eyes opened wide, seeing the familiar face of the CIA man step up to his table. Thessalonian extended his hand. Stefano took it. This was the first meeting that Thessalonian had had with the Sicilians that he did not have cotton wads stuffed in his mouth or made-up eyebrows. In fact, he had coordinated his appearance tonight to look tough and savvy, much closer to his real character than before. Mr. A. immediately noticed the change.

"You. Thessalonian. The man from the Fontainebleau."

The Chicago boss had not expected the same CIA man that had met them in Miami in July of 1960. He instantly regretted not having talked in greater detail to Rossini about the identity of the CIA contact.

"You look different."

Thessalonian sat down in the supper club booth.

"Well, it has been two years, Mr. Anacondini. Lots of things change in that length of time. Lots of things." Thessalonian let that statement hang for a moment.

Stefano Anacondini was not blessed with the old-school style of a Charlie Nuccia. He knew not the meaning of subtlety or hint. He charged forward like a dumb bull.

"What the fuck happened? Two years ago you guarantee a fucking deal with us on Castro. You call and tell me that Kennedy reneged, and that's the last I hear from you. Then his babyshit brother comes after all of us. The only good thing that happened since Kennedy became President is that the Feds drew back their surveillance on me a little and that was probably because Kennedy found out me and him were plugging the same broad ... no matter, what the fuck do you want now?"

Thessalonian relished the moment. Finally he was in a position to be himself with these dago bastards.

"This is the deal, Mr. A., Kennedy didn't just betray you, he's ass-fucked a whole bunch of others. People just as serious as you people, if not more so." He smirked, happy to have rudely awakened Anacondini and Rossini to the fact that they were not, as popularly believed, the toughest kids on the block. "And he's going to be hit."

Anacondini and Rossini looked at each other, shocked, as if expecting next a bolt of lightning to strike them or at the very least an earthquake. Thessalonian continued, "And there's something we need from you."

Thessalonian's scarred forearm dramatically reached across the table for Anacondini's drink, lifted it to his lips and sipped it; another subtle hint, demonstrating to the Chicago boss who was in control here.

"We have a shooter to whack the President and who'll take the fall, but we're going to need one of your people—someone, anyone—to take out our shooter after he's in custody ... A man that has nothing to lose and one whose connection to you is well camouflaged ... A man that could feasibly wear a nut's jacket or maybe be mistaken for a right-wing patriot, claiming he did it to spare Jackie the trial or some such nonsense."

"What's in it for me?" Anacondini asked after a moment's hesitation, whispering insecurely like the juvenile Orange Street gang member in his heart he still was.

"Points. Big fucking brownie points with Johnson. Do you understand me, Anacondini? Big fucking stroke!"

Gaetano Rossini hated what he was hearing. "This shit," he thought to himself, "is way over my head. Goddam the perils of being a middle man!"

Anacondini's interest and hunger were obvious to both Thessalonian and Rossini as he responded.

"Fuck, Thessalonian. I don't even have to think about that. A throwaway is no problem whatsoever. Just tell Rossini here when and where as soon as possible, and it's done."

Thessalonian leaned back in the booth and pressed his final point to the anxious, undisciplined Chicago Don.

"One other thing, Mr. A. No one, not Nuccia in New Orleans, not Romano in Tampa, nor any of the other families are to know about this besides us. Me—you—and Rossini. Understood?"

For the first time since his Sicilian wife divorced him, Stefano "Mr. A." Anacondini's ego felt at last rejuvenated. Who needs an old frigid Sicilian bitch anyway when I have friends like this man? Man, oh man!

"Understood, Thessalonian ... understood, understood, understood!"

Chapter Twenty-Two

May 17, 1962

"Lafitte's Westport Club."

"Betsy, is that you?"

"Yea."

"Hey, this is Mario from Chicago."

"Oh, hi, Mario, how ya doing?"

"Okay, Bets, Okay ... listen, is Vince around there?"

"No, I don't think so. Jake's here, you want to speak to him?"

"Yea, that'd be great, Betsy."

"Okay, hold on."

Seconds later.

"Mario, the Sissy ... what's doing up in snow country, buddy?"

"Hey, Jake, how's it hanging?"

"Swell. Still mean as a monkey. What's cooking?"

"Is Vin around, Jake—or do you know where I can reach him?"

"Hold on, let me ask Pops."

Mario waited on the Chicago end of the phone line as Jake Sincelli went to ask his father, Johnny Sincelli, Vince's whereabouts.

"Have you called his apartment, Mario? You know Mona's with him now and those two stay humping like rabbits."

Mario laughed.

"Okay, Jake. Listen, thanks. Take care."

"You, too, Mario."

Mona Spazek couldn't get enough of Vince these days. She suspected that he was going to start back traveling soon. Vince always held her a little tighter, made love to her a little more seriously when he was under pressure. She hugged him now as he slept.

It was 10:25 a.m.

It had been six days since Vince had met with Thessalonian at the Look See Bar in Kenner. Five days since he had talked with Charlie Nuccia about it. Charlie, as expected, had been furious about another seven month delay in Legerdemain, and for good reason. Robert Kennedy was accelerating his efforts to deport Charlie Nuccia for a second time and the top man of the New Orleans underworld was understandably worried.

Still, Vince had convinced his mentor that Thessalonian's plan made sense. He had even gone so far as to tell Charlie that without reservation he now trusted Thessalonian—Miles Barker—and that Charlie should rest assured that the best course—the only course—for Operation Legerdemain was being taken. Vince had also promised Charlie that he would speed his work on the parade route diagrams in the cities on Thessalonian's list so that they would be finished before December.

"Just remember, Charlie," Vince had told Don Nuccia, "Thessalonian knows who's boss. His balls are the size of peanuts. Trust my judgment on this. Trust me, Charlie!"

He had no idea now, as he slept, that his trust in the CIA man was about to be shattered.

The phone rang.

Mona answered, "Hello?"

"Hey, doll, this is Mario."

"Hey, Mario ... hey." Mona was glad to hear the voice of her old Chicago friend, but something in its strained, rushed tone discouraged conversation.

"You want to talk to Vince, Mario?"

"Yea, Doll, I'm sort of in a hurry."

Mona kissed Vince, who was still nestled in her arms, and nudged him. "Baby, wake up, it's Mario on the phone."

Vince slowly stirred, taking the receiver from her and mumbling into it..

"Hey, Sissy, what's up? What time is it?"

"Abut ten-thirty, Vin."

Mario waited a moment for Vince to collect himself.

"Vin, I've got to talk to you about something, something urgent. I'll be in New Orleans at seven p.m. tonight."

"Wha ... what's that, Sissy? ... Seven p.m. at Moisant."

"Yea, meet me, Vince, Chicago Pan Am flight. Got to go."

An empty dial tone buzzed in Vince's ear. Mario was gone.

It had all happened so suddenly.

Stefano Anacondini slapping Mario Pacissi open-handed across the face in front of a planeload of people. He had done that two days ago on their return flight from Los Angeles to Chicago. Not once, but twice.

To slap a Sicilian Mafioso across the face in this manner was a sign of the ultimate disrespect, an uno sgarro. Even if the man doing the slapping was the boss and even if that man was drunk, it was still an unforgivable personal offense.

Mario, after two days of agonizing, had decided to get out of Chicago permanently. Being humiliated publicly like he had been, Mario had concluded, was unforgivable. He felt he deserved better after all the loyalty and respect he had shown over the years to his father-in-law and the man's shrewish daughter, his wife. Mario knew that if he didn't leave now and make a clean break of it he would end up killing Stefano, and that was not a move he was prepared to make. So he had called his best friend, Vince Angeletta, hopeful that something could be worked out with Charlie Nuccia.

Normally the only way for a made Mafioso to leave one family and transfer to another was with the permission of the heads of the two respective families. Mario knew that Stefano would never willingly let him go, but Charlie Nuccia's tremendous power spoke loudly in interfamily dealings like this. If anyone could arrange it, the Top Man of New Orleans could.

Mario stepped off the Pan Am plane into the stifling humidity of a New Orleans early evening. It was 7 p.m.

Once inside the Moisant-New Orleans Airport terminal Mario spotted Vince. His New Orleans paisan was leaning against a concrete pillar, smoking a cigar, like a man without a care in the world.

"Damn," Mario thought, "I wish I were Vince just now."

Vince spotted Mario, threw his cigar away, waved and smiled, and began to walk towards him.

"Mario! Hey, man, are you okay?"

"Yea," Mario grinned, his characteristic warmth and ebullience momentarily evident as he kidded Vince. "Now what do I call you here? Is it Ralphie Bosco or Tommy Nunez or just plain Vin?"

"The latter," Vince laughed. "It's Vince "Angler" Angeletta at your service, Mr. Sissy. This is home."

They silently headed through the terminal parking lot to Jake's 1958 black Cadillac. Vince put Mario's luggage in the trunk and sat in the driver's seat. He looked at Mario seated next to him, seriously, before starting the car.

"Hey, Sissy, what is it, what's urgent?"

Mario looked out over the black expanse of swampland just beyond the New Orleans runway, his eyes glazing over and his throat constricting with emotion.

"Remember, Vin, you said if I ever needed anything to give you a call? One friend to another?"

"Sure," Vince acknowledged.

"Well, Vin, can you believe it? Mr. A. bitch-slapped me twice in front of a whole planeload of people the other day. He was drunk, but that son of a bitch knew what he was doing."

"You're kidding." Vince was astonished. Even though he had never been a big fan of Anacondini—having pegged the Chicago boss for a hypocrite and bullshit artist—to have slapped his own son-in-law was incredible. Charlie, as usual, had been right again; it sounded like Stefano had become a pazzo crazy bastard since letting his wife divorce him.

"No, Vin, I'm not kidding. Wish I were," Mario softly added. "It happened two days ago—we were flying back to Chicago from LA and he'd already drunk about a half a dozen of those little bottles of bourbon. He asked me to get him another one and I said, respectfully, that he ought to lay off. That's when the bastard hauls off and slaps me. Twice. Me ... me the one man who doesn't talk behind his back, the one man who always puts up with his bullshit. Christ, I'm the husband of his daughter, I ought to get a fucking medal just for that. She's just like him—temperamental—I've had it, Vin. I want to come to New Orleans, permanently." Mario managed a slight Mickey Rooneyish smile, turning to face Vince, hopeful.

Vince turned away, a sneer spreading across his usually romantic lips. He started the Cadillac before commenting.

"That's serious shit, Mario. Serious business. Charlie won't do it unless you have something to offer. Something real heavy. In matters like this he's all business. Unemotional. It has to be that way. Fuck, he'll probably have to clear the whole transfer through the commission, because you know Mr. A. will never go along with it on his own."

Vince began backing the heavy car out of the airport parking space, following the airport exit signs marked Airline Highway and Downtown New Orleans.

Whatever calm and reservation Mario had maintained on the flight down vanished now as he jumped across that Sicilian Rubicon and went for broke.

"I do have something to offer, Vin. Something huge." He was staring at Vince's shadowed profile as they pulled up to a red light. "They're going to kill the President, Vin, and Mr. A's supplying the shooter to shoot the President's shooter afterward. And no one's supposed to know; not Marco Romano and especially not Charlie Nuccia. How's that for heavy?"

The red light turned green and Vince Angeletta's face turned white and the black 1958 Cadillac, like an enraged swamp monster, screamed into the night.

"On May 13, Don Nuccia, Rossini met Mr. A. at his office in the Ammo Antilly in Cicero. I was there. He tells Mr. A. that the CIA wants a very private meet with him out in Los Angeles. Mr. A. was drunk and thought it had something to do with Castro, but Rossini made it clear that they had said: no Romano, no Nuccia, this time nobody. We fly out to Los Angeles that day and they have their meet at the Beverly Hills Supper Club the next night around 11 p.m. I was sitting at the table but the waitress handed Mr. A. a note and Mr. A. tells me to get up and go wait outside by the car. About an hour and a half later they come out. Mr. A. is pretty drunk by now and he's cussing me and Rossini like pigs. Rossini almost has to carry him out of the club. We get him in the car and he keeps mumbling 'I'm happy, happy, happy ... they're finally gonna whack him.' Finally, Rossini tries to politely shut him up but Mr. A. turns on Rossini and yells for him to stop bothering him and adds that the only thing Rossini has to worry about is finding a throwaway, when the time comes. We get back to the hotel, just me and Mr. A., and he gets even drunker. But before he passes out he lays out the whole scam for me. The CIA wants him to supply a shooter, a throwaway to kill the guy that's going to shoot President Kennedy. Sounded to me like they're planning on Kennedy's shooter getting arrested afterwards and they need somebody to take him out while he's in police custody. A nice tidy package."

"You say Rossini was trying to get Mr. A. ta shut up in front of you, like the CIA told them ta not speak a word of their arrangement, right?"

"Yes, Don Nuccia."

Charlie Nuccia turned to Vince.

"So thatssa it. Vin, what do you think?"

Vince was finding it hard to believe that a scared shitless Thessalonian would have the balls to double-cross him and Charlie Nuccia so blatantly. Considering this, he turned to Mario.

"Hey, Sissy, could you excuse me and Charlie for a minute? We need to hash this out. Go and tell one of the cooks to fix you a steak. They don't call this place the Steak Pit for nothing."

"Sure, Vin."

Mario stood up and walked out, leaving Charlie Nuccia and Vince Angeletta alone in the rear supply room of the Steak Pit Restaurant on Bourbon Street.

It was 10:00 p.m.

Vince ran his fingers through his black wavy hair a few times.

"Charlie, if it's Thessalonian that met with Anacondini, we're dead in the water. But I just can't imagine that being so. I mean, that guy seemed so fucking scared when I talked to him at the Look See the other day. He acts too scared shit to even look at me or you crosswise, much less double deal us. How could anybody be that good of an actor—and so fucking consistent?"

"I don't know, Vincenzo. But we must get an explanation for what Mario heard." Charlie looked to his most trusted solidato.

"We will get an explanation, Charlie, that we will." And as

an afterthought, "What about Mario?"

Charlie's manicured nails tapped delicately on the supply room shelf he was leaning against.

"I'll take him, Vin, but you've got ta find a place ta hide him. He's not ta go out on the streets for any reason and he must definitely not return to Chicago. You will handle that, Vin?"

"No problem, Charlie."

"And get ta the bottom of this, Vincenzo, before you travel ta any more cities on Legerdemain business."

Vince's arrogant nostrils opened wide, breathed in heavy the stench of dirty Steak Pit kitchen laundry.

"Lo considera fatto, Don Nuccia. Consider it done!"

Daniel Carthage had no doubt in his mind that the barrel of a small caliber revolver was stuck in his kidneys. It surely wasn't a penis, which he would have preferred.

It was 11:25 p.m.

Carthage listened, strict attention to the voice holding the gun.

"I've got some business to discuss with you now—about the bible man—there are three other men covering you."

Carthage took in the circumstances. He was sitting on the edge of a barstool in a private club catering to homosexuals on Bourbon Street. His face was well known in this particular club, he thought quickly, but he was personally unestablished here, which meant that none of the other customers knew him well enough to assist him if there was trouble. And trouble there would certainly be if he did not do what the man behind him with the gun had told him to do—now. His CIA training kicked in; calm the enemy, pacify the enemy.

Carthage stood up from the barstool. The man behind him wrapped his arm around the pilot-CIA operative as if they were lovers. The man guided Carthage out the door of the private club and into the shadowed recesses of a side alley.

Daniel Carthage had an unusual looking head of reddish-brown hair. He had been stricken in his late twenties by a disease that had caused him total baldness. The expensive toupee that he had bought in Paris years ago to conceal that baldness was the first part of his body to fall when the assault upon him began. Carthage felt sure his head had just been struck by a freight train. Barely conscious, he looked up from where he lay on the grimy cement into the face of his attacker. Into the face of Vince "Angler" Angeletta.

There were three other men standing behind Angeletta, none of whom Carthage could identify. He watched as Angeletta turned to the three men and said something to them in Italian. They all turned and walked away, appearing to have been dismissed. In Angeletta's hand the CIA man saw a .22 caliber pistol pointed directly at him.

"I think we have a problem with the Bible man—Thessalonian—your boss."

Dan Carthage, in his boggled mind, did his best to do an instant status review of Legerdemain. He, Cross and Bannerwell were deeply involved with orchestrating Oswald but they had had very little to do with the aspect of Legerdemain involving Charlie Nuccia and his people besides delivering messages to them occasionally like he had done with Angeletta the other day on the street corner. Theirs was a minimal involvement with the Sicilians. So what was Angeletta talking about—unless they've somehow uncovered the parallel orchestration of Oswald?

Vince continued. "The CIA approached Stefano Anacondini about taking out the Kennedy shooter after the Kennedy shoot. They met with him in Beverly Hills a few days ago. So this is what we want you to do. You contact Thessalonian and tell him to be at Lafitte's Westport Club tomorrow night—exactly at midnight."

Carthage tried feebly to protest.

"Angler, I don't know if I can reach him that soon."

Vince Angeletta went to his knees, made the side of his hand into a V and put it directly under the chin of Daniel Carthage. He then stuck the barrel of his .22 under the nose of the homosexual pilot.

"Let me put it to you like this, Carthage. You know Charlie Nuccia. You piloted for him a few times. You know how he operates. If that motherfucker Thessalonian does not show up at exactly midnight tomorrow night at Lafitte's Westport Club in Gretna, he's a walking dead man. There will be nowhere in the world he can hide from us. You make that very clear to that ivy-leagued pussy. Capisce, cocksucker, capisce?"

Carthage gargled. "Capisce ... Angler."

Vince, for punctuation, slammed the toupeeless diseased head of Dan Carthage into the side alley cement, and then as calm and as pacified as the CIA man would have wanted him to be, Angler Angelleta stood and walked away.

Chapter Twenty-Three

May 18, 1962

"Where have you got Mario, Vin?"

These were the first words out of Charlie Nuccia's mouth when Vince stepped into Charlie's rear office at Lafitte's Westport Club.

It was 11:30 p.m.

Charlie was prepared for their midnight meet with Thessalonian. He was suited immaculately with his favorite amber tie, and gold cufflinks and porkpie hat and was perched behind his massive mahogany desk like a fighting cock ready to literally rip Thessalonian to shreds if need be.

"He's at my apartment, Charlie, with Mona. I've made it my business to not let anyone know exactly where I live, so he's safe there. When I left they were talking about old times in Chicago." Then Vince added, "You did know, huh, Charlie, that Mario was the one who introduced me to Mona?"

The Top Man of New Orleans lifted a cigar out of his suit pocket and waved it in the air.

"Now that you mentioned it, Vin, I do remember. You and her are doing okay, Vincenzo?"

Vince had sat down in the low chair in front of Charlie's desk.

"Yea, Charlie, she's really something else. I think with a little more time she might even be another Rosalie. Can you imagine that?"

"That's good, Vin, very good. I'm glad ta hear it."

Charlie Nuccia did something he rarely did. He smiled at the prospect of Vince's happiness. It had been so difficult for Vince after Rosalie's death, Charlie thought to himself.

Vince had never felt closer to the man seated before him than he did right then. The concern Charlie was displaying for his most trusted solidato was sincere and that meant a great deal to Vince. Vince smiled back.

Charlie lit his cigar and motioned Vince to pull his chair closer. Vince pulled the chair so close to Charlie's desk that his knees were touching the front of it and the letters CN emblazoned there.

"Vin, Thessalonian's going ta have ta be broken tonight. We've got ta find out the truth from him once and for all, thatssa it. If he's playing it straight, then we keep going, if not, then," Charlie paused, "he's got ta go."

"Charlie, I'm a step ahead of you. I've got Jake waiting to take Thessalonian's body to the limepit if necessary," Vince answered.

"Good." Both men relaxed somewhat.

"Charlie, what does Mr. Johnny say about your deportation? Is he winning it for you?"

Charlie's pockmarked face scowled at the mention of his fight to stave off a second deportation.

"He's doing the best he can do, Vin. That fucking Robert Kennedy is hard at it, though. It's still a chess game."

"Too bad it's not Bocci ball, huh, Charlie? You sure would win it then." Vince grinned at his reference to Charlie's expertise at the Italian game of Bocci.

"Yea," Charlie smiled again, "Bocci would be better—much, much better. But then again, Vin," Charlie said, smiling an unprecedented third time, "tonight with Thessalonian will be our game, too. Called, you bet your life, CIA man ... New Awlins style!"

Thessalonian had been shaken when his Washington contact number had received a "whiplash" call yesterday from Daniel Carthage. The "whiplash" designation was used by Thessalonian's CIA operatives only in cases of dire emergency.

And, as Carthage had confirmed when Thessalonian had returned the call yesterday, an emergency situation was developing rapidly in New Orleans. The trust Thessalonian had built up with Nuccia and Angeletta over the last year was in jeopardy, and unless he moved quickly to placate the Sicilians, Contingency Legerdemain 2 would be lost.

The two New Orleans Mafiosos had demanded that Thessalonian meet with them tonight at Lafitte's Westport Club in Gretna. The CIA man would be arriving there in five minutes.

It was 11:55 p.m.

As the New Orleans cab Thessalonian was riding in made its way across the Jefferson Highway Bridge towards Gretna, he reassessed his movements since receiving the Carthage "whiplash" call.

First, Thessalonian had contacted Stefano "Mr. A." Anacondini and had informed him that there was a leak inside his Chicago family; that Charlie Nuccia had gotten wind of their secret arrangement and that if the Chicago boss did not put a lid on his leak before midnight tonight, their deal was off.

Second, Thessalonian had concocted, with documents, evidence pointing to the existence of another plot to kill Kennedy within the CIA's Directorate of Intelligence. Thessalonian was hoping to convince Nuccia and Angeletta that he was not the CIA party responsible for the overture made to Rossini and Anacondini in Beverly Hills a few days ago.

It will be a tricky sell, Thessalonian worried.

His gray eyes looked out the window of the cab as it pulled atop a gravel Mississippi levee road just minutes away from Nuccia's club. The levee road was desolate and surrounded by a smattering of swamp on either side. I wonder how many of Nuccia's enemies ended up in those lagoons, Thessalonian continued to worry ... and if I'm not careful ...

Mario and Mona were laughing about Vince.

It was 11:56 p.m.

"You should have seen him, Mario, when he told me his name really wasn't Ralphie Bosco. He was like a little boy confessing to doing something bad. Almost like he thought I was going to spank him or something. He's really cute sometimes."

Mario laughed again. He was proud of Mona. She had really come a long way from waitress to shopping center manager. Mario was hopeful that Vince could help him straighten out his life, too, like he had Mona's. But then, Mario chided himself, Mona's a beauty and well, I'm just short.

Mona poured them another drink from a half-empty bottle of Scotch. They were seated in the center den area of Vince and Mona's second floor French Quarter apartment. Vince had insisted that Mario stay put until further notice. Mona had volunteered to spend as much time as she could after and between work hours with Mario during his forced confinement. Of course, Mona knew nothing of the reasons for Mario's confinement, but accepted it as simply another fact of her life with Vince Angeletta.

The Scotch had relaxed them both, easing their stir-craziness. So much so that neither of them heard the footsteps coming up the outer fire escape nor down the building hallway. They were laughing too loud, reminiscing about Chicago.

"By the way, Mario," Mona asked coyly, "where did you get all those car salesmen you used to introduce me to? You know that I told Ralph—Vince—that I had him pegged for a car salesman when you first introduced us."

"Oh, man, I bet he loved that!"

"Oh, he did. Then he had the nerve to ask me how many of them I slept with. Ha! I didn't answer him, but just between me and you, Mario, I didn't sleep with any of them."

"Really?" Even Mario was surprised at that.

"No, they were all bums. I know they probably told you different, but I turned them all down. I mean these guys were real bums, Mario."

Mario laughed again.

The two sets of footsteps had reached the rear bedroom window and the front door as Mario's ebullient laugh subsided.

Carmine, Mona's old boss at the Sandhurst Shopping Complex and Mario Pacissi's replacement in the Chicago family as of yesterday, crashed into the heavy French front door with the force of an elephant. The sound of glass shattering could be heard seconds later as Gaetano Rossini muscled through Vince's and Mona's bedroom window. Both men were armed with silenced .44 magnum pistols as they converged swiftly on the den area.

Mario and Mona were taken completely unaware. Mario had not even had time to try a defensive move and Mona's screams were stifled by her own hand almost as soon as they erupted.

Carmine and Rossini were gloating like two cats with two mice on the line.

"Mario and Mona, fancy meeting you here. What a quaint scene. Excuse us for interrupting." He looked at Mona. "So what are you doing now, slut? You fucking Vince and Mario, too, maybe at the same time?"

"How did you find me?" Mario asked coolly, disregarding Carmine's provocation, still in a state of semi-intoxicated shock.

Carmine swaggered dumbly towards him like the oaf he was.

"Mr. A.'s not real pleased with you, old buddy. It seems you been running your fucking mouth. And as far as finding you, that was easy. You see Mona had to fill out a job application when she took the job at the Southport Shopping Center here in New Orleans and in doing so she had to put an address down—Vince's address—simple. So where is the fucking comedian, anyway, huh?"

"I don't know," Mario answered, then added courageously, "look, Mona has nothing to do with any of this. She doesn't know anything. I'm the one you want."

Carmine strutted behind Mona.

"That's true, Sissy, but no witnesses, you know how it goes."

In a flash of movement Carmine raised his silenced weapon to the back of Mona's head. She closed her eyes as if she knew what was coming—and it came!

The force of the muffled explosion literally tore the top of Mona's brain off. The large .44 caliber bullet entered at the parieto-occipital fissure and exited through her frontal sinus. Her silky thighs as well as the rest of her body flew forward, then crumpled on the den floor.

Mario rushed to her and got on his knees beside her. He was too traumatized to cry but an implosion of impotent rage did begin to rise in his bowels, to his intestines, and out of his small Mickey Rooneyish mouth.

He lunged at Carmine just as the Chicago Mafioso pulled again the trigger of his .44 caliber pistol. The rounds hit Mario directly in the left superior lobe and pulmonary artery of his heart. Gaetano Rossini also joined in the firing, hitting Pacissi in the left kidney, spleen and diaphragm.

Mario "the Sissy" died instantly.

Carmine and Rossini examined the carnage and looked to one another, confirming with a nod their successful kills.

They exited quickly.

Stefano "Mr. A." Anacondini, their Chicago boss, had spoken.

"Mr. Nuccia, I have uncovered another plot within the United States Intelligence community to kill Kennedy."

Charlie Nuccia did not react to this claim by Thessalonian. He just kept staring at the CIA man with his big brown expressionless eyes.

It was 11:57 p.m.

Thessalonian continued. "I have evidence documented here." Thessalonian reached down to the briefcase that he had laid at the foot of his low chair in front of Charlie Nuccia's desk. When he did Vince whipped out his British-made Sten machine gun that had been concealed on the top shelf of the bookcase hours earlier and yelled, "Don't even fucking think about it, Barker."

The CIA man froze, petrified, he sputtered.

"It just documents, Angler, substantiating what I'm saying."

"Just what are you saying, punk?" Vince spewed.

Thessalonian was angry at himself for allowing Angeletta to get the draw on him, but managed nonetheless to stay in character.

"It originated within the Directorate of Intelligence—my normal department assignment—but as I told you last year in Honduras, I've been on special attachment to the Missions and Programs Staff, Directorate of Plans, since two months before our Fontainebleau meet, so I've had very little contact with the Intelligence Directorate in that time. Therefore, someone was able to construct a rogue plot from within the DI without anyone noticing. Whoever's behind the rogue plot were the ones responsible for the meet with Anacondini-Rossini in Beverly Hills."

"Prove it," Vince demanded, still holding the Sten machine gun barrel near Thessalonian's back.

"What would be their motive?" Charlie Nuccia added with eerie calm.

Thessalonian was well aware at the moment that both Legerdemain and his life were at stake.

"Mr. Nuccia, Vince, you have got to understand that Kennedy has a lot of enemies in the intelligence community since the Bay of Pigs. From what I can discern there's a fairly sizable group leftover from Operation Pluto—the code name for the Cuban invasion—that hates the President. Now, if you'll allow me, I'll show you the documents to prove it."

"Just set the briefcase on Charlie's desk, Thessalonian. I'll open it," Vince ordered.

The CIA man sucked on the cotton wads in his mouth, rubbed a forefinger across his artificially darkened eyebrows and did as he was told.

Vince cradled the Sten in the crook of his arm and walked around Thessalonian to where the briefcase lay on Charlie's mahogany desk. Vince opened it carefully and removed from it a stack of documents. The documents were a compilation of Top Secret interagency memoranda with the CIA Directorate of Intelligence letterhead.

"Here, Charlie, see if you can make any sense of these."

Charlie Nuccia's teddy bearish, outlawish, heavy demeanor began plowing through the papers before him. Vince turned his hostile intentions and weapon back to Thessalonian.

After five minutes Charlie unbuttoned his immaculate suit coat and removed his porkpie hat. After ten minutes he loosened his amber tie, after fifteen minutes he unlinked his gold cufflinks, after twenty minutes he set the last of the official documents back into Thessalonian's briefcase.

Still with supernatural calm the Top Man of the New Orleans underworld lit a cigar. Vince's staredown of Thessalonian had not wavered.

"Vin, this stuff looks legit," Charlie said, directing the comments to Vince, then turning to Thessalonian, "Barker, if this is a con, it's an excellent one. You have had less than 24 hours ta prepare all this shit, and ta have prepared it in that short time would have been almost impossible. So let's say you're clean, how will this rogue plot affect us and Legerdemain?"

Vince eased the machine gun slightly away from the CIA

man upon hearing Charlie's supposition of Thessalonian's innocence. Thessalonian, in an attempt to capitalize on the momentary shift in his favor, began yet another performance for these Sicilians whom he despised.

"First, Mr. Nuccia, let me say a few things on my behalf. Like I told you last time back in November of '61 when I brought you the bad news of Kennedy's betrayal of the Castro arrangement: why would I have even showed up then if my intentions had not been genuine? Tonight the same applies. Why would I have showed up here at Lafitte's, unarmed, if I had anything to hide? It would be madness—insanity—on my part to try and scam you people. Clearly you must see that that is not my intention. I am merely trying to get my debt to you and my ass clear. I did guarantee the Castro arrangement—which was admittedly foolish—but done by me nonetheless. But you must understand, I am not God. I don't see all or know all. The U.S. intelligence community is a sprawling, worldwide network of closets. Each closet contains dozens of active covert operations at any given time. The whole system is prime for corrupt individual initiative. Obviously, that is what's happened here with this rogue operation." Thessalonian paused again, tactfully, like an ivy-leaguer at his doctoral dissertation. "As to how it will affect Legerdemain, that I don't know. It's entirely possible that this rogue operation, for one reason or another, will never happen. I believe that that should be our assumption and we should proceed accordingly with Legerdemain."

Vince tensed again, then interjected, "You know, Barker, it wasn't until after our meet at the Look See a week ago that I even began to trust you, and I expressed that to Charlie here. Now, I'm not so sure."

Vince turned to Charlie.

"Don Nuccia, I say we take this CIA motherfucker out now and forget about Kennedy," Vince again pointed the ominous looking Sten machine gun at Thessalonian. Thessalonian was sweating, grasping for some way to convince these ignorant guinea bastards that he was telling the truth. Charlie Nuccia was inwardly applauding Vince's terror tactics. The shrill ring of his desk phone startled him. Charlie picked up and listened.

"Yea ... yea ... yea ... yea ... we're on our way."

The Top Man stood, suddenly reached for his suitcoat, tightened his tie, relinked his cufflinks and reset his porkpie hat. He walked to the door and yelled for Jake across the expanse of Lafitte's. Jake lumbered through the club, stopping at the rear office door. Charlie issued Jake's instructions loud enough for Thessalonian to hear.

"Jake, guard this man," Charlie pointed to the seated, worried CIA operative whom Jake remembered from the Fontainebleau, "and if he moves so much as an inch, kill him."

Charlie motioned to Vince, "Vin, give Jake your gun. Come with me." The Top Man turned and began walking purposefully to the main entrance of his most lucrative gambling joint. He turned to Vince halfway there. "Vincenzo, somebody found Mario. He's dead," and added slowly with sympathetic tears in his eyes, "so is Mona ... I'm very, very sorry."

Chapter Twenty-Four

May 19, 1962

The New Orleans police captain ushered Charlie and Vince into the murder scene personally. It was 12:55 a.m. The bodies of Mario and Mona lay as they had fallen on Vince's French Quarter apartment floor. It was a gruesome sight. The police captain, who had been on the Nuccia family payroll for twenty years, spoke first.

"Two assailants, Mr. Nuccia: one up the fire escape, in through the bedroom, the other through the front door. Bullet wounds appear to be large caliber—probably .44 magnums—silenced."

"Who called you?" Vince choked out the question, kneeling beside Mona's mangled body.

"The apartment manager. When he heard the window and door crash—he said he didn't hear any shooting—when he told me the apartment was leased to the Fleur di Fleur Novelties Company, I called you," the police captain explained, looking from Vince to Charlie.

"Thank you, Captain," Charlie said as he bent his short stature double and grabbed Vince by the arm.

"C'mon, Vincenzo, we'd best be leaving. The press will be here soon."

Vince, weak-kneed and nauseous, walked down the apartment stairs like a hundred-year-old man. Charlie led him by the arm to Jake's Cadillac, parked by the Chartres Street curb. Charlie opened the passenger door for Vince, then got in the driver's side beside him.

After a brief term of respectful silence Charlie started the car and pulled away from the curb. He talked as he drove.

"Vincenzo, I know we're both upset right now but we still have responsibilities. We've got ta make a decision on Thessalonian."

Charlie looked to his solidato, who was like a son to him, as he expertly maneuvered the car past Bienville, Conti, and Toulouse streets.

"Vin, I don't think Thessalonian's responsible for Mario and Mona. Can you imagine what kind of balls the man would have ta have to be sitting in our office while one of his people ... " Charlie hesitated, searching for the appropriate words, " ... murdered them. Vin, I just can't believe the man has got that much courage or that much smarts."

"But, Charlie," Vince spoke again, forcing himself to in spite of his grief, "you were the one who said that's why they're called the intelligence community. They're intelligent."

"I did, Vin." Charlie looked sideways again at Vince as he steered down Canal Street. "But no one's that clever. I think it's impossible."

"Then what happened?" Vince whispered.

"Stefano took Mario out, Vincenzo. And Mona was unfortunately there, so they took her out, too. I hate ta say this, Vin, but Mario took his chances when he left Chicago."

"But how did they find out so soon where he was?"

Charlie was hurting for Vince. Hurting badly.

"There are hundreds of ways, and exactly which way we'll never know."

The Top Man's tone was one of resignation as he accelerated over the Jefferson Highway Bridge back towards Gretna and Lafitte's Westport Club.

He concluded, "I do believe there is another rogue plot ta kill Kennedy happening out there and that Thessalonian is not involved with it, and that we have ta forget about what's happened here tonight. Stefano owned Mario. It was his right ta take him out. Mona was a tragic, tragic accident—thatssa all, and finally, Vince, if we stop Legerdemain now and kill Thessalonian, her death and Mario's death will have all been for nothing."

Charlie pulled atop the gravel Mississippi levee road and stopped.

"I still want Kennedy hit, Vincenzo, before my second deportation if possible; as soon as we're able. But as I told you in Honduras, it is not an order, it's a choice, your choice. Are you still willing to take care of this for me?"

Vince "Angler" Angeletta's middle-aged five foot eleven inch frame was slumped now; his cheeks were more hollow than sunken, and his silvery brown-blue eyes were red and moist from the shock of losing his best friend and his lover in the same night. He was too ashamed at his pain to look up from the Cadillac floorboard.

"Yes, Don Nuccia. I will not fail you. Again ... Questo te prometto."

ONE YEAR LATER
June 26, 1963
The Schoneberger Rathaus,
West Berlin's City Hall
Berlin, West Germany

Early AfternoonToday in the world of freedom, the proudest boast is "Ich bin ein Berliner."
That line should go over well ...
... at least a whole lot better than Diem's political support in South Vietnam is going. It's deteriorated to nothing ...
... and his brother, Ngo Dinh Nhu, having to resort to force to quell Buddhist demonstrations ... outrageous!
And they still have the audacity to make demands on me, the President of the United States ...
... we ought to overthrow their non-reformable asses with a coup ...
Better yet, we ought to get the hell out of there ...
Today in the world of freedom ... hmmm ...
what freedom?

Chapter Twenty-Five

June 27, 1963

"I have a flash supplement from INFIX for you—Intercept Eagle," Clemer Dodd's voice wavered as he spoke into his MAMA WEST 030601 tie-in.

Major General Marion Armstrong III listened carefully to the Pentagon end of the 030601 line as the gruff voice resumed.

"Legerdemain Contingencies status is to be set as of now at Full Trigger Stage, repeat Legerdemain Contingencies status is to be set as of now at Full Trigger Stage ... do you acknowledge, Eagle?"

General Armstrong, prickling from head to toe, responded, "Acknowledge ... clear."

It was 7:00 a.m.

The words General Armstrong had just heard spoken through his 030601 phone line, originating from INFIX, the code named source representing Sosar Tomeen, meant that Legerdemain's activation status had finally been changed, after two years of Holding Pattern stage and one and a half year's Modified Holding Pattern stage, to Full Trigger Stage.

The General walked away from the maple cabinet housing the 030601 line and walked to his desk. He buzzed his aide, Corporal Forrestol.

"Corporal, get me Plato Smith on the line."

"Yes, sir, General Armstrong."

Within minutes the General's desk phone rang back. Plato Smith spoke through it.

"Ratchet ... what is it?"

General Armstrong gathered his thoughts and his nerve.

"Plato, I've just received a flash supplement from INFIX ... and Legerdemain is now at Full Trigger stage—do you read?—Full Trigger stage."

"Yes, I understand."

"Now, Plato, I need detailed status on Thessalonian and each Legerdemain Contingency."

"One moment." There was a brief ruffling of papers over the phone line.

"Okay, Ratchet ... Contingency LED-1 involving General Mancus and Captain Marsh: According to Thessalonian's latest surveillance reports General Mancus has been holding steady and has assumed a hands-off posture with Captain Marsh. Mancus spends most of his free time with his infirm son. Mancus has shown no sign of further mental deterioration since the Holt-Taylor incident. Captain Marsh, too, seems patient and steady. Marsh has been participating in all the low profile advanced marksmanship training courses available at Ft. Bragg. Contingency LED-2 involving Charlie Nuccia and his shooter: The shooter traveled from May to October of last year diagramming potential presidential parade routes: St. Louis, Detroit, Cincinnati, Dallas, Atlanta, Miami, Kansas City, Denver, Minneapolis, Little Rock. The Sicilians seem as determined as ever to conclude this piece of business. There is a notation here, however, that they have consistently complained about the time factor to Thessalonian. Nuccia is very concerned about the continuing prosecutorial hysteria of the attorney-general. Contingency LED-3 has been structured like a masterpiece. Thessalonian has really outdone himself with the Jimenez-Cuban shooters program. The shooter was raised in New Orleans; he can even trace an uncle that works for Nuccia. The shooter was sheepdipped by the ONI in Atsugi, Japan, did a fake defection to the USSR three years ago. Thessalonian arranged for the shooter's return, and building on the appearance of that defection and the shooter's questionable discharge from the Marines, Thessalonian has successfully portrayed the shooter as unstable with both Marxist pro-Castro linkage and anti-Castro Jimenez Cuban exile linkage. The man can truly fall many ways, which Thessalonian says he will. Marsh will escape after the shoot. Nuccia's man will escape after the shoot. Both to be dealt with later. But the Jimenez shooter will be taken out very publicly after his arrest by a loose-cannon, nut-type that Thessalonian has arranged for with another Sicilian faction."

"Then we are ready, Plato?" General Armstrong asked, very anxious to be done with Legerdemain.

"Yes, Ratchet, we are ready."

"Then it's time. Tell Thessalonian we are at Full Trigger Stage, to use his best judgment and to conclude. Any questions, Plato?"

"No, Ratchet."

"Then finish it as soon as possible!"

George Whitten was feeling more comfortable and more relieved than he had in two years.

It was 1:30 a.m. Central European Time.

Sosar Tomeen had summoned the senior analyst with the Pentagon's Program Planning and Budgeting Systems Office (PPBS) to Zurich from Washington yesterday. Whitten had been preoccupied on his overseas flight, concerned that Sosar had finally decided to implement an Immediate Zero Action order on Operation Legerdemain; the equivalent of an operational self-destruct. But upon arriving in Sosar's penthouse office in the IIPAC building on the Zollikerstrasse in Zurich, George Whitten had been pleasantly surprised.

Sosar, seated, a tumbler of whiskey in his three-fingered right hand, proceeded to instruct the architect of Legerdemain in his silky multilingual tone.

"George, we've been at Modified Holding Pattern stage long enough. According to reports, Kennedy has been totally unresponsive to General Armstrong's SACSA advisories as well as the Taylor-Rostow Report of November '61, both recommending the deployment of conventional U.S. forces into Southeast Asia. Plus I have here an unconfirmed report that the President's brother, the attorney-general, is advising him now to get out of Vietnam if the war is unwinable by any foreseeable South Vietnamese regime. Either way, John Kennedy's maintaining the status quo, special forces and intelligence involvement or complete withdrawal of U.S. military personnel is unacceptable to IIPAC. On the other hand, the dossier analysis/psychological profile you prepared for me late last year on Lyndon Johnson indicates that the vice-president's policies, as we had predicted, are perfectly in line with IIPAC objectives. Finally, I have never seen John Kennedy more indecisive; as evidenced by his inability to coherently sponsor a coup of South Vietnam's President Diem and his brother Ngo Dinh

Thu. I mean, it appears that the man is wavering uncontrollably, and every day this continues we at IIPAC are losing huge sums of money."

The lanky Sosar stood and looked out of his office window onto the darkening horizon of the Swiss city line. "Therefore, I have decided to put Legerdemain at Full Trigger Stage now, and as INFIX I want you to notify General Armstrong immediately. I take it that that will not be a problem, George? After all, you have had three years to iron out any cockhumping problems!"

George Whitten stiffened

"No, Sosar, there will be no problems. Legerdemain will be concluded by the end of the year No problems."

Sitting now, hours after his conversation with Sosar Tomeen and minutes after having communicated his INFIX message to MAMA WEST IIPAC for transmission to General Armstrong, George Whitten's broad face was indeed savoring the relief and comfort of Legerdemain's forward motion, basking in the brilliance and genius of his creation, manifested at last

Chapter Twenty-Six

FIVE MONTHS LATER
November 18, 1963

The little Italian Floral Shop Vince Angeletta had patronized the last eighteen months was prospering, if from nothing else but the Angler's business alone. He religiously bought four dozen roses a month from them and laid a dozen each, twice a month, on the graves of Rosalie Ann Sedoux Angeletta and Mona Spazek. He was standing in the St. Thomas Cemetery now, beside their adjacent tombstones.

It was 1:45 p.m.

From May to October of last year Vince, unable to attend to this ritual, had further enriched the floral shop by contracting them to set fresh flowers on the graves for him. Unable because, after Mario and Mona's funerals in May of '61, Vince had begun casing Thessalonian's presidential parade cities. In each, St. Louis, Detroit, Cincinnati, Dallas, Atlanta, Miami, Kansas City, Denver, Minneapolis and Little Rock, he drew dozens of maps and diagrams. Then using the largest library in each city he would research the geomunicipal layout and speculate on the most likely course for a presidential drive through. His primary focus being on the feasible routes between airports, city halls, monuments, and historical landmarks that were sniper suited.

It had been complicated work that Vince had taken to easily. He had finished with it by October, nearly two full months ahead of Thessalonian's timetable.

In January Thessalonian had sent word back to Vince, through Carthage, requesting that Vince rework his diagrams of Miami, Detroit, and Dallas. Vince did so in great detail, hopeful that Thessalonian had narrowed the kill zone to one of these three cities. By July, though, after Vince had completed the revisions, it was Charlie Nuccia who decided that hopeful wasn't enough. He ordered Vince to immediately set another meet with the renamed "Gli occhi debole di un pugnale"—the CIA man with the eyes of a weak dagger.

During the meeting at the Steak-Pit Restaurant in the French Quarter Charlie had raged at Thessalonian.

"Barker, there are ta be no more diagrams—no more plans—no more strategies—no more-no more!! Either Legerdemain is finished by the end of the year or you will be .. that I swear to you, Mr. CIA!"

The Top Man's ferocity had been sparked in late May by a report from one of his clandestine contacts within the New Orleans Office of the Federal Bureau of Investigation (FBI). That contact had informed Charlie that they had recently received a personal memorandum from J. Edgar Hoover expressing dissatisfaction with their investigation of the Nuccia family, whom the memorandum called "the most powerful criminal organization in the Gulf Coast states." Charlie was convinced that Hoover's sudden interest in him had been instigated by the blue-blooded hand of Attorney-General Robert Kennedy. Up until then Hoover's FBI had played only a minor role in Bobby's "Get Nuccia crusade."

So the Top Man's contempt for the Kennedys was at a peak. Vince had not seen his Don Nuccia so upset, so emotionally out of control, since Honduras in April of '61.

Thessalonian's reaction to Charlie's fury was equally uncharacteristic. The CIA man had still been his weak puppy self with his stupid-looking dark eyebrows quivering and his weirdly shaped jowls looking as uncoordinated as ever, but he did not argue with Charlie about risks or consequence like he had in the past. With amazing calm, he guaranteed Charlie that by the end of the year Legerdemain would definitely be finished, and that even then he was very, very close to selecting and scheduling, using Vince's research, a city for the hit.

But that was five months ago and now Vince was worried. Worried and bored. He was sick of whiling away the hours eating Italian Po' Boys at Castricone's with Jake, and playing Baccarat, Pinochle, and Poker at Lafitte's Westport Club.

He wanted it over. He wanted Legerdemain over now!

The "City of the Dead," St. Thomas Cemetery off of Esplanade Avenue, wrapped its early afternoon doom around Vince's impatience and grief. He cried a few tears for Mona and a few for Rosalie, then turned and walked out of the above-ground cemetery.

Daniel Carthage waited for him on the sidewalk near the cemetery entrance. He approached Vince on the balls of his feet, prepared to bolt if the crazy Sicilian made a threatening move towards him. He had never forgotten how the Angler had slammed his bald, diseased head into that alley cement a year and a half ago.

"Angler?"

Vince turned, instantly recognizing the fake reddish brown hair of Carthage. In a way he was glad to see Thessalonian's errand boy, maybe he had word.

"Yea, Carthage, what is it?"

Vince's silvery-brown-blue eyes were opened wide with expectation. He walked closer to the homosexual pilot.

"Vince, it's time. Here are the final plans from Thessalonian."

Carthage handed what looked like some sort of bonded government pouch to Vince. On the front and rear of the pouch, respectively, were the front and rear seals of the United States of America. The rear seal caught Vince's eye with its design and boldly etched Latin inscription—*Annuit Coeptis*—highlighted on it. He wondered what it meant.

Carthage added with finality, "You'll never be dealing with me again, Vince, but I will still be living in New Orleans. If we happen to see each other around, there must never be any recognition, okay?" he asked timidly.

Vince looked at him gravely, his five foot eleven inch muscular frame ramrod stiff, clutching the pouch with anticipation.

"Never's a nice word, huh, Carthage?"

He jabbed a forefinger in the direction of the intelligence operative's chest. "Like the raven, huh, motherfucker. Nevermore!"

Daniel Carthage wanted Legerdemain over, too, just as bad as Angeletta and was happy that this morning he had received from Thessalonian a whiplash call; the final order to execute.

It was 2:10 p.m.

He and Bannerwell and Cross had spent the last six months, according to Thessalonian's instructions, accelerating composition of the Cuban-Juan Jimenez connected character of Lee Harvey Oswald; from Oswald's affiliation with 544 Camp Street and Bannerwell's anti-Castro, anti-Communist League of the Caribbean and Friends of a Democratic Cuba located there, to 531 Camp Street, a side entrance to 544, where Oswald's phony pro-Castro, pro-Communist Fair Play for Cuba Committee was headquartered, to Oswald's erratic behavior, to his ordered use of pseudonyms like "Hidell", to his use of pseudonyms to buy weapons through the mail, to his mysterious-looking trip in September to Mexico City and finally to situating Oswald's employment in Dallas, at the exact spot Thessalonian had ordered; the Texas School Book Depository.

It had been an exhausting time and, yes, Carthage was ecstatic that within two weeks Legerdemain would be over.

And Dallas is where it would end. Dallas ... end game.

He walked swiftly down Esplanade away from St. Thomas Cemetery to a public phone booth he knew of nearby.

That poor sap, Lee Harvey, was waiting in Dallas for his call.

"Archer Marsh, the man you will be killing, John F. Kennedy, is larger than life—a legend, a God—impervious to the likes of you. The likes of white Alabama trash like you!"

It was 3:00 p.m.

These words, bellowing from his own subconscious, had haunted Captain Archer Marsh for two years. The Special Forces confederate Viking had tried to block them out but had failed, and now the words were making him even more restless.

Two years! Two years of combat inactivity was enough to cripple any professional fighting man, even one that had kept his marksmanship and physical condition in top form. It was just too long a time with the silence and isolation he had had to endure.

He hadn't heard another word of encouragement from General Marion Armstrong III through his permanent aide, Corporal Forrestol. Nor did General Mancus visit often. Mancus seemed to have lost all enthusiasm for Legerdemain after the Holt-Taylor incident. And as far as Thessalonian was concerned, that guy was invisible!

It had been just Archer Marsh, alone, constantly confined in barracks; like prison. He was nearing his breaking point, knew it, and figured it was time he told somebody about it.

The new Archer Marsh that had emerged after Forrestol's visit in April of '61 was rapidly becoming an old Archer Marsh. That flush of satisfaction he had once had to his face was now sallowed by the stress of waiting on Legerdemain. Even his blonde hair and blue eyes seemed less bright, less alive.

"FUCK this!" Archer Marsh yelled in frustration into his empty Ft. Bragg barracks.

General Alexander T. Mancus opened the Captain's front door as the word "this" faded.

"Fuck what, Captain?" the deputy commander of the Special Warfare Center at Ft. Bragg asked as he stepped lightly into Marsh's quarters.

Captain Marsh instantly forgot his grievances, noticing a lift in the usually lethargic stride of General Mancus. A lift unusual for a man in his early 60s.

"Oh, nothing, sir ... I, ah ... stubbed my toe. That's all," Marsh answered.

"Your toe?" The General actually smiled at that.

Marsh noticed a paper and what looked like a bonded government pouch in the General's right hand. The paper appeared to be an encoded mimeograph from his teletype. Could this be it?

The flush in Captain Marsh's face was returning now. The tall, slim General Mancus moved towards the Captain, lifting his headwear off, letting his white, strandy hair flow. The military man, who in Marsh's eyes had given Legerdemain credibility from the beginning, stood solemnly, inches away from him. He handed the government pouch with the front and back seal of the United States on both sides to Marsh, lifted the encoded mimeograph and began to read aloud from it.

"To Mancus—Marsh ... These are the orders for the resolution of Legerdemain. They are self-explanatory and clear. God has indeed ... smiled ... on our undertakings. Thessalonian"

"Goddamn the perils of being a middleman," Gaetano Rossini

spewed as he hung up the phone on the nightstand in the bedroom of his Hollywood home.

It was 4:00 p.m.

The two aspiring Hollywood actresses in bed beside him had roused and were wallowing all over his six foot frame with tongues and lips and crotches, desperately trying to impress this powerful Hollywood "strategist." Amazingly enough, one of the girls was even attempting to run her hand through his thick mass of greased black hair. He slapped her hand away, then grabbed the two nymphomaniacs by the necks.

"Do it-a to each other, I'll-a watch."

The usual exotic charm of Rossini's broken English had just become ugly. Nonetheless, the girls began licking and kissing; the thighs of one girl rubbing against the clitoris of the other, breasts squinched together, pink nipples pressed. He sat up and reached again for the phone on the nightstand, his eyes unblinking, intent on the sapphist sights before him. He dialed a number in Dallas. Someone answered, "Yea."

"This is Rossini. Miami's out, Detroit's out, Dallas is in. Just got the word personal from Mr. A. in Chicago. Go with that carousel man, the Jew, Jack Ruby "

Thessalonian had made at least two dozen trips to Dallas since June 27. That had been the day that all three contingencies of Legerdemain had gone to Full Trigger Stage.

Knowing that there would be no further delays had strengthened Thessalonian's position in July when Charlie Nuccia unexpectedly summoned him to New Orleans. It had felt good to unconditionally guarantee the Mafia boss and his shooter, Angler Angeletta, that by the end of 1963 Legerdemain would be finished. Still, he had been forced to stand and stomach a dressing-down by that short, Sicilian, Napoleon-fuck, called by his underlings the "Top Man", in the back room of some sleazy steak house the dagos owned on Bourbon Street. Man, was he going to enjoy killing those two after Dallas.

It was 6:00 p.m.

Thessalonian's day had been intense. First he had contacted Dan Carthage with a whiplash call ordering him to: a) deliver the bonded government pouch he had received two days ago to

Vince Angeletta, notifying Angeletta that the time to execute had come. Thessalonian had debated over the usage of the bonded government pouch with Angeletta, deciding finally that it was worth the calculated risk. The CIA man remembered his resolution in Honduras, "Do not underestimate the Sicilians!" Specifically detailed plans would be expected—plans with the imprimatur of an official yet unofficial Thessalonian ... making it appear that the CIA man had had to smuggle the papers directly out of his Directorate of Plans office where he had structured them. b) contact Oswald, currently employed at the Texas School Book Depository in Dallas, informing the ex-Marine, ex-ONI Operative, that he, Carthage, would be arriving in Ft. Worth with a final intelligence brief for him within the next 24 hours. c) make sure Bannerwell and Cross, Carthage's CIA cohorts in New Orleans, maintain a high profile during the next two weeks by making daily public, verifiable appearances.

Thessalonian was pleased with the efficiency his men, Carthage, Bannerwell and Cross had shown over the last six months. They had successfully completed composition of the Oswald character as well as successfully placed Oswald in Dallas as an employee of the Texas School Book Depository on schedule.

After his whiplash call to Carthage, Thessalonian had then teletyped General Mancus at Ft. Bragg, ordering him to give a bonded government pouch, the same type Angeletta had received, to Captain Archer Marsh; the only remaining member of SFG Team Legerdemain. The teletype indicated to Mancus and Marsh that the pouch, which had been delivered to the General two days prior, contained orders for the resolution of Legerdemain.

Finally, Thessalonian had contacted Stefano "Mr. A." Anacondini in Chicago and had told him that it was time for them to select their shooter to shoot Oswald and that that shooter must be located in Dallas. Thessalonian proceeded to give Mr. A. the necessary details and figured Anacondini would immediately contact Rossini in Hollywood. Someone would call someone else in Dallas. Oswald would fall.

Within 24 hours Captain Archer Marsh, triggerman for Contingency Legerdemain 1, Vince "Angler" Angeletta, triggerman for Contingency Legerdemain 2, Lee Harvey

Oswald, triggerman for Contingency Legerdemain 3, and an unknown triggerman supplied by the Chicago Mafia to shoot Oswald afterwards, would be in Dallas, poised.

The target/objective of Special Op Legerdemain, President John Fitzgerald Kennedy, would be arriving in Dallas on Friday morning, November 22.

Kennedy's multipurpose visit to Texas had been planned by his staff several months earlier. It would include visits to San Antonio, Houston, Austin, Ft. Worth, and finally what amounted to a Democratic campaign sweep through Dallas in hopes of mending the differences between two rival Democratic Lone Star power groups.

Thessalonian had contacted Plato Smith when he had first learned the details of the President's Texas trip through the presidential Secret Service itineraries he regularly received. He then submitted to his superior the Dallas presidential parade route that had been prepared by Angeletta, admitting to himself that the Sicilian bastard had done an excellent job on the diagram. Thessalonian assumed that Plato Smith then, using his own contacts with the White House staff, had influenced the logistics of Kennedy's schedule, enough to where the chief executive would be in Dallas in Delay Plaza on the early afternoon of the 22nd.

All Thessalonian had to do was make sure Marsh, Angeletta, and Oswald were there, too, then that Oswald would be captured directly after the shoot and that Marsh and Angeletta would escape, and that Oswald would be killed by Anacondini's man. Thessalonian would then be responsible for the elimination of Marsh, Mancus, Jimenez, Angeletta, Nuccia, Anacondini, and Rossini as quickly as possible thereafter. If, however, worst case scenario and Angeletta were to be captured, Thessalonian was positive the Mafioso would invoke his code of Omerta and silence. Regardless, Angler would be linked to the Nuccia family in New Orleans and Charlie Nuccia would take the red hot heat for the President's murder. There, too, Thessalonian was confident Charlie Nuccia would remain silent. Likewise, Thessalonian had ensured Captain Marsh's silence by providing him with a tab of cyanide for ingestion if arrested.

The remaining post-assassination details, like fueling the

confused investigatory fires of the Dallas Police Department, the FBI, the Secret Service, and the Attorney-General's office, would be handled by Plato Smith. From there Thessalonian could only anticipate that the real powers behind Legerdemain would offer him the sun, the moon, the stars, and the galaxy for his three years' dedication.

The Dallas hotel he was staying in was cheap, small, and rundown. He walked to the bathroom, methodically undressed, stepped into the shower, and, as usual, let the flow of water, this time rusty iron water, soothe the irritation of his burn scars. His thin lips gargled the brackish water without flinching, whispering repeatedly in husky incantations:

"Marsh, Angeletta, you're for me, but, little Oswald, you're the key!"

Chapter Twenty-Seven

November 19, 1963

"San Angelo Field—this is Cessna 631 Bravo—I'm twenty miles southeast of you—request landing instructions—over."

"Cessna 631 Bravo—this is San Angelo Field—land at runway two right—winds from southwest at ten miles per hour—approach on discretion—over."

It was 9:30 a.m.

Vince Angeletta's guts were as calm as a South Pacific typhoon. Next to him in the empty co-pilot's seat lay the bonded government pouch Carthage had handed him by the cemetery entrance in New Orleans yesterday. It contained Thessalonian's final instructions for Legerdemain. Included were Vince's parade diagrams of Dallas, drawn in August of '62 and revised in February of '63. The Mafioso was pleased that all his preparatory work had not been in vain, and impressed, too.

Thessalonian's package was incredibly detailed. There was a timetable, an outline of "worst case scenarios," even a list of situational attire, explaining the kind of clothes Vince was expected to wear and when.

Arriving in Dallas correctly was of the utmost importance. The instructions stated that Vince should fly into San Angelo, arriving no later than 10 a.m. on the morning of the nineteenth. Upon arrival he was to be sure to tell the field personnel caring for his plane that he was a claims adjuster for the Four Seasons Insurance and Credit Corporation. He was to be dressed in an inexpensive, conservative suit and would wear a pair of square eyeglasses. He was to carry as part of his luggage his black exercise bag. However, it was to contain only one weapon: a Mauser model 98K, heavy barrel, bolt-action rifle with a Zeiss scope; the exact same type of rifle that had failed him on the rooftop in Havana. This caused Vince some consternation, but the Mauser was an excellent sniper rifle, and Luigi Bertucci had knocked the hell out of the one in Cuba, so Vince put his superstitions aside. Thessalonian insisted in his instructions that Vince carry no handguns, so for the first time in years he was without his .22 Ruger pistol. And finally, Thessalonian had, in big letters, instructed Vince to bring his "special identification"; his Secret Service badge and wallet.

From San Angelo, Thessalonian had instructed Vince to rent a 1960 Dodge Polara car; the same make and model Vince had rented when breaching Kennedy's security at Ft. Bragg. The same make and model the Secret Service regularly used.

He would then drive to Dallas from San Angelo, arriving in the second largest city in Texas no later than 6 p.m. this evening. Once there he was to check into the prestigious Fairmont Hotel, just like any other traveling businessman. He was to be unassuming and forgettable with everyone; from the porter to the hotel clerk, just another average face for the next couple of days.

Tomorrow he would reconnoiter the area around Dealey Plaza, especially the grassy knoll area north of Elm Street. This is where Vince would be positioned on the afternoon of November 22.

Inexplicably, as Vince turned on the downleg of his approach to San Angelo Field, he felt that familiar deep-seated reserve of his kick in, just like it had over the Everglades and on that Havana rooftop in 1960. It strengthened his resolve and calmed the typhoon in his stomach.

Twenty feet—ten feet above ground—reducing power—wheels contact—flaps full up ... landing.

At least this time the U.S. military transport plane had served him decent food. They had called it a snack, but still it was more than the transport out of Laos had served him in 1960.

"Special Forces Group Legerdemain," he reminisced, "Holt and Taylor gone, I'm all that's left, Captain Archer Marsh, 77th SFG Abn, currently on reassignment but not for long."

It was 9:45 a.m.

He lovingly clutched the bonded government pouch in his lap. The U.S. military transport plane he was flying in was due to land at Barksdale Air Force Base in Bossier City, Louisiana within minutes. Marsh was wearing the same pair of big aviator sunshades he had worn on the day of Holt and Taylor's demise; not even a smidgen of remorse accompanied his recollection of that day. He had done what he had had to do, what had been best for him, simple.

His shades tilted downward and were looking at the government pouch in his lap. The Captain had Thessalonian's final orders, enclosed in the pouch, memorized. He was to take the 12:20 p.m. bus from Shreveport to Dallas. He was to be dressed like a college athlete and would check in to the modest Breezeway Hotel near downtown no later than 8 p.m. tonight. Day after tomorrow he would reconnoiter the Texas School Book Depository Building thoroughly, working from premarked blueprints of the building. He would be positioned in a corner fifth floor window on the afternoon of November 22nd.

Beside him lay his weapon, disassembled, in his travel bag. It was a specially fitted Remington .308 caliber. Transporting it in his luggage on the bus from Bossier City to Dallas, then checking into the Breezeway Motel with it, would be easy. Even leaving the Texas School Book Depository with it on the 22nd after the shoot looked easy according to Thessalonian's planning.

The rifle had been designed to disassemble and fit perfectly into a custom pair of baggy athletic pants Marsh would be wearing on Friday the 22nd. The pockets that had been sewn into the pants to accommodate the rifle pieces were hardly noticeable. With Marsh's bowlegged stride he would appear to be just another awkward college kid running from the Depository; trying to find out who had shot the President.

Thessalonian would pick up the team leader within yards of the Depository Building in a 1958 green Ford Fairlane station wagon and they would both calmly drive back to Barksdale Air Force Base in Bossier City, simple. If, however, there were any complications, Thessalonian had given Marsh a tab of cyanide to swallow, but a cocky Captain Marsh was positive that would not happen.

"Damn," Marsh thought, despite the seriousness of the moment, "the only thing missing now is Lola!"

Being homosexual, being bald, and being diseased, did not preclude Daniel Carthage from being an excellent pilot. He glided his Cessna 150 into the small, private airstrip in Livingston, Texas, north of Houston. As he made his approach, he surveyed the woodland area surrounding the airstrip. There was nothing there except an automobile parked off its northeastern side. That would be the vehicle Thessalonian had arranged for him to use for the next forty-eight hours.

It was 10:45 a.m.

After landing, Carthage had been instructed to drive straight to Fort Worth, arriving there no later than midnight tonight. He would check into a Fort Worth hotel called the Spur. The Spur, for the most part, lodged assorted rodeo people and Carthage, too, would identify himself as a rodeo promoter. The wide brim Stetson hat that Thessalonian had instructed Carthage to wear would easily cover his fake reddish brown hair, hair that would be remembered by witnesses if seen.

Tomorrow at noon Carthage would meet with Operative Oswald in his hotel room at the Spur and deliver to the ex-Marine the final intelligence brief on Legerdemain. Up until now Lee Harvey Oswald had been kept ignorant of many Legerdemain details, including its ultimate operational objective. Both Carthage and Thessalonian had invoked their "need-to-know" privilege, commonly used in intelligence operations, whenever the wiry clandestine agent expressed curiosity. But tomorrow he would have to be told exactly what Special Operation Legerdemain was all about. Sort of. He would be told that John F. Kennedy was a Communist agent and that the president must be assassinated in Dealey Plaza on Friday afternoon. Carthage knew that this would be a delicate sell, but felt confident that Oswald would, after some befuddlement, accept it at face value like a good soldier and do his duty.

Carthage supposed, however, that Oswald would ask questions. Questions that would have to be answered, like, "Why all the Cuban bullshit in New Orleans and all of my disjointed activity leading up to this?"

Lee Oswald in Carthage's opinion was not a stupid or weak man. His Russian experience proved that; two and a half years spent in deep freeze, speaking another language, living another culture, yet he had survived admirably.

At that point Carthage would answer with a half-truth, "Because, Lee, if by some terrible fluke you are arrested, your background must look Cuban-related, somehow, either sympathetic to Castro or angry over the Bay of Pigs and the plight of the Cuban exiles. That way the American people will be spared the revelation that their grand, young President was a Communist agent. Lee, yours is a sacred mission. The very fate of America will rest Friday on your shoulders. And if, worst case scenario, you are arrested, we'll get you out, just be patient and silent."

After throwing these seeds of divine mission into the man's mind Carthage would then have to go over the intricate details of Oswald's escape route from the Book Depository, stressing to Oswald that even though his arrest could be handled, he should try to avoid it at all costs. That he must think like a soldier on the battlefield from the second he shoots the President to the time of safe pickup by Thessalonian. If person or persons unknown were to attempt to hinder him, then he must engage and injure them, that's all. If possible, he should avoid killing any innocents.

Finally Carthage would guarantee Oswald that after he successfully concluded Legerdemain, he would be allowed to retire with full pension to any spot on the globe to live out the remainder of his life in want of nothing. "Maybe room there," Carthage thought, "for a few more seeds of divine mission and, like magic, a presidential assassin, after months in the womb, would emerge."

"About fucking time," Carthage grimly murmured, just as the wheels of his Cessna 150 hit Texas paydirt.

At 11:00 a.m. someone telephoned Jack Ruby. They had told the Jew, the owner of Dallas' Carousel Burlesque, to get his ass in gear, that a major order had come down from the boss in Chicago. Ruby dressed quickly and drove to meet this someone; this someone who Ruby knew to be Stefano "Mr. A." Anacondini's man in Dallas.

Mr. A.'s man poured him a martini and laid it out for him.

He told Ruby that he had been chosen to do a piece of work, a piece of delicate work, mainly because of his contacts within the Dallas police department.

Ruby was confused and said so.

"Don't be confused, Jackie," this someone had said, "there's nothin' to be confused about. On the 22nd when Kennedy's here he's gonna get whacked. They're gonna arrest a patsy. You're gonna get inside police headquarters and whack the patsy. Easy as pie."

Ruby's first thoughts were of being in prison for the rest of his life, then of what would happen to him if he didn't do what "Mr. A." had ordered. Then he stopped thinking, listened to the details, finished his martini, stood up, and shook the hand of this very important someone.

Driving away, he felt what he had always imagined his strippers felt when they were performing.

Dirty—naked—helpless ... and bare-ass exposed.

THREE DAYS LATER
November 22, 1963
Aboard Air Force One
Midair between Fort Worth, Texas and Dallas, Texas, USA
Late mid-morning

The Fort Worth Chamber of Commerce really outdid themselves with that breakfast this morning ... it was good of Connally to arrange it.

Saved me some embarrassment after T.C.U. backed out ... what pettiness, not wanting to give me an honorary degree because I'm Catholic.

I suppose the fact that I am President of the United States is insufficient ...

This is nut country! ... and I'll be most relieved when this trip is over ...

Almost as relieved as I was that the CIA finally did something right by orchestrating Diem's death in Saigon a few weeks ago.

Now maybe a responsible regime can be put in place in Vietnam ... one that we can assist from a distance—enabling us to pull out the majority of our people ...

Funny—Southeast Asia resembles Texas in a way.

Nut country ... both ... and I'm in the middle of each .. not an enviable spot.

Chapter Twenty-Eight

November 22, 1963

"Capitalism is an economic system, not a political system. It is unconcerned with the people's welfare. Its only concern is the continual flex and pump of the free market—those who attempt to inject social conscience into it are feebly misapplying its context. Pure capitalism—the buying and selling of goods—is of itself, in itself, and answerable to no one. It is as simple and as fundamental as urination or defecation or fornication. Of itself it exists, amoral, objective. And to be successful, Sosar, you, too, must be, like it, detached from the mundane, your worth as a human inextricably tied to your financial net worth. Besides, a healthy free market will cure all of society's ills, but that, Sosar, is not for you to worry with. Others weaker than yourself can quarrel over that. Your mission in life is basic: to accumulate capital. The more you have, the more of a man you will be."

"What great lessons Rocknawell taught me," Sosar Tomeen, the principle controller of Legerdemain, thought affectionately. "My mentor, my headmaster."

It was 4:45 p.m. Central European Time.

Sosar paced back and forth in his palatial Zurich office with a glass of soda water gripped in his three-fingered right hand. No matter how in-place every detail of Legerdemain seemed to be, the Chairman of the Board of the Inter Inpetto Armaments Corporation (IIPAC) was worried.

It was in stressful times like these that the old lessons of Rocknawell, his childhood headmaster, came back to him, and memories of Vanderbilt Boarding School, and memories of the loneliness, and just how much he had hated the loneliness. And today, especially, he was haunted by thoughts of prison. What if? What if? What if? What if? But when the panic stopped he knew he was protected—insulated; By the actual assassins—

Oswald, Marsh, Angeletta. By Thessalonian-CIA Field Control, by Plato Smith-CIA DDP Base Control, by General Armstrong-Pentagon Control, then by those close-mouthed Sicilians: Nuccia, Anacondini, Rossini.

"Yes, it will all be fine," he repeated to himself.

What gave Sosar Tomeen the most comfort was the mentality of America itself. He believed his fellow Americans to be a gullible and dumb lot, and that given a crazy like Oswald for a presidential assassin scapegoat, they would be satisfied. He also believed and knew as a researched fact that Hoover of the FBI would do anything to protect the image of his bureau; that he'd probably whitewash the whole cockhumping shoot and make the Secret Service and Dallas Police do the same—for the sake of appearances.

"That's it," Sosar concluded to himself, "that's what the American people are about; appearances, cosmetics, as long as they look to be prosperous and their cities are kept for the most part clean, they'll stay happy and unquestioning. They'll buy any lie they're told from an authoritative source. And that's what Legerdemain is; an empty deception, a sleight of hand, where the hand itself is the culprit ... not what it's holding or the cards it's shuffling, but the hand itself. Yes, it will all be fine."

As an added precaution, though, Sosar had decided to give the order to Whitten that none of the Sicilians were to be killed afterwards. That way, if by an unforeseen fluke America did not buy the Oswald-lone gunman scenario, the Sicilians would suffice as the next best scapegoat. The other loose ends Thessalonian could tie up as he saw fit.

Sosar Tomeen had been immeasurably impressed so far by Thessalonian, and would offer the CIA agent a high position within the IIPAC hierarchy after the completion of Legerdemain, which would be, Sosar anticipated, in approximately four hours.

"Rocknawell, my old friend, are you watching this trick?" Sosar called out, motioning with his glass of soda water now held in his left hand, raising his three-fingered right hand dramatically. "I'm going to turn the world over very, very soon ... like magic ... watch me!"

At 11 a.m. Thessalonian stood on a tarmac at Dallas Love Field and watched Air Force One taxi towards him. His dead-fish gray eyes and black microdot pupils were unblinking and unwavering in their stare, contrasting noticeably with the applauding Texans in the tarmac crowd surrounding him. He was confident, though, that none of these noisy imbeciles would notice his frozen gaze.

It was imperative that Thessalonian see with his own eyes the president disembark from the 707. If for some reason the President had changed his mind about motorcading through Dallas, which he had the absolute authority to do, Thessalonian had to know immediately. That way he could notify Angeletta, Marsh, and Oswald so they could disappear, otherwise all these assassins would be waiting foolishly for nothing. And the longer the contingency assassins were in place the greater their chances of being discovered. If that happened, Kennedy would quadruple his security in future trips, thereby quadrupling the difficulties in assassinating him.

The plane ramp lowered and after a three-minute delay Jacqueline Kennedy, the First Lady, appeared, followed closely by President John Fitzgerald Kennedy. The crowd around Thessalonian went wild.

The high cheekbones of the CIA master operative went a little higher as he animated a wide grin. He, too, began yelling and clapping, looking just as idiotic as everyone else, but then it was easier for a normal looking, cheering man to nonchalantly step backwards, out of and away from the tarmac gathering.

He walked quickly towards the airport terminal and parking lot and his 1958 green Ford Fairlane station wagon parked there. Dealey Plaza and history were both anxiously anticipating his arrival.

Lee Harvey Oswald's nerves were shot.

It was 11:50 a.m.

Each passing moment brought the President, who Carthage

had classified a few days ago as an active Communist agent, closer and closer to Dealey Plaza, closer and closer to the street below the sixth floor corner window of the Texas School Book Depository, where he was positioned.

Oswald had worked at the Depository since October 15th, but it was not until his last Wednesday's meeting with Dan Carthage at the Spur Hotel in Fort Worth that the full reasons for his employment at the Depository were disclosed. Carthage also provided Oswald an explanation for the ex-Marine's calculated Cuban-cause-related, psychologically unstable behavior during the past year and a half. But instead of clarifying matters, his CIA co-controls explanation had only confused Lee Harvey more.

Oswald turned his head and goose-necked towards the cardboard box to his left. Propped against it was a 1938 6.5mm, bolt-action, clip-fed Mannlicher-Carcano rifle. Turning back to the slightly opened sixth floor corner window three feet in front of him overlooking Elm Street his whole wiry body shook with trepidation, a single suspicion germinating, then quickly maturing inside his head.

"Carthage made a big deal Wednesday of the sanctity of this mission, calling it a divine mission, yet neither he nor Thessalonian put me through any marksmanship courses in preparation for it; not even an easy one, and this rifle here is outdated as hell. Damn, this is going to be an incredibly difficult shot and to further complicate it, Carthage said that I must wait until Kennedy's limo is exactly ... there." Oswald peeked out the crack of the window at the precise spot Carthage had indicated. "Damn, I could fire sooner and it would be easier. And what if I miss and hit Jackie or Connally? They can't all be Communists."

At the internal utterance of the word Communists, the full absurdity of that claim in connection with Kennedy became apparent to the ex-ONI operative. Lee Harvey Oswald knew at that instant he had been scammed—set up—to take a deadly fall. But instead of leaving the sixth floor of the Depository then, he became paralyzed with fear; fear of Thessalonian, Carthage, fear for his wife, fear for his child. His mind began jolting possibilities, options, right and left, front and back. Only one course made sense to him. He would shoot and miss, shoot and miss. After all, they had not prepared him. He would be blameless.

His nerves were beyond shot now—they were dysfunctional—he was dysfunctional.

"Divine mission ... my ass," he cursed aloud.

Terror had seized him and began involuntarily trickling, warm and yellow, down his leg.

Captain Archer Marsh, piece by piece, pocket by oversized pocket, lifted the specially fitted .308 caliber Remington rifle out of its concealment. He then locked the barrel nutbolt and the metal tubing that served as its stock handle together. He clipped the trigger housing and Colt scope on next, took a handkerchief from underneath his baggy athletic pants beltline and spread the three shells it contained in front of him. He grabbed the handkerchief, wiped his brow and blonde hair and loaded the weapon. He pressed his big aviator sunshades firmly down on the crook of his nose. The Special Forces officer and team leader, without a team, was secure.

It was 12:18 p.m.

Lastly—ritualistically—he removed a cellophane wrapper from his sock. It contained the tab of cyanide Thessalonian had given him. He unwrapped the cellophane and set the pill down on the windowsill.

"As if," Archer Marsh silently pondered, "as if I would actually swallow it, just like I never swallowed Thessalonian's red scare Communist bullshit about Kennedy. What a bunch of dog puke. Sex maniac, maybe. Gangster friend, maybe. But Communist? Fuck you, Thessalonian. And Corporal Forrestol, speaking ever so sincerely for General Marion Armstrong, 'This nation's very survival is on your shoulders.' You mean your very survival, don't you, fellows? And Holt and Taylor—poor stupid punks—unable to conceive of such a power. Just remember, all of you, my promotions, bonuses, and exorbitant pensions and save the pigshit lies for someone else."

He lifted up and rechecked the trajectory from his fifth floor corner window at the School Book Depository to the exact spot on Elm Street Thessalonian had instructed him to fire at. Thessalonian had been very insistent on this detail, marking it in red on the map included in the bonded government pouch materials. Archer Marsh knew that he had better have it right seeings as how he had had a campfire with the government pouch last night.

He heard the crowd noise swell from the direction of Houston Street ...

And his twenty-inch biceps swelled with it—

And his penis—

And his balls—

The bitter country boy's time .. had come.

He looked like a Secret Service man, like an Italian Dick Clark, with his black conservative, very government-like suit, tie and shoes on, just as he had looked when he had breached Kennedy's security at Ft. Bragg and Cape Canaveral. The square eyeglasses that he had worn since arriving in San Angelo were in his suit breast pocket along with his Secret Service badge and wallet. His black exercise bag laid opened at this feet. In his hands was a Mauser Model 98K, heavy-barrel bolt-action rifle with a Zeiss scope.

It was 12:23 p.m.

Vince stood behind a fence on the edge of a parking lot on top of the grassy knoll north of Elm Street. He could hear and see through the cracks in the fence the presidential motorcade approaching. He spotted Kennedy's steel blue limousine immediately, taking an instant account of the numbers and positions of the real Secret Service men surrounding it. He looked ahead thirty yards to the exact shooting spot Thessalonian had emphasized in his final plans. Plans contained in a bonded government pouch that Vince had, on a last minute impulse, stashed instead of destroyed.

Again his deep-seated reserve pumped. He became perfectly calm, just as he had been on that rooftop in Havana in 1960. He raised the rifle to his shoulder and aimed the crosshairs of his Zeiss scope directly on the handsome profile of John Kennedy.

The steel blue limousine moved closer, appearing to float on the exuberant uproar of the crowd.

Twenty seconds—Vince's furry eyebrows squinched.

Fifteen seconds—his arrogant nostrils stopped breathing.

Ten seconds—his left silvery-brown blue eye closed, his right eye sighted.

Five seconds—the palms of his vital and potent hands gripped

Zero seconds—he pulled the trigger. The rifle fired.

CRACK!

CRACK!

CRACK!

The President jerked—a bullet penetrating five and a half inches below his collar line—around his sternomastoid—his throat—there were other shots—the President jerked again, a bullet through the fourth ventricle of his brain. More shots—Jackie was bobbing up and down, other people were ducking—blood—wind—noise—more shots.

Within ten seconds it was over.

The exuberant uproar of the people became shrill now—disorganized—as the presidential motorcade sped off.

Vince quickly picked up his three shell casings, shoved the weapon into his exercise bag, and began to walk towards his Secret Service look-alike rental car parked in the grassy knoll parking lot. He opened its car door, threw the bag in, closed it, and turned around just in time to see a Dallas Police officer running towards him, sidearm drawn, crying out frantically,"FREEZE, MISTER! FREEZE, POLICE! DON'T MAKE A MOVE!"

Vince froze, then calmly said, "I'm with the Secret Service, Officer—I'm reaching in to get my identification."

Vince pulled out his Thessalonian-supplied Secret Service badge and wallet from his suit breast pocket, unfolded it, and held it at arms length in front of him.

The Dallas Police Officer looked Vince in the eyes, lowered his weapon, and said, "Okay," then ran off farther across the parking lot towards the railroad tracks where there was even more pandemonium.

Vince hurriedly got into his Secret Service look-alike auto and split, a feeling of blood clotting in his brain and of CIA acid being poured through his rectum.

"Who in the motherfuck fired those other shots?" he asked himself.

"Who?"

⌖ ⌖ ⌖ ⌖

"King Kennedy, King Kennedy, King Kennedy—Big—Fucking—Deal!" Archer Marsh sputtered, without realizing it, as he half ran through the lobby of the Texas School Book Depository.

It was 12:31 p.m.

His baggy athletic pants were loosely jostling around him; the metal of the disassembled .308 caliber Remington knocking against his bowed legs. Everyone else was running, too, out of the Depository to see what all the fireworks was about, and to see why the presidential motorcade had sped up and driven away so quickly. Captain Archer Marsh, though, instead of running down Elm Street towards the underpass and the railroad tracks, turned left away from them, still in a half-run as if disoriented. He headed towards Houston Street where Thessalonian's 1958 green Ford Fairlane station wagon with Thessalonian at the wheel would be waiting. The corners of his blue eyes grimaced from the weight of the pieces of his concealed rifle, also subconsciously from anger.

He was certain that he had heard other shots being fired at the same time he was firing his. Some seemed to have come from above him in the Depository building, others from the grassy knoll area north of Elm Street. This disturbed the Special Forces Captain tremendously but for now the threat of capture and a cyanide death disturbed him even more. The naked Lola tattoo on the calf of his right leg spread wide with each tense step.

Thessalonian had some explaining to do. The cool CIA-DDP man, who had reminded Marsh of a motorbiker at their initial briefing, was up to his scarred neck in duplicity with Mancus and Forrestol and Armstrong.

The more his adrenaline boiled the more he wished he could take them all out to Kalioke Swamp, cut all their throats, and bash each of their skulls in. With that comforting image in mind the first waves of enjoyment and killing power began flooding his senses.

He had just shot en-titled royalty—a legend—a God ... King Kennedy.

Yep, little ole Archer Marsh ...

White Alabama trash—
No more!

Lee Oswald, after his wildly inaccurate presidential shooting spree, had decided with extreme reservation to follow Thessalonian's pre-set escape route. Except for one small detail; he needed a weapon to protect himself, or at least to blow his brains out if arrest was imminent. His Italian Mannlicher-Carcano rifle would be of no use to him, seeing as how he had no more ammunition for it, and had been ordered to leave it behind in a sixth floor Depository storage room anyway.

It was 12:37 p.m.

He remembered what Dan Carthage had told him: "We can handle your arrest just be patient and silent. But once you shoot the President and are making your escape, pretend you are a soldier on the battlefield, injure anyone getting in your way, but, of course, avoid killing any innocents."

"What strange diametrically opposed orders," Oswald thought. "Arrest no problem but still take out anyone that gets in your way, but leave your sniper rifle behind. Of course, avoid killing innocents. Of course, of course!"

It was then, as he stepped into a taxi a few blocks away from the Depository, that his sensitivities and paranoia overedged even more with the realization that he had heard other shots fired at the President besides his. He may have shot to miss, but who's to say the others had? What others? Who were they? Why had he not been briefed on them? What if the President was dead?

"Damn."

He paid the driver, stepped out of the taxi, ran to the flop house that he had maintained for the last few months, and grabbed his .38 caliber Smith & Wesson pistol from his dresser drawer. His rendezvous and pickup point with Thessalonian, the Texas Theater, was within walking distance. He decided to walk—not run—to it.

His brain, though, clicking overloaded, stopped him cold.

"But if Thessalonian and Carthage have double-crossed me, why go to the theater? Why not go off in a whole other direction, change the escape plan? If it turns out I'm wrong about them, I'll just tell them later I had no choice."

Oswald now became physically ill. He could feel the maggots of his prolonged dysfunctional state eating away at his gray matter like a drunk, sick from having one-guzzled a fifth of Russian vodka.

Nonetheless, the ex-Marine, ex-ONI operative, current CIA operative, began walking, not running, out of the flophouse towards the Texas Theater as if on remote control, his internal buttons responding automatically to his operational orders.

Besides, for Lee Harvey Oswald a disordered world and a chaotic life in hiding would be impossible. Death would be preferable to that.

"Damn ... damn it all!"

The Dallas Police car pulled slowly alongside him. Oswald pretended not to notice at first. He just kept walking, not running. It was 1:15 p.m.

The officer called out to him. He had to stop. He walked closer to the police car—like a soldier on the battlefield. Words were exchanged. The policeman—T-I-P-P-E-T on his name badge—stepped out of the car.

"Injure anyone getting in your way, Lee," Carthage had told him, "Arrest can be handled, but—"

Lee Oswald fired four .38 caliber Smith & Wesson rounds into Officer Tippet's spleen, left kidney and the thalamus-hypothalamus of his forebrain. Tippett fell.

Lee stupidly pocketed his weapon and kept walking a little faster now ...

"Of course, avoid killing any innocents ... "

Of course!

"Dallas Police Department. This is the Dallas Police Department emergency line ... Hello?"

"Hello?"

"Yes ... this is the Dallas Police Department. May we help you?"

"Yes, the man who shot the President ... "

"Yes ... yes ... hello ... hello .. please continue."

"He's hiding at the Texas Theater. Third row from the rear."

Click.

Tud-tud-tud-tud-tud-tud-tud-tud

"Hello ... hello ... hello ... please continue ... hello, hello?"

Lee Harvey Oswald sat in the Texas Theater—third row from the rear. It was 1:50 p.m.

He wanted to die.

Thessalonian should have been here by now.

A scuffling in the rear. House lights up. Men approaching.

Closer.

Closer

Hands on his shoulders.

Hands on his arms.

He made a fist with his hands and hit and hit and hit.

Hands yanking him.

Hands shoving him.

Handcuffs on him.

"I'm just a patsy in all of this ... don't you see ... just a patsy ... a damned ... pppaattsssyyy!"

INTERLUDE

November 22, 1963 to Present

Slip
Bowline
Triple Half Hitch

Knotted tight
as a rat's ass

Nobody'll snitch

Thessalonian

November 22, 1963
1:00 p.m. CST, Parkland Memorial Hospital, Dallas, Texas USA, President John Fitzgerald Kennedy is pronounced dead.
2:40 p.m. CST, Aboard Airforce One - Love Field, Dallas, Texas USA, Vice President Lyndon Baines Johnson is sworn in as President of the United States.

November 24, 1963
1:20 p.m. CST, Dallas Police Headquarters, Dallas, Texas USA, Jack Leon Ruby (Rubenstein), owner of Dallas' Carousel Burlesque, shoots and kills Lee Harvey Oswald, suspected presidential assassin, on orders from Stefano "Mr. A." Anacondini, Chicago Mafia boss.

November 25, 1963
9:10 a.m. CST, Barksdale Air Force Base, Bossier City, Louisiana USA, Captain Archer Marsh, Team Leader of Special Forces Group Legerdemain, boards U.S. military transport plane for return flight to the Special Warfare Center at Ft. Bragg, North Carolina. Before takeoff, as Marsh is locked into the transport fuselage, potassium cyanide pellets are dropped into acid, producing hydrogen cyanide gas, and is introduced into the aircraft ventilation system by Legerdemain Field Control, Thessalonian. A trapped Archer Marsh dies of chemical poisoning within ninety seconds.
1:11 p.m. EST, U.S. Army Special Warfare Center, Ft. Bragg, North Carolina USA. The on-base home of General Alexander T. Mancus, deputy commander of the Special Warfare Center, is set ablaze by paramilitary operators on orders of Thessalonian. General Mancus and his infirm son are incinerated.
2:26 p.m. EST, The White House, Washington, D.C. USA. President Lyndon Baines Johnson approves NSAM-273. A plan ordering for the comprehensive study of methods to increase U.S. military activity in Vietnam.

November 28, 1963
8:36 a.m. EST, Safe House, Key Largo, Florida USA.
Cuban Revolutionary Directorate leader, Juan Jimenez, is shot in the back of the head by paramilitary operatives on orders of Thessalonian. He dies instantly.

December 9, 1963

8:50 a.m. EST, Supreme Court Building, Washington, D.C. USA, The Warren Commission established by President Johnson and headed by Chief Justice of the United States, Earl Warren, to investigate President Kennedy's assassination, receives its first five volume report from the Federal Bureau of Investigation (FBI) concerning the events in Dallas on November 22. Unbeknownst to the Commission, FBI Director J. Edgar Hoover, who is officially in charge of the investigation, has ordered his agents to accredit evidence substantiating the Oswald (lone gunman) and Ruby (lone avenger) theory and to discredit/convolute evidence leading to the contrary. Hoover's overriding concern is the credible public image of his bureau.

December 11, 1963

11:00 a.m. EST

Central Intelligence Agency (CIA) Headquarters, Langley, Virginia, USA. Legerdemain Field Control, Thessalonian, is ordered by his Central Intelligence Agency Directorate of Plans (CIADDP) superior, Plato Smith, to not kill any of the Sicilian Mafiosos involved in Legerdemain. Thessalonian argues vehemently against this but is overruled. Plato Smith also orders Thessalonian to be in Zurich, Switzerland at a specified address in two days. No further information given.

December 13, 1963

3:30 p.m. CET, Inter Inpetto Armaments Corporation (IIPAC), Central Office, Zurich, Switzerland. Sosar Tomeen, Chairman of IIPAC, meets with Thessalonian. No mention of Operation Legerdemain is made, but Thessalonian is offered a vice-presidency with IIPAC, as well as a high six figure annual salary. Thessalonian accepts. For IIPAC's records, Thessalonian reveals his true name—Victor Thomas Ingels.

December 20, 1963

9:00 a.m. CST MAMA-WEST IIPAC Communications Relay, Isla de Providencia. The Senior Classified Communications expert for the North American Division of IIPAC, Clemer Dodd, disturbed over the assassination of President Kennedy and the flurry of suspicious communiqués transmitted through his

MAMA-WEST IIPAC system during the last month, decides to begin his own secret investigation into the "030601-Legerdemain" tie-in. He is determined to uncover "Intercept Eagle's" identity and to gather evidence, if any exists, of Intercept Eagle's culpability in the president's murder. He structures a plan whereby he will be transferred from his Isla de Providencia outpost to the Zurich Central Office of IIPAC. He predicts that his access to classified materials there will be limitless.

January 10, 1964
7:00 a.m. EST, The White House, Washington, D.C. USA.
President Johnson approves the Pentagon's OPLAN 34-A, graduating the U.S. military presence in Vietnam.

January 25, 1964
10:15 a.m. CST FBI Office
New Orleans, Louisiana USA, Calogera "Charlie" Nuccia, Sicilian boss of the New Orleans underworld is questioned, in a perfunctory manner, by representatives of the New Orleans office of the FBI, as to his whereabouts on November 22, 1963. His alibi stands.

March 13, 1964
2:21 p.m. CST, Lafitte's Westport Club, Gretna, Louisiana USA.
Vincenzo "Angler" Angeletta, former principle money courier (spalloni) for the Nuccia organization becomes Charlie Nuccia's top assistant/advisor in all family business. The closeness of their relationship, however, is kept secret.

August 7, 1964
9:00 a.m. EST, The White House, Washington, D.C. USA.
President Johnson and Congress approve the Gulf of Tonkin resolution, which serves as a Declaration of War against North Vietnam, allowing for the full combat commitment of U.S. conventional forces.

September 24, 1964
10:00 a.m. CST, The Supreme Court Building, Washington, D.C. USA. The Warren Commission investigation is completed and the Warren Report is published. Its conclusions:
A) Lee Harvey Oswald shot the President.

B) He was not connected with any conspiracy of any kind, nature or description.

November 3, 1964
Lyndon Baines Johnson is elected the 36th president of the United States.

December 11, 1964
4:30 a.m. CST, Ochsner Medical Facility, New Orleans, Louisiana USA. Guy Bannerwell, ex-FBI agent turned private investigator and one of Thessalonian's three former CIA operatives in New Orleans, dies of heart failure.

January 3, 1967
10:00 a.m. CST, Parkland Memorial Hospital, Dallas, Texas USA. Jack Leon Ruby (Rubenstein) is pronounced dead of cancer. He dies without ever having been moved officially to a federal jurisdiction or without ever having confessed to or revealed his or Stefano "Mr. A." Anacondini's role in Oswald's murder.

February 22, 1967
8:35 a.m. CST, Fontainebleau Hotel, New Orleans, Louisiana USA. Daniel Carthage, the second of Thessalonian's three former CIA operatives in New Orleans and subject of a recently undertaken New Orleans district attorney's office investigation into the Kennedy assassination is found dead. Carthage's death, made to look like a suicide (certified cause: massive brain hemorrhage due to drug overdose), was actually an execution contracted by Victor Ingels (Thessalonian), now Vice President of Sales for IIPAC. Ingels, acting independently, believed the homosexual pilot and most involved operative participant in Legerdemain would be vulnerable to police interrogation.

March 1, 1967
9:05 a.m. CST, International Trade Association Bldg. New Orleans, Louisiana USA. Clay Cross, president of the New Orleans International Trade Association and last of the three former Thessalonian CIA operatives in New Orleans is arrested on a

warrant issued by the New Orleans District Attorney's Office. Cross is charged with participating in a conspiracy to kill John F. Kennedy with Oswald and Carthage (both now deceased).

January 31, 1968
5:00 a.m. Vietnam Time, U.S. Embassy, Saigon, South Vietnam. On Tet holiday, the largest and most ambitious North Vietnamese offensive begins with an attack on the U.S. Embassy. Dozens of important South Vietnamese towns and cities are attacked simultaneously.

February 12, 1968
9:07 a.m. Vietnam Time, Military Advisory Group (MACV) Headquarters, Saigon, South Vietnam. General Westmoreland, commander of all U.S. forces in Vietnam, both conventional and non-conventional, requests an additional 206,756 U.S. troops from President Johnson.

March 13, 1968
7:20 a.m. EST, The White House, Washington, D.C. USA. President Johnson only partially grants General Westmoreland's requests, asserting that the tide of American public opinion is now shifting against the U.S. military presence in Southeast Asia.

March 31, 1968
8:05 p.m. EST, The White House, Washington, D.C. USA. Lyndon Baines Johnson in a televised speech to the nation announces that: "I shall not seek and I will not accept the nomination of my party." His aggressive U.S. militaristic resolve against North Vietnam was weakening, therefore he had been advised by certain special interest groups (including the defense contractor consortium of Brandtest and Set, General Technologies, Inc., BlairCorp, and IIPAC) to exclude himself from the upcoming presidential campaign. Already exhausted from the apparent futility of the war effort he conceded to those interests.

June 5, 1968
9:12 p.m. PST, Embassy Ballroom - Ambassador Hotel, Los Angeles, California USA, Robert Kennedy, Democratic presi-

dential candidate and still ongoing nemesis of Calogera "Charlie" Nuccia, is shot several times after giving a speech at his California Primary victory celebration. A lone gunman, Sirhan Sirhan, is arrested.

June 6, 1968
10:30 p.m. PST, Good Samaritan Hospital, Los Angeles, California USA. Robert Kennedy is pronounced dead.

June 8, 1968
8:00 a.m. CET, Inter Inpetto Armaments Corporation (IIPAC), Central Office, Zurich, Switzerland. Sosar Tomeen introduces Victor Ingels (Thessalonian) to George Whitten, the architect of Legerdemain. For the first time, Operation Legerdemain of '60, '61, '62, and '63 is discussed openly between the three men. Tomeen is not displeased by Robert Kennedy's death, considering RFK's publicly expressed anti-war sentiment, but is concerned over any possible investigatory backlash the young Kennedy's assassination may have on Legerdemain. Therefore, he orders Whitten and Ingels to conduct an investigation into Robert Kennedy's murder and determine if any of the still living principles of Legerdemain, especially Charlie Nuccia, were involved.

November 5, 1968
Richard Milhouse Nixon, Republican presidential candidate, is elected the 37th president of the United States, with huge political and financial aid from defense contractor consortiums like Brandtest and Set, General Technologies, Inc., and IIPAC.

December 6, 1968
5:00 p.m. CET, Inter Inpetto Armaments Corporation (IIPAC), Central Office, Zurich, Switzerland. George Whitten and Victor Ingels present their conclusions on the Robert Kennedy assassination to Sosar Tomeen: A) There were no Legerdemain principles involved; B) Sirhan Sirhan was acting alone or possibly as an incited agent for a group of OPEC-anti-Israeli interests, who were concerned over the young Kennedy's position on oil depletion allowances, and/or his stated intention to sell fifty phantom jet fighters to Israel.

March 1, 1969
12:45 a.m. CST, Louisiana State Court, New Orleans, Louisiana USA. Clay Cross is acquitted by jury trial of the charge of participating with the now deceased Oswald and Carthage in a conspiracy to kill John F. Kennedy.

June 8, 1969
8:00 p.m. EST, The White House, Washington, D.C. USA. President Nixon announces to the American people that he has ordered the withdrawal of 60,000 U.S. troops from the 543,000 stationed in Vietnam and that he intends to arrange, if possible, a cease-fire in hopes of negotiating with the North Vietnamese a lasting peace. Privately he informs his military-industrial supporters that troop reduction is the only viable course to assuage a growing American anti-war movement.

December 11, 1972
1:10 a.m. CST, Ochsner Medical Facility, New Orleans, Louisiana USA. Clay Cross dies of complications during surgery.

January 27, 1973
11:00 a.m. CET, 8 Ave General Leclerc, 94 Choisy-le-roi, Paris, France. The Vietnamese Embassy delegation announces the signing of the Vietnam Peace agreement. The signatories are Le Duc Tho and Henry Kissinger.

February 16, 1973
9:20 a.m. CET, Inter Inpetto Armaments Corporation (IIPAC), Central Office, Zurich, Switzerland. Clemer Dodd, after a decade of secret investigation into the MAMA-WEST IIPAC 030601 tie-in, decides that he has accumulated sufficient evidence on the major figures of Operation Legerdemain to secure an indictment from an American Grand Jury. He has uncovered the Legerdemain roles of General Marion Armstrong III, who acted as Intercept Eagle, Plato Smith, who was Legerdemain's CIA-DDP control, Victor Thomas Ingels—then code-named Thessalonian— who was Legerdemain's field control, the identity of each participant in the three contingencies of Legerdemain, and lastly, George Whitten and Sosar Tomeen, the architect and principle of Legerdemain. Dodd fears, how-

ever, that during the last month his undercover investigation may have been accidentally uncovered by a co-worker. Alarmed, he decides, instead of presenting his material to the IIPAC infiltrated American government, to contact the one Kennedy triggerman still alive, Vincenzo "Angler" Angeletta, in hope that the Nuccia-Angeletta Sicilian contingent, bitter over their blatantly manipulated role in Kennedy's death, will take revenge—legal or otherwise—against Tomeen and his men. Dodd cynically concludes that even the legitimate elements of the American government would, upon receipt of his evidence, seal it in the National Archives. Knowing that this could easily be arranged under the all encompassing guise of national security only reaffirms Dodd's decision to approach Vince Angeletta instead. Clemer Dodd decides to take a leave of absence immediately and reserves passage on a Pan Am flight from Zurich to New York to Chicago to New Orleans.

February 22, 1973

11:15 a.m. CET, Inter Inpetto Armaments Corporation (IIPAC), Central Office, Zurich, Switzerland.. Sosar Tomeen and Victor Ingels (Thessalonian) meet to discuss the disposition of an IIPAC Senior Classified Communications expert who is suspected of spying against the company. They become very concerned when reviewing the man's record, discovering that the man, Clemer Dodd, was the MAMA-WEST IIPAC 030601 tie-in operator during Legerdemain. Sosar Tomeen becomes exasperated over this and other cockhumping loose ends of Legerdemain and orders Ingels to tie them all up, thereby sanctioning the deaths of Clemer Dodd, General Marion Armstrong III, his aide Corporal Forrestol, Plato Smith, and even his old comrade George Whitten. Tomeen insists, however, that Nuccia and Angeletta must stay alive to deflect and divert any future investigations into Kennedy's death. Maintaining that, second to Oswald, the Mafiosos are the perfect scapegoats. Ingels again argues vehemently against this as he did with Plato Smith in 1963, but Tomeen is adamant. Tomeen does concede, however, that the other Sicilians, Anacondini and Rossini, may in the future become expendable.

February 25, 1973
8:33 p.m. CST, Lafitte's Westport Club, Gretna, Louisiana USA. Clemer Dodd, after days of searching the New Orleans area for Vince "Angler" Angeletta, finally locates him at the Baccarat table of Lafitte's. Dodd's first words to Angeletta are: "Thessalonian's real name is Victor Thomas Ingels and I know where you can find him." Angeletta shuffles Dodd out of Lafitte's quickly. Clemer Dodd proceeds to tell Angeletta the results of his secret decade-old investigation. Clemer Dodd gives Angeletta three briefcases full of documentation to support his accusations. Vince Angeletta is stunned.

February 26, 1973
11:00 a.m. CST, Lafitte's Westport Club, Gretna, Louisiana USA. Vince Angeletta meets with Calogera "Charlie" Nuccia to discuss Dodd's information. Their decision is to hide Dodd's three briefcases of documentation in the same Dallas safety deposit box where Vince stashed Thessalonian's government-pouched final assassination plans in 1963 and to wait for further developments.

March 13, 1973
2:41 a.m. EST, Madison Hotel, New York, New York USA. A panicked Clemer Dodd, still on official leave of absence, phones Vince Angeletta in New Orleans. Dodd tells Angeletta that he has detected surveillance the last several days and that his investigation may have been uncovered and that, if it has, he is sure that his execution has been ordered. He warns Angeletta that the Mafioso, too, may be in danger.
8:15 p.m. CST, Lafitte's Westport Club, Gretna, Louisiana USA. Vince Angeletta informs Charlie Nuccia of Clemer Dodd's phone call. Charlie orders Vince to disappear for an unspecified length of time. Vince agrees.

March 15, 1973
7:48 a.m. EST, Madison Hotel, New York, New York USA. The body of Clemer Dodd is discovered in the shower by hotel housekeeping, the apparent victim of a suicide. The shower is still running, Dodd's left wrist is slashed vertically and a razor blade is lying on the floor nearby. He was murdered hours earlier by Victor Ingels (Thessalonian).

May 8, 1973
6:10 a.m. EST, Brookland Heights, Washington, D.C. USA. General Marion Armstrong III and his aide Corporal Forrestol are murdered in what appears to be an estate burglary. Several of General Armstrong's estate valuables are stolen by Victor Ingels (Thessalonian) after he murders the two men to support the burglary claim.

July 2, 1973
7:22 p.m. EST, Tower Pines, Alexandria, Virginia USA. The body of Plato Smith is discovered floating face down in his swimming pool, an apparent drowning victim. A drowning aided, forcibly, by Victor Ingels (Thessalonian).

September 14, 1973
11:05 p.m. CET, Inter Inpetto Armaments Corporation (IIPAC)Retreat, Gstaad, Switzerland.George Whitten, the architect of Legerdemain, dies of a heart attack. Unknowingly tranquilized earlier in the evening, Whitten was fast asleep when Victor Ingels (Thessalonian) administered to him an intravenous injection of insulin, causing the ex-OSS man instant death.

May 10, 1975
9:00 p.m. EST, Congressional Chambers, Capitol Hill, Washington, D.C. USA. The Senate Select Committee to Study Government Operations with respect to Intelligence Activities, known as the Church Committee is formed. Their primary mandate is to investigate the alleged 1960 CIA plot to hire underworld figures to assassinate Fidel Castro and the plot's relevancy, if any, to the assassination of John F. Kennedy.

July 19, 1975
6:30 p.m. CST, Oak Park, Chicago, Illinois USA. Stefano "Mr. A." Anacondini, now retired, is shot to death in his basement kitchen by Victor Ingels (Thessalonian). The murder, finally approved by Tomeen, was necessary because of the Church Committee's intention to subpoena Anacondini.

September 7, 1975
10:13 p.m. CST, Tally's Bar, Grand Isle, Louisiana USA. Vince "Angler" Angeletta, in hiding since March, 1973, is certain that a man is following him. Vince, after waiting three hours inside the bar for the man to leave, decides to make a move. Vince leaves the bar and waits for the man, who exits soon afterwards. Vince grabs the man and shoves him down in his best "Angler" fashion. He knocks the man senseless and pulls him out to a wooded area away from the parking lot. Vince rifles the man's pockets for identification, discovering only a single business card and about a hundred dollars in the man's wallet. The card reads: GO Investigations—Richmond, Virginia. Vince, remembering that 13 years ago in Honduras, Thessalonian had given him and Charlie, in conjunction with the phony name of Miles Barker, a Virginia address. Vince's uncontrollable paranoia having been fed by too much liquor during the night deduces that the man works for Thessalonian, now Victor Ingels, and that he has been sent to kill him. Vince, rashly, without taking precautions or thinking the scenario through, turns the man over, and pulls out his ever-present .22 Ruger from the small of his back and shoots the man in the base of the skull. Exactly fifteen seconds later a redneck voice out of the shadows orders him to throw down his weapon. Vince laughs at how similar the redneck voice speaking to him now is to the voice of the redneck boss who had murdered his father in 1937. Vince realizes then just how drunk he is and what a terrible mistake he has made. He is arrested, given no bail, and charged with murder.

December 10, 1975
9:30 a.m. CST, Louisiana State Court, Grand Isle, Louisiana USA. Vincenzo "Angler" Angeletta is found guilty of second degree murder and sentenced to 30 years, no parole, to be served in Angola State Penitentiary, Angola, Louisiana.

September 12, 1976
9:00 a.m. EST, Congressional Chambers, Capitol Hill, Washington, D.C. USA. As an outgrowth of the Church Committee work, the 94th Congress establishes the House Select Committee On Assassinations.

October 15, 1976

4:26 p.m. EST, Biscayne Bay, Miami, Florida USA. The dismembered body of Gaetano Rossini, formerly Stefano Anacondini's representative in Hollywood, is found floating in a chain-weighted oil drum. His murder was contracted to independents by Victor Ingels (Thessalonian). Weeks prior Rossini had willingly testified before the House Select Committee on Assassinations.

February 17, 1979

9:00 a.m. EST, Congressional Chambers, Capitol Hill, Washington, D.C. USA. The conclusions of the House Select Committee on Assassinations are publicly announced. They are: A) Oswald did shoot and kill JFK as the Warren Commission deduced. B) Oswald did, in fact, act as the tool of a much larger conspiracy.

January 10, 1980

10:30 a.m. CET, Inter Inpetto Armaments Corporation (IIPAC) Central Office, Zurich, Switzerland. Sosar Tomeen announces publicly to a group of international business correspondents that IIPAC as of January 1, 1980 has been rated the third largest armaments conglomerate in the world. Privately to Victor Ingels (Thessalonian), now Vice Chairman of IIPAC, the 64-year-old chairman admits that if it had not been for Johnson's escalation of the Vietnam War and the subsequent U.S. defense budget increased spending for conventional forces during that period, IIPAC would not have survived.

June 15, 1983

8:00 a.m. CST, Seagoville Federal Correctional Institute, Fort Worth, Texas USA. Calogera "Charlie" Nuccia reports to prison to begin serving a seventeen-year sentence for wire fraud and bribery charges. Charlie Nuccia, now 77 years old, is stricken with Alzheimer's Disease and is not expected to survive his prison term. Johnny and Jake Sincelli take control of the Nuccia organization with Charlie's blessing.

Present

Vince Angeletta, himself dying in prison with cancer and suffering from years of accumulated guilt over having allowed his mentor, Charlie Nuccia, to be manipulated by Thessalonian, decides that the least he can do is confess his sinful failings to a trusted priest. He contacts a former New Orleans underling, Carlo Cefalu. Cefalu, under federal investigation, blackmails Father Joseph Prio into tape recording Vince's confession in hopes that the old Mafioso will reveal valuable secrets to the priest. Secrets Cefalu can use to bargain himself out of trouble with the Federal authorities.

Book Two

Present

Eat my young
Eat my old
throw me a kiss afar
on my knees
wanton
violate me, war

Nicholas Plauche Chapter

Chapter Twenty-Nine

In Angola State Penitentiary, Angola, Louisiana, USA

Scratch—Scrape, Scrape
Scratch—Scrape, Scrape
Scratch ...
Scratch ...

The middle-aged fingernails of Father Joseph Prio were red and chipped. The underside of the confessional crucifix hung around his neck was clawed irreparably. He stroked his tough gray-black beard. He removed his wire-rimmed glasses and rubbed the emotional shock from his brown-black eyes. He fiddled dumbly with his receding gray-black hairline while his tongue flicked maniacally between the space of his two front boyish teeth. He was overwhelmed.

He thought of Carlo Cefalu, then of the tape recorder hidden in the satchel lying next to his chair. He looked down at the satchel then up to the old man seated next to him.

Vince Angeletta was in a stupor, grieved. Not from having helped murder the President of the United States so many years ago, but instead from a perception of having failed his patron, Charlie Nuccia. He was staring at his hands as he had for hours.

Father Prio felt empathy for Vince's soul—not a Sicilian scummed soul like Carlo Cefalu's—but a human soul, twisted by mythical Sicilian tradition, loyalties, and beliefs.

"And who am I to judge, anyway? To demand penance?" the priest asked of himself harshly, "My soul is as lost as his, the victim of its own immorality ... Whiskey Bay ... the death of Scarlet Leblanc."

Father Prio hesitated, then stood as if suddenly palsied with a terminal illness. His mind clicked, then decided that for both him and Vince now only one form of penance would do; total public exorcism.

"Vince," Father Prio said wearily, as he began pacing in the prison visiting room, "we are not so different, you and I."

These words brought the old triggerman around. Vince lifted his silvery brown-blue eyes and wiped the dribble from his lips, smearing a portion of it into the whiskers on his cheeks. He looked hard at the priest.

"How's that, Father Prio?"

"Call me Joey, Vince."

"Joey?" Vince Angeletta asked, his eyes alert now, locked intently on this man of the cloth before him. A man, supposedly Carlo Cefalu's trusted priest, who was saying things that Vince did not understand or like.

"Yes, and I have some confessing of my own to do and I want you to listen closely, and I want you to understand. And afterwards, Vince, we will share the penance, and maybe one day the absolution."

Vince's character lines frowned gravely at this. "What the fuck is he talking about?" The emaciated Mafioso began wringing his hands again.

Father Prio removed the confessional crucifix from around his neck and laid it on the prison visiting room table. He reached into his jacket hung on the backside of the chair for a handkerchief. He used it to wipe the sweat from his forehead and upper lip. Father Prio then reached again to his jacket for a pack of cigarettes. He pulled a cigarette out of the pack and lit it. The priest by these acts had transformed himself into a civilian. Vince was terribly confused.

"My visit here today, Vince, was coerced. Yes, I am parish priest and church administrator for St. Cecilia's Catholic Church on Lake Pontchartrain ... and yes, Carlo Cefalu and I have known each other for many, many years; as a kid I even ran with Carlos' street gang. Ironically that was the same time your Operation Legerdemain was running, between '60 and '63. But in 1963 I

disassociated myself from him. Then last week I received a letter from him addressed to Father Joey Prio. I knew the minute I saw the envelope it was from Carlo, because for over 25 years now no one has addressed me as Joey, not even my church friends. He wanted to meet with me. I agonized over whether to or not, but after re-examining my professional responsibilities I relented. That meeting took place at Mama Maria's last Friday. He showed me your letter."

"What's wrong with that? That's what I told him to do," Vince interjected impatiently, his mental processes including paranoia now in high gear.

The hurricane temperament of Father Joseph Prio swelled.

"Look, Vince! I asked you to listen to me, dammit! And I mean it. If you want to die in peace, my Sicilian confessee, you'd better hear me out!"

Vince Angeletta, astonished by this outburst, shut up. The priest continued.

"I was coerced—blackmailed—into coming here today, because like you, Vince, I have sinned greatly."

Father Prio closed his eyes wishing desperately that he were back in his study at St. Cecilia's, with its age-encrusted wetbar and couch and chair—alone in his refuge—at peace within his cell. He inhaled on his cigarette deeply, longingly.

"Back in '63, Vince, while still a teenager, when you were closing in on Kennedy, I was high-rolling it. I was respected within Carlo's gang because of my skill as a burglar. Even Carlo, the bully's bully, didn't push me around. He even went out of his way to show me a good time. God knows I wish he hadn't."

Vince had stopped wringing his hands now. He sat tense, bewildered, motionless.

"One weekend Carlo sets up a little party. His girl Alicia Jordan and another young girl, Scarlet Leblanc, rode with us over to Whiskey Bay. Back in '63 that's where all the kids went to fool around. Carlo even arranged a boat for us. He had brought a bag of marijuana, plenty of liquor, and off we went. At about sunrise we got there and launched. The girl, Scarlet, starts coming on to me and I'm loving it. Carlo pulls into this cul-de-sac in the swamp and the party begins."

Father Prio's voice had become bland, emotionless, in no way representing the near broken-down state of his anguished spirit.

"Vince, we had what amounted to an orgy on the boat. The girls were all over me and Carlo like hungry animals. The more sex we had, the more stoned we got."

The priest paused, catching his breath, hoping that he wouldn't get sick like he had at Mama Maria's. He inhaled again on his cigarette.

"Scarlet was a beautiful girl. A French girl, probably a lot like your Rosalie, Vince. She had such a beautiful body, and knew exactly how to use it. Then the most horrible thing imaginable happened."

Father Prio—Joey's—voice dropped a register as he stopped pacing and resumed his seat next to Vince. It seemed to Vince that the priest's color was changing.

"She was fascinated with the .22 pistol I carried. She laid my naked body down on one of the boat cushions and put the gun right next to my erection. I was so stoned by this time and wasn't very clear about what she was doing. She'd suck on the gun barrel for a while, then on my erection. She was licking the gun like it was another erection. Carlo couldn't control himself. He moved up behind her, got on his knees and penetrated her. She went wild and began sucking both the gun barrel and me with such fury ... "

Father Prio choked.

"The pistol went off, Vince, in her mouth. I had been too stoned to remember it was loaded. Blood went everywhere."

The priest sat back, unable to face or return Vince's stare.

"Carlo took care of everything from that point on. We sank her body—what was left of her body—with weights, and Carlo paid Alicia off. Luckily, Scarlet had very little family, so the police inquiries into her disappearance were never extensive. But that ended my association with Carlo. It ended my life. I enrolled in the seminary shortly thereafter and have for over twenty-five years been atoning for that tragedy; the tragedy of Whiskey Bay 1963."

Vince relaxed, his fear of Father Prio's motives replaced now by the realization that the priest was as scared of eternal darkness as he was.

"Okay, Joey, that's a bad thing that happened to you and if it means anything, I'm sorry it happened," Vince paused. "But why did Carlo want you to come hear my confession? Why, of all people, you? What's the scam?"

Father Prio reached down to the satchel and lifted it up. He wrestled with it, opened it, and removed the tape recorder from it. Vince's silvery brown-blue eyes bulged.

"The scam, Vince, is that Carlo's in a lot of trouble in New Orleans with the Federal Task Force. He used Whiskey Bay to blackmail me into getting your confession on tape. He knows how close you were to Nuccia and how important a man you were in Nuccia's organization. He figured you'd have lots of valuable information, information he can use to get himself off the hook with the Feds. It's all on tape, Vince, your confession ... and mine."

Vince quickly, impulsively, lunged for the tape recorder with every ounce of feeble strength he could muster. Father Prio let the Mafioso have his way. Vince stopped the recorder and removed the long-play cassette tape. Father Prio waited till Vince had the cassette securely in his hand before making his appeal.

"Vince, when will it end? When will it ever end for both of us? When will we ever be men enough to make it right?" Father Prio stood again, his color returning now, along with his determination to impose a penance of total public exorcism on himself and the old Mafioso. "You were manipulated, Vince—you and Charlie—you were used by forces who are so entrenched in this country as to be almost invulnerable but who does the public peg Enemy Number One? You and your kind, Vince. When, in truth, there are so many more evil, more sinister. Like Sosar Tomeen and Thessalonian. Both of whom are probably alive and well, living in the lap of luxury in Switzerland, laughing about how they pulled off the crime of the century; not just against Kennedy, but against the American people. My God, Vince, the Vietnam War made IIPAC billions, and it probably wouldn't have happened if Kennedy had lived. We're talking about the deaths of thousands of young men, Vince. Thousands of young, innocent men. And for what? To feed the Goddamned bank accounts of some arms industrialists."

Vince gritted his brittle, old man's teeth and grimaced.

Joey kept talking.

"And you are in a position to expose them. Just with what information Clemer Dodd gave you, not to mention the final assassination plans that you said were stashed along with

Dodd's package in that Dallas safety deposit box. True, by doing so you would have to reveal your role and Charlie's in the murder, but you are both dying anyway."

Father Prio stopped, allowing Vince to fully absorb that reality.

"It's time, Vince, for both of us. I, too, intend to answer for the death of Scarlet Leblanc—to publicly reveal the incident and to suffer the consequences ... but not before I help you, my friend."

The priest concluded with finality.

"And being the priest who has heard your confession, this penance of total public exorcism I impose—no, demand of you—Vince. Listen to me ... it's time. America has suffered enough. Close the wound. You're the only man alive who can."

IN MAMA MARIA'S RESTAURANT, NEW ORLEANS, LOUISIANA, USA

One week ago Father Joseph Prio had entered this same spicy, informal Italian Cajun restaurant and underworld sit-down spot, located two blocks off of Prytania Street in the garden district of New Orleans.

"So much has happened since," Father Prio remarked to himself under his breath as he approached the entrance to Mama Maria's.

He was dressed as he had been last week—in cleric black—which was incongruent today with the new-felt vibrancy in his soul; a soul liberated when Vince Angeletta had agreed to publicly expose Operation Legerdemain.

So, feeling much less God-forbidden and much less like a sick, unwormed Louisiana dog, Father Prio entered the restaurant. Neon signs advertising the specialty of the house—hot pasta crawdads—shadowed the priest's face.

"Evening," he said to the hostess.

"Evening," she returned. "Mr. Cefalu is waiting for you," she added with a certain degree of reverence, not for the priest but for Carlo. To the staff at Mama Maria's Carlo Cefalu was still a star.

Carlo was sitting at the same small red and white checkered table where last week Father Prio had felt his old street temper flare and its subsequent pus-like adrenaline rush through him. The priest was scared, very scared, but his was a righteous fear now, a hero's fear.

Fat Carlo's back was to the wall, with only his left profile visible. He was wearing a yellow alligator sport shirt, brown slacks and a pair of white slip-ons. Father Prio speculated that Carlo had probably just come from a late afternoon of golf at the Lakeshore Country Club; golf, the priest recalled, being Carlo's one civilized passion.

"What say, paisan?" Carlo greeted as Father Prio sat down in the opposite wooden chair.

Carlo was holding a demitasse cup of espresso close to his mouth. He drank, then rubbed a napkin across both his sneering lips and the tip of his beaten nose. There were no phony handshakes this time, no seemingly sincere gestures, there was only hostility. Carlo, without skipping a beat, edged his pompadour hair with its platinum streak close to Joey. He wanted to be in Joey's face from the git go.

"Awright, hothead ... what the fuck have ya got?"

Father Prio was tempted to smile. Taking Carlo down a pubic hair at a time as he had anticipated was going to be a pleasure. The priest returned Fat Carlo's hostility.

"Carlo, let me explain something to you," Father Prio began, as tightly wound as an electric guitar string, "what we have here is a business deal—an arrangement—I'm not going to let you keep degrading me or continue dealing with me as if I were a fool. And if you keep trying to, I'm going to have to knock the hell out of you just like I did in 1959."

Vince had advised Father Prio on this approach. Vince had explained that to submit to Carlo's intimidation would be disastrous for the priest, that a new school Mafioso like Carlo only understood two things: business and strength; that even though Carlo possessed incriminating information on him he was not necessarily in control of the situation, for Carlo needed the information Father Prio possessed just as desperately. That, Vince concluded, established an interdependence—a business—a premise for an arrangement.

Carlo didn't respond immediately but did sit back and folded his beefy arms across his chest.

"Ah ... so the holy ass has gone and caught himself an

attitude. That's fucking great! That means ya must have found out something up in Angola to strengthen ya position. I'm all ears, Joey." Carlo's Brooklyn-Dixie Orleans accent bit sharply on Joey.

"Give me a cigarette," Father Prio told Carlo.

"Give you a cigarette? Sure, Joey, sure."

Carlo lifted his gold cigarette case from his back pants pocket and opened it. He removed a cigarette, handed it to Joey and even lit it for him; like a gentleman beast, made over.

"I taped Mr. Angeletta's confession, Carlo. He talked for hours. In fact, if he had talked much longer, my cassette tape would have expired."

Carlo's stomach bounced like whale blubber when he laughed. He laughed now, just a little.

"Very smart, Joey. I always knew ya were smart. Now, how about giving me the tape?"

It was Father Prio's turn to laugh now, just a little.

"I have no problems with that, Carlo ... except—"

The word "except" cliff-hung Carlo.

"Except what? Listen, ya piece of ... ah fuck, never mind ... ya owe me, Joey."

"Except," Father Prio continued, " ... I re-recorded the master and made four separate tapes from it. The first tape I'm prepared to give you tonight."

Carlo's face turned as red as one of Mama Maria's hot crawdads—boiling.

"What the fuck ya prepared to give me? Ya prepared to give me?"

"That's right, Carlo. And that's that. You can expose Whiskey Bay. You can kill me. You can get some of your goons to beat me. But I'm only going to give you what you have to have. Like I told you last week, I am a priest and have been for over 25 years now. Mr. Angeletta trusted me to receive his confession, and I will betray only as much of that trust as I have to. Besides, maybe one tape will be all you'll need to get the Feds off your back. If not, then I'll give you the second tape. If still not enough, then the third tape, and finally, if you convince me it's absolutely necessary, I'll give you the fourth tape."

Carlo rebutted, enraged.

"No, let me tell ya what I'M gonna convince YA of! That it is in ya best interests to give me all four tapes—now!"

It looked like Carlo was reaching down to tuck his shirt in or adjust his belt, but then his hand did not reappear. His face contorted.

"Joey, I've got a .38 caliber revolver pointed at ya fuckin' nuts and I swear, if you don't give me all four of those tapes in about sixty seconds, I'm gonna blow ya sack off!"

Father Prio, near panic, looked around. There were other late night diners seated nearby. Carlo was bluffing.

"Who in the hell do you think you're dealing with, Carlo? You're not going to shoot me because there are too many witnesses here. And even if you did, a .38 revolver can't be silenced, so the shot would make a tremendous amount of noise. They'd arrest you and charge you with attempted murder—or," Father Prio noted with more than a touch of uncertainty, "murder."

"That's the way ya got it figured, huh, Joey? Are ya forgetting I got a lot of friends in this restaurant?"

"All these customers can't possibly be your friends," Father Prio argued.

Carlo laughed a lot now, loudly.

"Ya see that woman over there—the broad with the frizzy hair? Well, her old man is indebted to me on a loan for about a hundred fifty grand. She's the vig—the interest. Every Friday night she whores for me to keep me from whackin' her husband. And the guy she's with, that's a prominent local banker. He likes to be tied and whipped and popped in the ass with a dildo. And the two guys over there looking like Popeye and Bruno. They're mine. And lastly, the family sitting towards the front; I just helped their son get out of jail. The district judge who sentenced him is a degenerate gambler, owed me for some Jefferson Down racing vouchers. As far as the staff and employees here," Carlo paused, gloating. "Need I say more, you dumb pompous bastard? This is my world ya in—my territory—NOW, I WANT THEM FUCKIN' TAPES!"

A huge, coppery spit of fear had wedged in Father Prio's throat. He wanted to gag, to run, like a sick dog again, with his tail between his legs. Instead he laughed—loudly, just as Carlo had.

"Wasn't it you, Carlo, who told me last Friday night that in your world now there isn't any honor anymore and that it's just, to quote you, 'one big fucking free-for-all'?"

Carlo didn't answer. His gun hand stayed under the table.

"You really think that everyone in here is going to keep his mouth shut about your murdering a priest? Before their eyes? Again, Carlo, you must take me for a fool. Sure, a couple of them might clam up, but all of them? No, Carlo, I don't think so and like you said last week, there isn't any statute of limitations on murder "

"Ya got thirty seconds left, Joey. And as far as what ya think I can—or can't—get away with, it's of no interest to me. Twenty-five seconds."

"Okay, Carlo, you may not care now, but you will later," Father Prio countered, doing his best to follow the script he and Vince had written.

"You see, Carlo, there's a fifth tape, and if anything should happen to me, that tape is going to get delivered to a very important someone."

"Joey, ya got fifteen seconds. What ya lawyers gonna do? Deliver it to the Feds? That ain't proof of nothing."

Father Prio decided it was time to give Carlo a taste of his own spit

"No, Carlo, my lawyer has instructions to deliver, if I should meet an untimely death, the fifth tape with an accompanying letter to Mr. Johnny Sincelli, and if he's not available, to his son, Jake Sincelli. I hear they're both real nice fellows."

Before Carlo could respond, Father Prio continued sarcastically.

"Have you by any chance heard of these two, huh, Carlo? The elder Sincelli was Charlie Nuccia's consigliere for years and years. Now he's the boss of New Orleans. In fact, I think he's your boss, too. And Jake, why Jake was Mr. Nuccia's driver and personal bodyguard ever since the cradle. You know, Carlo, I've heard that since they took over Nuccia's organization in 1983 they've killed at least a dozen New York wiseguys, a crew of heavy hitters that were trying to move in on their New Orleans action. They wiped them out. You know the lime-swamp routine, and I think one or two were even going to turn states evidence. Those got special treatment: penises cut off and stuffed in their mouths. And I bet that the Sincellis would wipe you out the same way if they were to find out you were trying to make a deal with the Feds. Especially considering that you're using information obtained from their old friend, Vince Angeletta, to do it."

Carlo's fat face was draining, from boiling red to chalk white. His sneering mouth was almost sniveling. There was movement under the table. His hand appeared back on the table empty. His voice was subdued, a gentleman beast again, madeover, defeated.

"I always knew ya were smart, Joey. Ya win. Let's talk about the first tape."

Father Prio exhaled, feeling as giddy as a kid's balloon with the air rushing out. He had narrowly escaped death, but he had won. So had Vince.

"Here's the first tape," Father Prio said, reaching down, retrieving it from the inner lining of his black nylon sock. He laid it in the center of the red and white checkered table.

"Now, Carlo, let me tell you what it contains."

Father Prio put his hands together on the table with his forefingers touching. He was recalling every nuance of the story he and Vince had decided to put to Carlo. They had over-dubbed and re-recorded the master tape of Vince's confession onto four separate tapes, providing just enough information on each to titillate the federal authorities. It was their way of testing the waters before swimming, their way of seeing how deep Operation Legerdemain had been.

According to the late Clemer Dodd there had been two Pentagon contacts: Armstrong and Forrestol; six CIA contacts: Smith, Thessalonian/Ingels, Carthage, Cross, Bannerwell, and Oswald; four U.S. military Special Forces contacts: Mancus, Marsh, Holt, and Taylor; two Cuban contacts: Juan and Margareta Jimenez; ten Mafia contacts: Romano, Bertucci, Anacondini, Pacissi, Ruby, Nuccia, Angeletta, Johnny and Jake Sincelli, and Rossini; and two IIPAC controllers: Whitten, the architect, and Sosar Tomeen, the principal.

Father Prio and Vince reasoned that with twenty-six people involved the chances of a leak to a mistress or an associate was not only possible but probable. Even though no one besides Armstrong, Smith, Thessalonian/Ingels, Whitten, and Sosar

Tomeen had known Legerdemain's full extent, it would be safest to proceed slowly and very, very carefully.

Therefore, the first tape of Vince's confession only alluded dramatically to the plot. Vince could be heard crying on the tape, as if in agony—Legerdemain ... Legerdemain ... .It was just babble but credible enough babble to spark the curiosity of the authorities.

"What in the world would make a hardened Mafia man cry like this?" Father Prio and Vince predicted they would ask. It was powerful yet vague stuff.

"Carlo, Mr. Angeletta was extremely upset over something in his past. He referred to it as 'Legerdemain'; a sleight of hand of some sort. He referred to it as if it might have been a contract killing."

"What the fuck ... Ledger ... what?" Carlo asked, mystified.

"Legerdemain. When you listen to the tape you'll hear him talking around it. Then he'll skip over to something else, about the Bible; the Thessalonians segment of the Bible. It's very incoherent, but I suspect it's major material. So my suggestion to you is to start off by mentioning just the word Legerdemain. There's no telling where it might lead. See what they say."

"Whoa, Joey," Carlo's mind was not following, "Is Vince crazy?"

"No, not one iota," Father Prio emphatically assured Carlo. "He's just upset over his lifetime of evil, and I believe this Legerdemain was the most evil of his deeds." Father Prio paused, knowing he had to give Carlo more. "He said that Legerdemain—whatever it was—happened in the early '60s. He said something about parades and the Top Man, which I presume is what Charlie Nuccia used to be called. Then Cuba and some guys named Bertucci, Marinello, Jimenez, and Romano, and shooting a short-wave radio to bits. Then horseback riding through the jungle and a landing strip in Pinar Del Rio. Then the Top Man getting deported. Then Honduras. He mentioned there a Bible salesman, which is probably somehow connected to the Thessalonians reference, and about this Thessalonian covering its back, willing to help them get vendetta."

"Vendetta, what?" Fat Carlo was fascinated now. "On who, what?"

Father Prio retreated. He had given Carlo enough.

"I don't know. But I advise you to listen to this first tape thoroughly. It's incredible stuff. And again, if I were you, I'd hit the Feds with the word Legerdemain. Legerdemain. I think they'll bite."

"No tellin' where it might lead, huh, Joey?" Carlo grinned stupidly.

Father Prio stood, letting the tape lay where it was on the table.

"Carlo, after you've talked to them, call me. We'll take it from there. But do not mention tape on the phone, refer to it as our square deal. Remember that: square deal, the whole business, just like my father's store used to be called: Sal 'toto' Prio's 'Square Deal' grocery. Agreed?"

"Yea, Joey. Sure. And ya will be hearing from me about our little 'square deal.'"

Carlo pocketed the tape, then added belligerently, "That, my old Whiskey Bay fuck buddy, ya can count on!"

IN THE BROADWATER BEACH HOTEL, BILOXI, MISSISSIPPI, USA

"Room 1-0-1-1, this is it, Nick," Mike McKinney whispered, pointing.

Nicholas "Nick" Plauche, Assistant United States Attorney for the Eastern District of Louisiana, half expected McKinney and himself to be gunned down or blown up or garroted or stilettoed at any moment. Bravely he knocked on the hotel room door.

The door opened slightly and a heavily accented voice asked, "Who are ya?"

"Nick Plauche and the man you spoke to on the phone who you made the arrangements with ... Mike McKinney ... a co-worker."

"Okay," Carlo confirmed.

The door opened wide but neither Nick nor Mike entered.

"And who are you?" the Assistant U.S. Attorney asked the broad back of Carlo Cefalu, with mock suspicion. Carlo turned, unamused.

"What do ya mean? I'm fucking Santa Claus. Now come on in ... and close the door, will ya?"

Plauche and McKinney exchanged nervous smiles, scanned the room and entered, satisfied that the fat man before them was indeed Carlo Cefalu, high-ranking member of the Nuccia/Sincelli organized crime family of New Orleans. They closed the hotel room door behind them and walked in slowly.

"Well, aren't you going to search us? You told us to expect it," Nick asked Carlo.

Carlo looked tired and not in the mood for bullshit.

"Forget about it. Ha, if I can't trust ya, who can I trust? Come on, sit down."

Carlo had spent the last forty-eight hours listening to Vince's tape. The old man's wanderings had exasperated Carlo. On the tape, Vince would go at random from speaking English to Sicilian—which Carlo didn't speak or understand—then off one tangent onto another. It had been a laborious two days and nights for Carlo. He had picked out the most repeated names and phrases that Vince had used, listed them and intended to explain each of them as best he could to Assistant U.S. Attorney Plauche. He just hoped that the prosecutor was as straight a shooter as everyone said he was. If he was, then there was truly no telling where Vince's information might lead.

"Fuckhead Joey may have pegged it right," Carlo reluctantly conceded in his thoughts.

A copy of Joey's first tape, a copy that Carlo had re-recorded for himself, and a cassette tape player lay on the bed closest to Carlo. A pencil and sheet of paper lay on the hotel table beside him.

Carlo's yellow alligator sport shirt and brown slacks were wrinkled now, with tomato sauce stains on the midsection of his shirt as well as on the tips of his white slip-on shoes. His platinum-streaked pompadour was matted and disheveled. He looked like a slob.

The Broadwater Beach Hotel room was kind of slobbish itself; not cheap, but nondescript all the same. There were two king-size beds, both uncovered, thin hotel towels scattered about, and green shag carpet that needed vacuuming on the floor. The room's design style was at least ten years out-of-date. Interior decoration was something Nick always paid attention to. His wife, Annie Plauche, was one of the best interior decorators on the Gulf Coast.

Nick and Mike sat on the uncovered bed farthest from Carlo. McKinney took out a writing pad and pen from his jeans pocket. Nick reached into his jeans pocket, too, removing from it a leather tobacco pouch the size of a wallet. He unzipped the pouch and lifted a small corncob pipe from it. Nick dipped the pipe back into the pouch, filling its bowl with a special blend of cognac and cherry tobacco. Nicholas "Nick" Plauche had smoked a corn pipe for over twenty years now and at thirty-nine years of age was unlikely to stop anytime soon. "Why?" he would tell anyone idle enough to listen, "Because smoking a pipe in Nam saved my life."

Nick's pipe story was always a popular conversation piece at the Vietnam Veteran conventions he and Annie attended. They had attended one last week in New York City and as usual, Nick's storytelling accompanied.

On September 19, 1968 PFC Nicholas Plauche had been assigned point guard duty. His 25th Infantry Division platoon was on a recon mission in Dau Tieng. Nick had just returned the night before from a week of R & R in Saigon. While in Saigon Nick had decided to become a pipe smoker just like his Uncle Marlow had been. Marlow Hebert was a coon-ass fisherman from Cameron, Louisiana who along with his wife, Eva, had raised Nicholas. Besides, with only 126 days remaining in his Vietnam tour, Nick had decided that he deserved the indulgence. Plus, he enjoyed the taste of fine tobacco. Always had, ever since having sneaked around with Uncle Marlow's pipe as a kid.

Nick's Saigon trip had exhausted him and he was unable to stay awake at his guard post. Shortly after lighting his first pipe bowl of the night he dozed off.

Later he'd bolted awake to the smell of burning fatigues and flesh; his own. Seconds after brushing the smoldering tobacco off his body he detected movement twenty yards in front of him in the bush; a dozen enemy soldiers at least.

He'd shook his platoon leader awake with just minutes to spare.

A fire-fight ensued; the most intense Nick had experienced in 239 days of combat duty. His platoon, however, thanks to the burn of spilt pipe tobacco, survived intact, no casualties, no deaths.

So to Nick Plauche, pipe smoking was good luck. He puffed on his bowl now.

"Carlo, we're here per your request. What have you got?"

Carlo Cefalu looked up from the hotel table where he had been making some final notes and eyeballed the two Feds in blue jeans. He was least impressed with the skinny one: Mike McKinney. McKinney wore his brown hair in a ducktail cut and looked ratty, untrustworthy. Plauche's co-worker had the washed-out look of a junkie Carlo decided, and was put off by him. Nick, however, looked as solid as a Baraterria pirate; about six feet one inch tall, one hundred ninety pounds, and smoked a corncob pipe; a nice hokey but effective touch, Carlo mused. Plauche had short, blackish-red, almost auburn hair, with a thin rogue's mustache cut even with the spread of his lips. His baby-blue eyes were startling.

"This man looks very much like someone I can fucking relate to," Carlo concluded.

"Mr. Plauche, I'd prefer to speak to ya alone."

Nick relit his bowl, puffed again, then responded.

"Carlo, I can't do that because you are currently the subject of a federal task force investigation. How do I know that this isn't a setup? If I were to speak to you alone, you could claim you bribed me, paid me off, and it would be my word against yours. Sorry, Carlo, Mike has to stay. At least until we develop a more trusting relationship."

Carlo began to sneer at this but stopped himself quickly. This Plauche had an honest, straight-shooting tone about him. Carlo liked it.

"Okay, Mr. Plauche, Mr. McKinney, this is where we start."

Carlo was tempted to light a cigarette but thought better of it; he wanted no distractions. The fat Mafioso stood and gathered up the cassette tape player and Vince's tape off the bed. He set them on the hotel table and reseated himself.

"What I have here is a tape. The voice on the tape is Vincenzo Angeletta, sometimes called Angler. He was Charlie Nuccia's right-hand man until he was arrested and convicted of murder in 1975."

"Wait a minute, Carlo," Nick interrupted, "Angeletta was

the main money man—the main spalloni—for Nuccia, not his right-hand man."

Carlo was surprised at Plauche's knowledge.

"I'm glad ya know who he is—or rather who he was—Mr. Plauche. That's going to make this all much easier." Fuck it, Carlo relented, he had to have a cigarette. He reached for one in his gold cigarette case. "This is the deal. Vince started me out in the rackets back in the mid-60s. I was on his crew. He and Charlie for some reason were real cool about the closeness of their relationship. Nobody knew—not even the Sincellis—how strong Vince was. From '64 to when Vince disappeared in '73 Charlie consulted Vince on everything. Vince was like a son to Nuccia. Ya know, Vince's daddy had been murdered and Charlie never had any sons of his own, so they were a perfect match from the beginning. Vince would sometimes say things to me about Charlie. I mean to tell ya, these two, they loved each other. Believe me, not even Giuseppe Nuccia, the top man's brother and underboss had as much weight as the Angler. This I know firsthand. Anyway, Vince has been in Angola for years now and a few weeks back he writes me a letter, wants to make a Catholic confession. Ya know, all of us Sicilians are raised Catholic, so it's a very natural inclination, especially if ya know ya dying. And Vince is dying. The big 'C' he says. So I get a priest who's a friend of mine to go do Vince's confession. My priest, as a personal favor to me, tape records it."

Nick removed the pipe from his mouth. He was disturbed by this.

"Isn't that sacrilegious, Carlo? I'm not Catholic or anything, but if I were, I'd imagine that'd bother me."

"No, it don't bother me. Look, I'm in a position where I've got to make moves and eat shit if necessary. It's all part of the game."

Nick did not comment. Unfortunately, to the U.S. Attorney's Office, information was information.

Carlo continued.

"Vince had a lot to say, but these, as far as I can figure, are the most important points of his confession." Mike McKinney readied his pen. "Back in the early '60s something went down, something Vince keeps referring to as Legerdemain."

"Legerdemain? Sleight of hand?" Nick clarified.

"That's it, Mr. Plauche, sleight of hand. It had something to do with Cuba. The names Vince mentioned, along with Charlie Nuccia's, were Manuel Marinello, Luigi Bertucci, Marco Romano, and Juan Jimenez. It sounds to me like Vince had to make a fast getaway from Cuba. He talks about horseback riding in the jungle and a landing strip in Pinar Del Rio, and about shooting up a short-wave radio."

"Carlo," Nick Plauche interrupted, "all of that is ancient history. It's a well-known historical fact that around 1960 the CIA hatched a plot to assassinate Castro. It's also historical fact that certain Mafia people were involved; primarily Anacondini and Rossini out of Chicago and Romano out of Tampa. Sounds to me that Vince could have been involved, too."

"Yea, yea ... I know, I know. But hold up, it gets better," Carlo maintained.

Maybe it was lack of sleep but talking about what he had been listening to for forty-eight hours was beginning to excite Carlo.

"Vince goes on then to Honduras—where Charlie was deported to in 1961—and that Thessalonian, the Bible salesman, was scared shitless."

"Th-ess-a-lon-ian?" Mike McKinney questioned, making sure he got the name correctly. He was writing everything down, verbatim.

"Yea, Thessalonian ... and that Thessalonian offered to arrange ... offered to help them get vendetta."

"Arrange what, Carlo? Vendetta against whom?" Nick asked, his interest intensifying.

At that instant Carlo surprisingly stood up, threw his cigarette butt into the hotel room's dirty green shag carpet and smashed it with his shoe. Annie Plauche would have been appalled.

"Intercept Eagle, Mr. Plauche. And that," Carlo firmly added, "is all I have to say for now."

In In Annie Plauche's Interior Self-Design Studios New Orleans, Louisiana, USA

"Hello."

"Hi, honey."

"Hey, Nick, don't tell me. I know. You've got to work late tonight. It's a grave matter of national hypocrisy and you alone as the last guardian of the republic must fight off all the revolting peasants and midgets! Oops, here come those little guys now ... run away, run away!"

"Cut it out, Annie. Instead of marrying you I should have booked you doing standup in Vegas. Could've made a fortune."

"Hey, I'm still available. Just waiting for an offer. Any offer."

"Well, I'll make you an offer right now, an offer you can't refuse."

"Nick, you must've been talking to gangsters today. You're beginning to sound like one."

"Who me? Of course not. Midget peasants maybe, but gangsters—no way!"

"Uh-huh, I'll bet. What's the offer, kiddo?"

"Dinner at the Glass House—9 p.m.—then maybe a roll in the hay afterwards."

"Stop it, you brute ... Okay, if you insist. But it has to be as good a roll as it was last week at the Waldorf."

"Better ... mmmmm ... lots better. I love you, Annie."

"Me, too, you crazy man. See you at nine, and don't be late."

"I won't."

In the Office of the United States Attorney, Eastern District of Louisiana, New Orleans, Louisiana, USA

"Word it as a formal request for data—not an informal query—to the Organized Crime Information Center—OCIS—ditto: ... Legerdemain ... Thessalonian ... Intercept Eagle ... parenthesize; regarding 1961 to 1965 activities of organized crime subjects—Calogera 'Charlie' 'Top Man' Nuccia and Vincenzo 'Angler' Angeletta—as a side note, reference the names: Manuel

Marinello, Marco Romano, Luigi Bertucci, and Juan Jimenez. Process it, Mike. I'll sign it."

Mike McKinney looked at Nick with uncontrollable curiosity. "What do you think this is all about, Nick?"

Nick had spoken little to his staffer on the drive back to New Orleans from Biloxi. McKinney knew, though, that that was Nick's way; holding his thoughts tightly until he had them all figured out, except with Annie. With her he was an open book.

Nick underplayed his answer.

"Don't know, Mike. I do know that the CIA's Operation Mongoose was happening at about the same time as Vince says he was in Cuba, early '60s. Mongoose was full of Mafiosos trying to assassinate Castro. Maybe Vince was one of them."

"What about the vendetta thing?" Mike asked, then proceeded to answer his own question. "You know the first thing I thought of?"

"What?" Nick asked innocently.

"John Kennedy."

Nick shuffled his feet, boyishly, as if to say, oh golly gee whiz, that never crossed my mind; which it had the minute Carlo had opened his mouth.

"Kennedy ... Kennedy ... Why Kennedy, Mike?"

"C'mon, Nick, you know what they've said in the gossip columns over the years. That Nuccia is the prime suspect in President Kennedy's assassination. Never could pin him, though. Can you believe they barely even questioned him after the thing?"

"What's the linkage?" Nick questioned.

"Linkage? Well, JFK fucked Nuccia and his pals with his less than overt action at the Bay of Pigs. With that they lost tons of future casino monies in Havana. Then Brother Bobby's crusade against Nuccia, the unions, sounds like vendetta motive to me. Enter the missing link, Vince Angeletta, then Oswald and his ties to both Nuccia and New Orleans."

Nick had heard enough of McKinney's simplistic notions.

"Let me set it up," Nick paused, sliding his corn pipe between his teeth, "Charlie Nuccia's eating pizza one day. He says, OK, dis here Kennedy fuck and his brother are startin' to piss me off. I dink I'll call Rocco and tell him to call Dutch and git his crazy nephew fuck to whack dem Boston hot shits. So what if dey can trace him to me. I'm invincible. I feel in me guts dat John Kennedy will be in Texas in November '63. I'll tell de crazy fuck to just take him out! Then Nuccia ever so slowly takes another bite of pepperoni and anchovies and mumbles through gnarled teeth, 'We is bigger than U.S. Steel!'"

McKinney's naturally pallid complexion turned Tabasco red now, around the edges. Plauche kept on.

"Look, Mike, all I'm saying is that for years I've been hearing that Nuccia killed Kennedy bullshit, but I've never bought it. At least, not Nuccia by himself. For starters, whoever did the job on John Kennedy had to have access to information that Nuccia couldn't have gotten within a million miles of. Besides," Nick had tired of their conversation and wanted to end it; he had better things ahead of him tonight to think about, like dinner out with his lovely wife and a session of hay rolling afterwards, "Cefalu is desperate. He's grabbing at straws, probably just teasing us so we'll delay the issuance of his indictment. And what better mystery to whet our appetites with than with Charlie Nuccia ... and," Nick whispered in his best conspiratorial tone, "Intercept Eagle—meaning Intercept Kennedy! Sure, and I'm Oliver Wendell Holmes."

"You're right, Nick, you're right," Mike agreed, still bitter at having been embarrassed.

"Then again," McKinney thought, "thicken the mustache, lighten the hair and there could be a resemblance. The late Oliver Wendell Holmes, great Supreme Court Justice, and the always-so-sure-of-himself Nicholas 'Nick' Plauche, God's gift to the U.S. Attorney's Office. Didn't Holmes smoke a pipe?"

In the Glass House Restaurant, New Orleans, Louisiana, USA

Annie Plauche had arrived two minutes before nine. No Nick, as usual. Annie was consistently amazed at how a man as intellectually efficient as Nicholas Plauche could be so socially inefficient with time. He had arrived forty minutes late for their wedding on June 15, 1970, had arrived fifteen minutes late for his graduation from Loyola University in New Orleans on May 17, 1975, and even twenty minutes late for his first court case in 1977.

"Time," Nick had postulated to Annie on many occasions, "is an abstract ... yesterday, today, tomorrow exist together all at the exact same millisecond of infinity. We should not encumber it with artificial calculation."

She would flash a charming, knowing smile at his bullshit and reply, "A late mate, that's what you are, kiddo, and shouldn't that have been insemination, artificial insemination?"

Annie smiled her startling smile now, between sips of strawberry daiquiri, thanking her stars that tardiness was Nick's worst failing. In every other area her husband was a dream.

The two had met in South Vietnam in October of 1968, a month after Nick's fire-fight in Dau Tieng. Annie Elizabeth O'Merly was working as a registered nurse for the Volunteer Physicians to Vietnam Program in Bac Lieu. She had volunteered for the program rashly after having a turbulent affair in New Orleans with one of the founders of the program, an American Medical Association (AMA) physician. Annie felt it appropriately ironic to join the volunteer effort after her affair with the physician in New Orleans ended in July. A part of her wanted to be as far away as possible from him, another part still wanted connection.

Her petty lovesick ruminations faded, however, almost as soon as she landed in Saigon. This was war and nothing in Annie's past experience had prepared her for it.

Annie O'Merly had come from a solid middle-class Irish Protestant family in Chalmette, Louisiana and loved love, boys, cheerleading, and stray dogs. Death, dying and disfigurement were as foreign to her as the language these small yellow people spoke, but she was overwhelmed with compassion for them nonetheless. Most, she realized early on, knew nothing of Communism versus Democracy, only of life versus death, rice versus no rice.

By the fall of 1968 she had become to these little people much more than just a beautiful nurse. She represented to them, more accurately than all the guns could, the greatness of America. Her benevolence towards the natives, however, had in the beginning rankled Nick Plauche. Their first words spoken to one another in the Bac Lieu hospital hallway were abrasive.

"Why don't you work for the U.S. Army Medical Services Corps instead of here, taking care of them?" Nick had asked her.

"Why don't you just mind your own business, Private. How do you say that?" Annie looked down at her clipboard with the supply order Nick had given her. "Plo-chee?"

"Plauche," he corrected.

"Whatever," she added briskly.

Nick's tenacity, though, bore fruit that day. He questioned, flattered, and flirted with Annie until her defenses thinned. She was pleasantly surprised to learn during her afternoon station break that this obnoxious but good-looking Plo-chee was a native south Louisianian, too.

From there their friendship grew, as did their love.

Annie left Vietnam when Nick's tour was finished. They married a year and a half later in New Orleans.

Nick was a dutiful, considerate and loving husband whose only flaw was his conception of time.

"A late mate, but a great mate, that's Nick," Annie mind-chatted as her lips pressed her daiquiri for another sip.

Fifteen minutes later Nicholas Plauche blasted in. He looked excited and was smiling. Annie hoped that he was smiling because of her. She had dressed provocatively for her husband tonight and was feeling magnificently sexy, glowing, even, about it.

Annie O'Merly Plauche was five feet eleven inches tall. With heels she came close to meeting Nick's six foot one inch frame. She had shoulder length fox-brown hair which she had fussed over like a debutante, earlier in the evening. Like Nick, Annie had a riveting pair of baby-blue eyes. Her lips were full, showcasing a smile as dazzling, as harmonious, and as exact as piano keys. The sensual sincerity of her eyes and smile combined made for one very, very sexy lady. Nick was still smiling as he bent over the table to kiss her cheek and sit down.

"Baby, you look absolutely stunning."

"Not bad for a middle-aged woman, huh, kiddo?"

Nick's thin mustache was stretched from ear to ear in appreciation of his wife.

"Hey, Annie, I don't know if I can keep my hands off you. It's not going to be easy."

The girl, Annie O'Merly inside the woman of Annie Plauche, loved this adulation. She actually blushed.

"You know you're late again, Nick. Isn't that watch with the buzzer that I bought you last Christmas supposed to tell you when you're late?"

Nick signaled for a waiter and requested menus and a wine list before answering. He settled back, took out his tobacco pouch, and reached for his wife's hand.

"Annie, baby, I'm sorry I'm late but something really interesting is happening at the office."

Annie and Nick's blue eyes, like magnets, connected.

"Let me put it like this," Nick paused. Even though he discussed U.S. Attorney business with his wife, he was never too specific about pending investigations. It was almost like a fantasy game they played.

"There is an old man sitting in prison. He wants to confess his sins. A priest hears his confession, but another man gets the priest to tape the old man's confession. The old man used to be powerful, and without knowing he's being taped mentions, albeit vaguely, some details of his past crimes. The possibility exists that he was involved in either or both attempts on Fidel Castro's life and in the assassination of John Kennedy."

Annie blinked.

"You're kidding, right, Nick?"

"Not a bit, baby. A few hours ago me and Mike did an emergency formal query to the OCIC—Organized Crime Information Center. Right before I left to come here we got a response. Never, and I mean never, Annie, have I seen a response come in so quick."

"Oh, Christ, Nick, I'm getting chills on this one. What in the world did they say?"

Nick paused again as the waiter returned to the table. He politely asked the waiter for a few more minutes, then answered Annie in a tone both thrilled and intrigued.

"It read ... OCIC ... Available Information on X #1 and Available Information on X #2—accessible—but it key coded a complete N/A—not available on either subject in conjunction with query reference of 'White Star,' 'Pluto,' 'Mongoose,' 'Plato,' 'Mancus,' 'SFG Team LED,' 'Cuban Revolutionary Directorate,' and/or the covert operational names the old man mentioned on the tape."

"I don't understand, Nick. What does that mean?"

"It means that I can get all the information I want on these two subjects—entire books, if necessary, on them—but, if the operational names of 'White Star,' 'Pluto,' 'Mongoose,' 'Plato,' 'Mancus,' 'SFG Team LED,' 'Cuban Revolutionary Directorate,' and/or the other names the old man used are punched in as part of my inquiry in regard to these two men, then there is no information available. None. And, Annie, I don't know what the other terms mean, but Operation Pluto was the code name for the Bay of Pigs invasion and Operation Mongoose was the code name for the Castro assassination attempts in the early '60s. So just by the names the old man mentioned being on the same list as these ... well, what he was involved with must have been huge and very classified."

Annie's chills had turned her stomach. She squeezed Nick's hand.

"Listen, kiddo, no joking around now, but if this old man in prison was involved in any of these monstrosities, his spilling his guts now is going to make somebody real angry and no telling what else. Tread softly, Nick. I mean soft. I mean as soft as on point in VC territory."

Nick, realizing he had upset his wife, changed the subject delicately.

"How about this? You take me home tonight and teach me what soft means. You can rub your fingertips lightly over my skin, my chest, my face, all over, then you can turn around on top of me and we'll lick each other softly ... softly ... so softly."

Nick was caressing his wife's palm with his middle finger softly. She was definitely blushing now. She smiled her enchanting smile.

"You late, wonderful, irrepressible brute ... you ... you should be shot."

"Let's hope not, Annie," Nick bristled in his best roguish manner, "at least not until I've tasted you, my love. All of you. Every drop!"

In the Inter Inpetto Armaments Corporation (IIPAC) Central Office, Zurich, Switzerland

COPY - FAX

Formal Request for Data - - - (RFD) - - - (RFD) - - -
To: OCIC - Organized Crime Information Center
United States Department of Justice
Washington, D.C.

RE: 1961-1965 Activities of Subjects
Calogera "Charlie" "Top Man" Nuccia 91/New Orleans
OCIC #91333
Vincenzo "Angler" Angeletta 91/New Orleans
OCIC #91704

RE:LEGERDEMAIN
THESSALONIAN
INTERCEPT EAGLE

RE: Also - RFD - Request for DATA-GENERAL
<no time frame - side note reference>

Manuel Marinello
Juan Jimenez
Marco Romano 131/Tampa
OCIC #13144
Luigi Bertucci 131/Tampa
OCIC #13182

Michael McKinney	Nicholas Plauche
Staff Processor	Authorized Sender
U.S. Attorney's Office	U.S. Attorney's Office
Eastern District of Louisiana	Eastern District of Louisiana

COPY FAX

Formal Reply - - - (FR - RFD) - - - (FR-RFD) - - -

To: U.S. Attorney's Office
Eastern District of Louisiana
Michael McKinney - Staff Processor
Nicholas Plauche - Authorized Sender

RE: Information N/A - not available - on subjects
Calogera "Charlie" "Top Man" Nuccia 91/New Orleans
OCIC #91333
Vincenzo "Angler" Angeletta 91/New Orleans
OCIC #91704
with classified RFD reference

	I		II
	"White Star"		"Intercept Eagle" **
	"Mongoose"		"Plato"
	"Pluto"		"Thessalonian" **
**	"Legerdemain"		"Mancus"
			"SFG Team LED"
			"Cuban Revolutionary Directorate"

without classified RFD reference - All data transmittable - on subject OCIC #91333 and OCIC #91704 activities 61-65

RE: Also - Manuel Marinello - no record
Juan Jimenez - no record
Information N/A as above Marco Romano - OCIC #13144 - 131/Tampa
Information N/A as above Luigi Bertucci - OCIC #13182 - 131/Tampa

The man with "Gli occhi di un pugnale"—the eyes of a dagger—scanned rapidly the two FAX copies before him.

Victor Thomas Ingels, Vice-Chairman of the Inter Inpetto Armaments Corporation (IIPAC) was dismayed.

It began yesterday.

It had been logged in as a "Whiplash" call—emergency—dispatcher registered as an operative with Ingels "Skirt of Tasses" network, Justice Department, Washington ... - - - - RE (Regarding)—LEGERDEMAIN - THESSALONIAN -INTERCEPT EAGLE - - -!

"Incredible—absolutely incredible!" Ingels thought, wishing now that his old age had bestowed upon him before this its gift of senility.

But it hadn't.

Close enough to eighty years old to stop caring, Victor Thomas Ingels, formerly Thessalonian, was in excellent health, excellent wealth, and still in love with his good life.

Until now.

Luckily his "Skirt of Tasses" barrier network had worked.

In 1976, after the Rossini murder, Ingels had bought several choice disgruntled federal employees in typical IIPAC fashion to monitor the vast array of ongoing U.S. Justice Department criminal investigations.

They had been instructed to "Whiplash" Zurich immediately if the following words, terms, phrases, codes or references surfaced:

White Star
Mongoose
Pluto
Legerdemain
Intercept Eagle
Plato
Thessalonian
Mancus
SFG Team LED
Cuban Revolutionary Directorate

They had also been instructed to computer insert and block any adjoining or subsequent context inquiries where these words, terms, phrases, codes or references appeared.

Thus, when Legerdemain, Intercept Eagle and Thessalonian all popped up on the informational probe from New Orleans the reply designation of N/A—not available—popped up too—automatically—and Zurich had been notified immediately!

Ingels anxiously rubbed his wrinkled throat scars and high cheekbones and focused on the two names appearing at the bottom of the New Orleans U.S. Attorney's Office Formal Request For Data (RFD):

Michael McKinney - Staff Processor; Nicholas Plauche - Authorized Sender.

Ingels hastily wrote the two names in a compact black memo pad, initialed an N.O. next to them and punched on his interoffice intercom.

"Judy," his still husky and hypnotic voice bellowed, "I need you to get me the Skirt of Tasses file right away."

Ingels clicked the intercom off, leaned back in what he jokingly referred to as his vice-emperor's chair and began planning. His mind functioning as methodically and precisely as ever. First, he would have his Tasses network do a complete check on McKinney and Plauche in an attempt to answer the following:

A) How did they uncover Legerdemain?

B) How much have they uncovered?

C) Is theirs a routine investigation or priority?

D) If priority, why?

E) Are they vulnerable—bureaucratically, financially, sexually, psychologically?

F) How can their probing be stopped?

Victor Ingels, now wealthy International businessman, formerly Thessalonian, master covert operative and assassin, reached for another intercom-like device before him.

A full minute later he spoke into the mechanism.

"Sosar, is that you? I have some news ... incredible .. news!"

In the Plauche Residence, Marrero, Louisiana, USA

Annie O'Merly Plauche's long, bare, luscious legs lay spread from one corner of the brass bed to the other.

Nicholas was on his knees between them. A soft session of hayrolling was underway.

Annie and Nick's lovemaking had always been intensely satisfying. They shared a mutual outlook on sex, believing it to be the ultimate form of communication between man and woman. Besides Annie's AMA physician and a few high school romances for Nick neither had had much premarital experience with it. So both their sexualities had matured over the years equally. Annie and Nick enjoyed each other's bodies with a sincere, healthy uninhibitedness.

Now Nick's fingertips touched softly on the tips of Annie's nipples as his tongue licked around her womanhood in effective polyrhythms. Annie sighed, gasped, moaned, arched her back, and climaxed.

Tonight's session had lasted for more than an hour. Afterwards as they lay, bodies spent, Annie voiced her concern.

"Kiddo, baby, I'm upset," she said as she played with Nick's short blackish-red hair and thin mustache, "about what you told me earlier, about this old man's confession."

Nick was staring at their wicker bedroom ceiling fan, marveling at how the texture of it mixed so well with the rest of the room. Annie was such a talented designer, he concluded.

He turned to his right and looked out their open bedroom window into the dark west bank of Marrero. As the sounds of crickets creaked in he tried to assuage his wife's fear.

"Annie, I love talking to you in general terms about my work, but the fact of the matter is some cases are complex ethically and practically. This is one of those cases. I doubt seriously it'll lead anywhere, Miss O'Merly, so don't fret, okay?"

Annie, still naked and lying draped across her husband, shot back, "Then tell me, Mr. Everything-is-under-control, how are you going to proceed with it from here?"

Nick and Annie's blue eyes met again, as if magnetized. He answered.

"The best way is probably to do a second check on the other classified phrases and code words not mentioned by my old confessor—the ones whose meaning I'm unsure of—like White Star, Plato, Mancus, SFG Team LED, and Cuban Revolutionary Directorate. I'll see where those lead."

Annie quickly added, "How far are you going to involve Mike in all of this? You know how jealous he is of you. I keep telling you that and you just keep ignoring me."

Nick looked away, "Mike's okay. I think you're wrong about him. He may not be the most conceptually intelligent individual I've ever met, but he does have integrity."

Annie shook her head in total disagreement, "No, he doesn't, Nick. He's a back stabber. I'm telling you. He reminds me of D.D."

D.D. (Donald Daniel) Sebastian had been Nick's personal nemesis during Nick's Vietnam experience. It had all started when Nick and six other grunts had formed a secret brotherhood—a clique—within their 25th Infantry Division platoon, two weeks after the Dau Tieng incident in 1968. They had named themselves the War Babies and had looked out for one another. After Vietnam several of them went into business together. Others served as best men at fellow War Baby weddings. All stayed in touch and made a point of attending the same Veteran conventions, like the one last week in New York to reunite and reminisce. Nick considered himself a close friend to all six men, except D.D. Sebastian.

D.D. was a loud, obnoxious fool with never a kind word or gesture for Nick. D.D.'s animosity towards Nick was unreasonable and unjustified and his cutdowns of Nick behind Nick's back were legendary. So much so that the War Babies had considered excluding D.D. from their club more than once, but Nick had never allowed them to.

"No, Annie, I don't think there could ever be another D.D.," Nick answered, refusing to acknowledge any similarity between Mike McKinney and D.D. Sebastian.

"I hope you're right, Nick. I really do," Annie replied.

Nick wrapped his arms around Annie, kissed her and began to rock her back and forth. She smiled her magical smile.

"I'm sure I am, honey. Now just lay back and relax about it. Here, I'll even sing you to sleep. Rock-a-bye babbyyy—eeee ... in the treeee ... tops ... ."

Annie giggled at Nick's exaggerated warbling, then put her forefinger to his lips, silencing him.

"Let's listen to the crickets instead."

Chapter Thirty

In Saint Cecilia's Catholic Church, New Orleans, Louisiana, USA

"Joey, we got to talk about another 'Square Deal'. I just got a call from the people and they want more."

Carlo Cefalu sounded out of breath. Father Prio tensed.

"What did they say, Carlo, exactly?"

Carlo hesitated, clearly self-conscious about talking over the phone.

"They said that our first meeting was interesting, but that they would have to have more in order to help me. Do ya understand, Joey? They said that they checked with Washington and that Washington was very interested, too!"

Father Prio mentally noted Carlo's use of the word "very." The priest would tell Vince that, so far, his story had been "very" well received.

"Okay, Carlo, when's the next meet?"

"Two nights from tonight."

"Then meet me in Jackson Square in front of St. Louis's Cathedral at three p.m. tomorrow afternoon. I'll have the second 'Square Deal' for you."

"Yea, okay, Joey ... 'Square Deal' ... at 3 p.m. tomorrow. Done."

"Done!"

In the Michael McKinney Residence, New Orleans, Louisiana, USA

(FR-RFD)
All Classified N/A Not Available - White Star
Plato
Mancus
SFC Team LED
Cuban Revolutionary Directorate

Mike McKinney was unhappy. His and Nick's second check

today of the other FR-RFD terms besides LEGERDEMAIN, THESSALONIAN and INTERCEPT EAGLE had been fruitless. So without hope of any further movement, Nick had instructed Mike to re-contact C.C.—Carlo Cefalu—and pressure the slobby Mafioso to give them more. Carlo had agreed to do so two nights from tonight at 9 p.m., same place; Broadwater Beach Hotel, Biloxi, Mississippi, Room 1011.

But McKinney's misery didn't end there. In fact, Mike's disappointment over the progress of this investigation was just another in a long series of job frustrations. Mike McKinney hated Nick Plauche. He hated his good looks, his secretive manner, his wristwatch buzzer that buzzed at all hours, and mostly his dumb corncob pipe! And he'd give plenty to fuck that fine bitch, Nick's wife, Annie.

Educationally he was superior to Plauche, yet he was Nick's staffer, not the other way around. Mike felt that Nick was always condescending with him as if Nick really did believe himself to be God's gift to the U.S. Attorney's Office. Furthermore, Michael McKinney had come from a proper upper class upbringing whereas Nick Plauche had been raised as a stepchild by some coon-ass fisherman in Cameron, Louisiana.

The entire situation was unacceptable. The stress of it was the main reason Mike looked unkempt these days. His paleness, ratted-up hair, and skinniness, were all symptoms of the same affliction; disgust with his station in life.

Mike threw the FR-RFD printout on the floor by his TV and stepped into his bathroom. His bachelor's pad was rented just as his 280Z Datsun automobile was leased. He owned nothing, he had nothing, he felt like nothing. He gargled more than a cup of mouthwash, almost choked on it, then spewed it out violently.

Michael McKinney was a man nearing the end of his rope, the edge of his precipice, the limit of his endurance.

He whimpered, gargled, choked, and spewed again, ...

... and again,

... and again.

In the Inter Inpetto Armaments Corporation (IIPAC) Central Office, Zurich, Switzerland

Victor Ingels's compact black memo pad with the names Michael McKinney and Nicholas Plauche written in it was lying on a foot table in front of Sosar Tomeen, Chairman of the Board of the Inter Inpetto Armaments Corporation (IIPAC). The foot table was situated in front of a purple settee exactly five feet to the right of Victor's vice-emperor's chair. Ingels was slouched in the chair, bringing his boss Sosar up-to-date.

"The Whiplash call came in from one of my 'Tasses' network people in Washington. With it came a copy of the Formal Request For Data (RFD) from the New Orleans U.S. Attorney's Office. Shortly thereafter I received a copy of the formal reply to their request for data (FR-RFD). I then initiated a check on the two signatories of the RFD in New Orleans: Michael McKinney and Nicholas Plauche; came up with some interesting details. You want them in writing or oral?"

"Oral," Sosar answered, his tone as silky and multilingual as ever.

Victor Ingels straightened up, then decided to stand. He examined Sosar closely before proceeding. Sosar Tomeen, even though younger than Ingels, looked at least ten years older. The chairman's tall, lanky frame was bent and shrunken now, as was his three-fingered right hand. It hung limply at Sosar's side, the victim of a rare crippling bone disorder. His once long otter-brown sideburns and Van Dyke beard were thinned and withered with age, as were his owlishly fat cheeks.

Sosar Tomeen's mental faculties, however, remained as formidable as ever. Ingels continued.

"Nicholas Plauche; modest upbringing by step-parents Marlow and Eva Hebert in Cameron, Louisiana. Joined the army in 1968. Served one tour of duty in Vietnam. Received commendation, Army Medal of Merit, for exemplary conduct in the 25th Infantry concerning an incident in Dau Tieng, September '68. Married in 1970. Went to Law School at Loyola University in New Orleans. Graduated 1975. Post-graduate studies at Louisiana State University. Received full law degree and began practicing law in 1977. Started working for

U.S. Attorney's office, Eastern District of Louisiana in 1978. Became Assistant U.S. Attorney in 1981. Highly respected by his co-workers for his instinctive intelligence and astuteness. Top candidate for U.S. Attorney post within a few years. Has a reputation as a solid, ingenious, and honest prosecutor."

Sosar nodded his comprehension, "Go on, Victor."

"Michael McKinney, assistant to Mr. Plauche, from one of the wealthiest families in New Orleans. Total of twelve years legal schooling divided between Harvard, Columbia, and Georgetown. Involved in some sort of cheating scandal at Georgetown. Forced to return home to New Orleans and start at the bottom of U.S. Attorney's office in 1983. Allegedly an impatient, unpleasant, and burned-out young man."

"Sounds like he's the cockhumping man for us," Sosar interjected.

"Yes, I agree, Sosar. Let me run my idea by you, see what you think."

Sosar, with considerable physical effort, nodded again and mumbled something about needing a whiskey but that his doctor had sworn him off it.

Ingels/Thessalonian spoke rapidly.

"We know who's behind this, just by a process of elimination. It is either Charlie Nuccia or Vince Angeletta or both. All of the others are dead. The last reports I've received on Nuccia indicate that the 'Top Man' is consumed with Alzheimer's Disease at the Seagoville Federal Correctional Institute in Texas. There are days he can hardly remember who he is, much less who he was. Sosar, I doubt seriously it's Nuccia leaking this."

Sosar painfully nodded a third time in agreement, and Ingels continued.

"Angeletta, however, is certainly still capable of busting Legerdemain wide open. At least we've heard nothing on him to indicate otherwise. So my bet is that it's Angeletta. Sosar, I advised you to kill those two many years ago but you wouldn't allow it, and maybe you were right. Considering the speculation about conspiracy that's come down over the last twenty years, with Nuccia alive he's been able to take some of the heat. If we had killed him way back when, then more questions might have been asked."

"Yes, I was right, Victor, in holding you at bay. Alive and well, Nuccia has come in very handy. But now, things are different. With Nuccia dying and Angeletta in prison for life, neither of them have anything left to lose. And who knows, maybe they do have something put away to substantiate their wild claims. Apparently they've already got a cockhumping U.S. Attorney's attention."

It was Ingels's turn to nod and respond.

"This is what I propose then. We talk to this Mike McKinney, find out how far the U.S. Attorney's Office has gone, then enlist his covert aid in sabotaging this Plauche fellow. Offer McKinney the world. Then finally after we've halted their investigation, make arrangements at long last to take out Angeletta and Nuccia once and for all, just so we're not bothered again."

"This is a cockhumping pain in the ass, isn't it?" Sosar noted with firmness, then suggested, "I think you should handle this personally, Thessalonian, if you're up to it. That way, no more cutouts, no more loose ends. It'll be finished absolutely."

Sosar didn't seem to notice his casual use of the retired code name Thessalonian. Ingels did.

Sosar kept at Victor/Thessalonian relentlessly just as he used to with George Whitten, the architect of Legerdemain, during strategy discussions of this nature.

"What is the background on Plauche's wife?"

Ingels sorted through the information that had been provided by his "Skirt of Tasses" network in Washington.

"Annie Elizabeth O'Merly, born in Chalmette, Louisiana, met Plauche in Vietnam. She is a successful Interior Designer in the Gulf Coast area; owner of Interior Self Design Studios. It is rumored that she and Nick have a very close, very happy marriage. Hmmmm ... that's important."

"Yes, it is, Victor. That's why I asked. She may be the weak spot with this Plauche."

"Exactly my thoughts, too. I suggest however, Sosar, that we concentrate first on enlisting McKinney; see just how baitable and bribeable he is. Do a situational analysis on Plauche's investigation, then figure out the best way and the best manner in which to stop it."

Sosar didn't nod this time at Ingels's comments, nor did he

interject or inquire. Instead the Chairman of IIPAC crossed his lanky, misshapen legs, stared straight ahead and coldly issued a final decree concerning Legerdemain.

"I want this cockhumping ghost of an operation laid to rest before they lay me to rest. Do what you have to do to accomplish that. If that means an Assistant U.S. Attorney's blood must be on our hands, so be it. A president's blood already is, so why not a federal prosecutor's. Rid me of this cockhumping ghost, Thessalonian. Do you read me, my master spy?"

Sosar Tomeen, as ancient as Satan, turned to Victor Ingels now, accentuating in mid-air with his ugly, deformed, limp three fingers, "Kill this ghost ... KILL IT!"

In Front of Saint Louis's Cathedral, Jackson Square, New Orleans, Louisiana, USA

Father Joseph Prio could not understand why St. Louis's Cathedral was such a hot tourist attraction. His own St. Cecilia's was much more modern and luxurious. Of course, St. Louis's was larger and did have the better location, and being world famous did not hurt its popularity.

"Oh, well," the priest sighed, "I'm just jealous."

But jealousy was not Father Prio's business today. His business was a second square-deal for Carlo Cefalu, a second tape of Vince Angeletta's confession. This overdubbed tape was clearer than the first. Its hints and allusions more like facts. Vince could still be heard crying dramatically in a few places, "Legerdemain ... Legerdemain," but its specifics were more legible, its dates more exact.

"July 22, 1960—meeting at Fontainebleau Hotel in Miami. Present were Charlie Nuccia, Romano, Bertucci, Pacissi, Stefano 'Mr. A.' Anacondini. Jake and Johnny Sincelli and Vince representing La Cosa Nostra and Thessalonian representing the CIA. Contract settled on Castro.

"November 11, 1960—final attempt made on Castro's life by Vince. Vince kills Bertucci. President Kennedy reneges on Castro contract. Thessalonian offers Nuccia to set up President Kennedy for assassination. That is Thessalonian's way of covering himself, his way of answering to Nuccia, Romano and Anacondini for President Kennedy's double-cross. Nuccia rejects Thessalonian's initial offer. Vince barely escapes Cuba alive.

"April 13, 1961—Nuccia deported to Tequicigalpa, Honduras by Attorney-General Bobby Kennedy. Thessalonian meets Nuccia in Tequicigalpa, still willing to set up President Kennedy for Nuccia; -to clear his debt so Nuccia can get vendetta on President Kennedy. Nuccia accepts. Vince takes contract on President Kennedy at the behest of Nuccia. Operation dubbed by Thessalonian as Legerdemain."

"Yes," Father Prio concluded to himself, sure of his and Vince's strategy thus far, "this should really get the Feds going."

The priest lifted his dark sporty glasses off the rim of his nose and wiped them off. First on his handkerchief, then lightly on his blue jeans. Joey was not dressed as a priest today, just in case Carlo was being followed.

Carlo Cefalu at that instant rounded the corner of St. Peters Street from Chartres, perspiring like a solar still. His two bodyguards from Mama Maria's that he had referred to as Pope and Burn were behind him. Carlo couldn't have been more obvious if he had worn a button stating, "I am in the Mafia—arrest me!"

He was wearing the same Nina Cheroot suit and Burn leathers, custom-fitted, that he had worn at that first meeting with Father Prio at Mama Maria's. His bodyguards, Pope and Bruno, had huge bulges sticking out from their left underarms. Popeye wore a big, sleazy pimp's gold chain, and Bruno was just big, towering over Carlo in both height and body mass, which was quite an accomplishment in itself.

As Carlo neared he became animated.

"Joey, paisan, so good to see ya!"

He hugged Father Prio like a long lost cousin.

Father Prio had to ask.

"Carlo, why the bodyguards? They look like they have machine guns under their suits. What are you afraid of?"

"Why, Joey," Carlo said remaining in character, playing the long lost kin to the hilt, "how do I know ya haven't contacted one of the Sincellis already? If ya have, I'm dead meat!

Now I don't think ya have anything to gain by doing that, but who knows, Joey? Ya are one smart son of a ... " Carlo was poised, ready to finish the insult, then paused and thought better of it. "Holy man, son of a holy man!" Carlo's whale blubber of a stomach thumped with a snicker.

"Now, how about that second square deal, my dear friend?"

Father Prio reached down, pretending to lace his shoe, into the inner lining of his black nylon sock for the second cassette tape. Before handing it to Carlo, the priest advised, "Carlo, I don't know if you are making copies of these tapes or not, but if you are, my only suggestion is to be very careful not to out-clever yourself. I think too many copies of these tapes lying around could be very dangerous. Capisce, my long lost cousin?"

Carlo's mouth did one of its diabolical sneers as he hugged Joey.

"Don't worry ya pretty little head over that. Just like in Whiskey Bay with Scarlet and Alicia, Carlo will take care of everything. Trust me!"

Father Prio pushed away from Carlo's stink, rubbed his tough gray-black beard and attempted to match Carlo's demented grin, thinking as Carlo and Popeye and Bruno turned and walked away towards Jackson Square and the Riverwalk, "If you only knew how Vince and I are using you, you Sicilian scum ... if you only knew."

Father Joey Prio then turned himself and quickly made his way towards the milling crowds and anonymity of Bourbon Street.

Passe good time!

Par—ty!

Party!

In the Office of the United States Attorney, Eastern District of Louisiana, New Orleans

"May I speak to Mr. Michael McKinney, please?" said a voice, husky and hypnotic.

"Hold, please."

"Hello, this is Mike McKinney."

"Ah, Mr. McKinney. I am from Georgetown University."

"Georgetown? Yes, who is this?"

"Let's just say I am someone, Mr. McKinney, who has always believed in your innocence and who, with the stroke of a pen, can clear up the little problem you had a few years back."

"I don't know what you're talking about. Besides, I never had any problem at Georgetown. And if I had, it would have been cleared up a long time ago. Who is this?"

"This is your future, that's who it is. We have to meet. There is no danger in meeting. You can always say, if questioned, that you were doing undercover work for the U.S. Attorney's office. You really have nothing to lose. Then again, maybe the information I have on you is wrong. Maybe you are happy with your little job there, content to be at the bottom of the barrel. Yes, maybe I was wrong."

"No, wait, who is this? I can't just meet you. I don't need any more problems. I mean I just can't. But if you tell me who you are."

"As I said, sir, I am your future. I'll be in touch."

Mike McKinney could only stammer desperately into the empty line.

"Who is this? Wait, wait. Who is this? Who is this?"

In the Michael McKinney Residence, New Orleans, Louisiana, USA

All day long Nick Plauche had had McKinney preparing for tomorrow night's meet with Carlo Cefalu. They had worked up a list of questions for Vince Angeletta. They intended to give the questionnaire to Carlo to give to his priest friend to ask Vince. How the priest would manage this was anybody's guess, but Plauche insisted that they try, nonetheless.

McKinney stepped into his rented bachelor's flat, still preoccupied with the mysterious and disturbing phone call he had received earlier in the afternoon.

Of course, he dare not confide in anyone about the call for fear that the Georgetown cheating incident would be resurrected and he crucified even more. As it stood, his influential family had stepped in and covered his involvement, preventing real disaster. Otherwise, he would never have been allowed to practice law, even as the low man in the U.S. Attorney's office.

Mike McKinney stepped once, then twice, flicked on the overhead in his apartment and realized suddenly he was not alone. There were four of them; three standing and one seated.

It had been many years since Victor Thomas Ingels/Thessalonian had had the opportunity to work his theatrical magic. As in the old days his look had been coordinated tonight for specific results.

He was seated, gripping an ivory-knobbed cane similar to the one he had carried to the Camino Hotel In Tequicigalpa in '61, and to his meeting with Nuccia there. The rest of his attire bespoke wealth and power. Ingels's blue bold pinstripe shirt and his empire blue slacks had been designed by Fluser. His grayish-brown tie and gray socks and shoes were Lauren as was the expensive black cashmere long coat draped over his shoulders, European style. He wore a diamond horseshoe pinky ring on his left hand and a large gold Stephen's class ring on his right. Lastly, a presidential Rolex watch adorned his left wrist.

Ingels's dead-fish pair of gray eyes and black microdot pupils glowered unwaveringly at Mike McKinney. The other three men, all confident-looking intruders, were strategically positioned in the den area to cover any irrational move McKinney might make. Their look, too, was calculated, custom-designed, menacing. They were all professional IIPAC paramilitaries; well-paid, world-class muscle.

Mike McKinney's mouth was agape with fear and wonderment. His normally washed-out complexion was completely rinsed out now. He looked deceased.

Ingels was amazed at how this young man looked more like a mortician, walking death naturally, than Thessalonian had ever been able to years ago, even with cotton wads in his mouth and darkened eyebrows.

"Don't be alarmed, Mr. McKinney, we are not here to harm you. On the contrary we are here to help you."

McKinney regained some of his gumption, realizing that the husky and hypnotic voice speaking to him now was the same mysterious and disturbing voice that had spoken to him on the phone earlier in the afternoon.

"Who in the living fuck do you think you are? I'll give you—all of you—exactly ten seconds to clear out or I'm calling the cops. I mean it!"

Ingels motioned to two of the paramilitaries. They moved quickly, like bushwhackers, up to the U.S. Attorney staffer, grabbed him and carried him to one of his cheap kitchen chairs that had been arranged to sit a few feet in front of Ingels.

Ingels's voice became nastily patronizing.

"Now, we're not going to have any of that, are we, Michael? Can I call you Michael?" McKinney didn't answer, but did rub his arms where the paramilitaries had manhandled them. "Let's talk like adults. Don't you think it's time you started handling your life and career like an adult instead of like a self-pitying child. Yes, Michael, I know all about Georgetown. What pettiness for them to threaten you with expulsion. Didn't you or your family understand what their game was? Didn't any of you realize that their sole objective was to squeeze out of you all a sizable endowment. And to think you and your loved ones actually bought it. Like two-bit marks in Atlantic City. Mostly you! How stupid could you have been? To get caught running a $500 per answer page service. Mike, what a disappointment you must be to your family. And with so many years of education! You dumb child. Any one of these three violent men here would have had more savvy than that."

Mike McKinney was shocked to his toes by this brutal, honest assessment. How could this old man know so much of his past? So many of his thoughts? Mike asked himself.

"There is still hope. There is still hope for you, my child. But—but—you'd best grow up—RIGHT NOW!—RIGHT NOW!" The power of the old man's shouts startled Mike.

The staffer felt his head nodding more from disorientation than real comprehension. He felt his entire being falling ... falling ... as if under the old man's spell. He began crying, not knowing why or what for, not knowing anything. The old man with the unflinching, luminous eyes consoled him, patting Mike's shoulder with a scarred arm.

"There, there, Mike ... there, there ... there, there. Listen to me, Mike, listen to me closely. There is a way out for you. A way to begin anew. And I have that way. Listen to me now.

Listen." The old man's voice had once again lowered itself to a steady, hypnotic tone. "During the last few days you and Nicholas Plauche have stumbled upon ... well, let's put it this way: you and Plauche have stumbled upon history in the form of LEGERDEMAIN, INTERCEPT EAGLE and THESSALONIAN."

Ingels reached into his cashmere coat pocket and retrieved the two Copy Fax printouts, RFD and FR-RFD, that had been wired to Zurich from his "Skirt of Tasses" network, then continued.

"I know all about this, Michael, as evident by my possession of these copies of your 'Formal Request for Data,' and the 'Formal Reply to your Request For Data' from the Organized Crime Information Center in Washington," Ingels was talking very slowly, as if speaking to a retarded child. McKinney was reacting as if comatose. "I'm sure you realize how powerful I must be to have access to this information. Therefore, you must realize that I have the power to clear the Georgetown incident up completely and place you in any number of this country's outstanding law firms, where any and every thing you desire, personally and professionally, could be provided to you."

"I understand ... I understand," Michael kept repeating as if echoing a supernatural incantation.

"Good, very good, Mike, but I must know the circumstance and status of Plauche's investigation. From what source did the original information come? How far has it progressed? Where is it going to next? I'll need to know everything and every move Plauche makes, for the duration. You will leave nothing out, not the smallest detail. Am I making myself clear, Michael? You mustn't fail me. You must perform expertly, never making Plauche suspicious. We will start tonight—now. And just to show you my good faith, Michael, here ... " Ingels motioned to one of his paramilitaries who reached for a duffel bag lying at his feet, "is $100,000 in cash, in small, easily depositable bills. I've even made the effort to tie them up in $9,000 bundles, so no tax forms will have to be filled out. You know a $10,000 or less transaction is not recorded. Here, Michael."

"Lord have m-m-mercy," Mike stuttered. Seeing and feeling the money almost made him cry again. Happy tears.

"Yes, I'll do it. I hate Plauche, anyway. The cocky bastard. I'll do what you want. I swear it. And I am efficient. I am. You'll see." Mike looked up from the duffel bag back into the aged man's powerful eyes.

"But, sir, what do I call you. Please, I must have a name to call you. Please. Please?"

For Victor Thomas Ingels only a perfectly symmetrical name would do.

"Thessalonian, my child. Thessalonian!"

IN THE BROADWATER BEACH HOTEL, BILOXI, MISSISSIPPI, USA

Carlo Cefalu was not difficult to find. Especially not for Thessalonian. He simply took into account certain details that Michael McKinney had given him. Like when McKinney and Plauche had first met with Cefalu at the Broadwater Beach Hotel, there had been a cassette tape player and a tape lying on the bed. McKinney said that Cefalu looked disheveled and was writing notes on a sheet of paper like he had been awake for quite some time deciphering the contents of the tape; a tape presumably originating from Vince Angeletta and an as yet unnamed priest who had recorded Vince's confession for Carlo.

Therefore, Ingels/Thessalonian figured that the odds were good on Cefalu arriving at the Broadwater at least twenty-four hours prior to tomorrow night's second meeting with Plauche and McKinney to decipher either more of the same tape or other tapes.

The next move was simple then. Ingels, his three paramilitaries, and McKinney drove to the Broadwater Beach Hotel, arriving near midnight. Ingels's paramilitary with the most indistinguishable face then checked into the hotel for all five men and they waited.

Ingels had insisted on McKinney accompanying the IIPAC entourage to deepen the dead-looking, weak-minded attorney's involvement and to keep an eye on him for the first few hours after their initial introduction and interrogation. Even though Ingels/Thessalonian was convinced that he had secured McKinney's loyalty, he had to be sure.

Four hours later a late model Cadillac pulled up to the

Broadwater Beach lobby. A man fitting the description of Carlo Cefalu, fat, gorilla-like, with a streak of platinum in his hair, registered.

The Ingels's paramilitary who had stationed himself in a corner of the hotel's front parking lot lifted a two-way radio transmitter to his mouth and spoke into it.

"Burma, this is Sumatra. Pig is here."

A second later, "This is Burma received. What room?"

The paramilitary slid down into the rented Chevrolet seat and watched closely as "Pig"—Cefalu—got back into his Cadillac and drove toward the rear of the hotel. He waited until Carlo stopped, got out, went to his trunk, lifted a suitcase from it, and entered the room, before driving slowly past to get the room number.

The paramilitary, code-named Sumatra, spoke again into his radio with combat precision, "Kid was right. Pig in 1-0-1-1."

McKinney had predicted that Carlo would check into Room 1011. He had told Ingels that that was the pre-arranged meeting room but that Cefalu might check into another room then transfer to 1011 shortly before meeting him and Plauche.

Ingels turned to McKinney, "So far, so good, Michael. Now, you understand things may get rough during the next hour. Are you man enough to handle it?"

Mike McKinney, bought and paid for, anticipating the bright future he had always dreamed of and certainly deserved, shucked at Thessalonian's concerns. "To hell with Cefalu. He's a dirtbag."

"Good," Ingels thought, "Very good."

Minutes later the paramilitary Sumatra picked everyone up—his two teammates, Ingels, and McKinney—and drove back, without headlights, parking near the entrance of Room 1011. The three paramilitaries exited the Chevrolet, quickly, quietly.

Two were equipped with bolt busting and lock removing devices. They were all dressed in black and heavily armed. It took exactly two relatively light slams and the three men were in.

Carlo had fallen asleep on the farthest bed with his Nino Cerruti suit half on, half off. The room, the bed, and Carlo smelled like liquor. It was obvious Carlo had spilled some gin onto the hotel room's dirty green shag carpet.

Cefalu barely had time to resist, but did have time to wish he had brought Popeye and Bruno, his bodyguards, with him tonight. Within a clap the paramilitaries had jerked Carlo's pompadour back, secured a rag across the Mafioso's sneering mouth, handcuffed his wrists, and chained his ankles.

The paramilitary Sumatra, who had been on stakeout in the parking lot, went to the entrance of the room and motioned an all-clear to Ingels and McKinney, still waiting in the Chevrolet. He then replaced the bolt and lock so as not to draw any undue attention. Thessalonian and McKinney walked into the room.

Carlo's eyes, sobering now, fixated on the impressive and intimidating figure of Victor Thomas Ingels/Thessalonian. They then looked over to Michael McKinney with recognition, as if to say—I knew you were a mousy shit punk from the beginning.

Thessalonian motioned to Carlo's suitcase lying on the floor. The paramilitary nearest to it, code-named Indonesia, raised it to the hotel room table and opened it. Out of it he pulled two half-full bottles of gin, a cassette tape player and three cassettes. Thessalonian moved, with cane in grip, towards the table. He examined the cassettes carefully. All were titled:

V.A. Number One Original
V.A. Number One Copy
V.A. Number Two Original

It seemed that Thessalonian's entire body twisted with loathing at the sight of these tapes as he mumbled ominously, "After so many years, so many years, you arrogant dago Sicilian bastard your time has come."

Ingels then turned and directed his immediate attention to another dago bastard, one that he didn't know so well, gagged and cuffed and chained on the Broadwater Beach Hotel bed. He began forcefully.

"Mr. Cefalu, I'll not fuck around with you. No need to. You are a serious man. You understand these things. We want to know about the priest. We want to know who he is, what he looks like and where we can find him. And lastly, as a point of curiosity, why is he violating his sacred vows by taping Angeletta's confession for you? I doubt he is doing it out of a friendship with you as you've claimed. Now, for this information, all investigations against you by the U.S. Attorney's office will be dropped and you will cease to be a target of the Federal Task Force. To make it understandable to your goon's mind—you'll be cleared. Are you following?"

The fat body of Carlo Cefalu had stopped squirming on the bed. It was apparent that Thessalonian's words were getting through Carlo's inebriation.

The third paramilitary, code-named Triad, as gently as possible, removed the gag from Carlo's mouth. All three paramilitaries had made a point of concealing their numerous firearms, each carrying a Luger 07 semiautomatic and Czech Skorpian machine pistol, from Cefalu's line of vision. They wanted the Mafioso to feel safe, under the circumstances, and willing to converse.

"Let me see if I got this right. Ya are a big enough man to clear me for good—(burlch)—all ya want to know about is the priest?"

"I am and I do," Ingels acknowledged.

Cefalu tried to prop himself, positioning himself to, in his terminology, eat shit. Carlo began doing just that.

"That's fucking fine with me. He ain't no friend of mine. Father Joseph Prio is his name ... Joey. He's parish priest for St. Cecilia's (burlch) Catholic Church. He's got a black beard with some gray in it, little pussy eyeglasses, wire rimmed, and he's going bald. (burlch) As far as why he's taping Joey's confession ... See, many years ago Joey—that's what I used to call him—Joey ran with my street gang. Hell of a burglar. I mean he could break into anything. Anyway, I took him on a party trip with a few girls to a place called Whiskey Bay. This place is about one hundred fifty miles west of Pontchartrain. Got to be the most deserted, secluded spot in Louisiana (burlch). There was a freak accident. One of the girls was blowjobbing his gun and it went off in her mouth. Blew her head off. I covered for him. So when Vince wrote me and told me a few weeks ago that he was dying and wanted a priest—a priest he could trust—to give a confession to, I saw it as a way to collect an old debt from Joey and get some info to help me with the Feds."

Thessalonian, still standing, felt every nerve end of his approximately 80-year-old body tingle.

"Did you say Angeletta is dying?"

Carlo nodded, then added, "Cancer."

"All right, go on, Carlo," Ingels encouraged after a slight hesitation.

"That's it. I forced Joey to tape Vince's confession, and he did. But then he comes back to me, real cute like, and says he made four tapes, no five, out of Vince's confession. Said he was going to piece them out to me."

"And what made you go for that?" Ingels asked.

"Had no choice. He said the fifth tape would go to Johnny and Jake Sincelli if he was hurt. And being with the government, which ya must be, ya know the Sincellis run the show in New Orleans. Could have got me whacked real quick. They still hold Vince in high regard."

Ingels was taking in each bit of data like a demonic computer.

"Why did Vince approach you in the first place about a priest?"

Carlo answered quickly, as if belatedly realizing he had left something out.

"Oh, yea, see, Vince was my sponsor into the Nuccia family. He helped me become a made man. He used to be my capo until he disappeared in '73."

Thessalonian picked up the cassettes.

"What is this V.A. number one copy, Carlo?"

Carlo began squirming again, regretting now that he had duplicated the tape. "Ya see, I made an extra tape for me of the first tape Joey gave me, but I wasn't going to make a second tape copy of the second one. Don't know who ya can trust anymore. Was just playing it safe, I swear," he lied.

Victor Ingels/Thessalonian appreciated the pathetic irony of this, especially coming from a Sicilian street hood like Cefalu. He turned away from "Pig" Carlo and motioned to his paramilitary, Sumatra. This time, though, his signal appeared more definite, more end-of-story like than the others.

Carlo noticed the difference, too, and reacted.

"Hey, where are ya going? What is this?"

Sumatra pulled from his leg holster his Luger semi-automatic, attached a silencer to it so quickly that Carlo had only seconds to ponder his fate. Sumatra pressed its barrel down against the side of Cefalu's pompadour, above the cochlea and tympanic membranes of the ear, and proceeded to turn Carlo's platinum hair lock red.

Bloody—Dead—Red!

In the Inter Inpetto Armaments Corporation (IIPAC) Central Office, Zurich, Switzerland

"Judy, is Victor on the line?"

"Yes, sir."

Ingels in clinical fashion briefed Sosar. Sosar digested Thessalonian's update voraciously, then summarized.

"Why didn't the cockhumping priest just tell Carlo to get lost completely? He could have, using the Sincellis as a threat. But instead he pieces the tapes out to Carlo, knowing that this Carlo is going to the Feds, giving the Feds just enough to get them interested. Angeletta, just as we suspected, is leaking Legerdemain. He and the priest were playing Carlo for a chump, using him to get Vince's story to the authorities, a bit at a time. That way they could explore the territory before moving. Smart, real smart. And now this Plauche is interested. Thessalonian, we'd better pull the plug on this before it goes any further, on the priest, on the U.S. Attorney and his staffer, on Angeletta, and just for good measure on Nuccia, too. Opinion?"

"No, Sosar," Thessalonian voiced, "I concur with prejudice."

Chapter Thirty-One

In Saint Cecilia's Catholic Church, New Orleans, Louisiana, USA

Father Joseph Prio awoke before sunrise with the lucky hand of God on his shoulder.

The priest had been ordered by his bishop to rendezvous this morning with a group of important prelates visiting New Orleans from Paris. Father Prio was to escort the prelates on a tour highlighting all the interesting French-Orleans cultural parallels, i.e., the French Quarter, the French Market. A boring task, indeed, but one that did require Father Prio's undivided attention from first light on. He had left his cherished sanctuary at St. Cecilia's two hours before Ingels and his three paramilitaries arrived.

After driving back to New Orleans from Biloxi, dropping a stunned but totally implicated Michael McKinney off at his flat, then instructing him to go to work and act as if nothing had happened, the four men in their rented Chevrolet drove straight to the church six blocks from Lake Pontchartrain.

In accordance with Sosar Tomeen's instructions a few hours earlier, Father Joey Prio was to be eliminated, preferably before the body of Carlo Cefalu was discovered at the Broadwater Hotel. Due to time considerations and the disadvantage of breaking light, Ingels and his men had been forced to leave Carlo as was, handcuffed, chained, with a gag drawn down around his neck, and a Luger slug in his brain.

They hoped it would be at least six to seven hours before housekeeping discovered the fat Mafioso's body, and at least late tonight or tomorrow before the gangland style slaying made the news.

Ingels instructed paramilitary Triad, who was driving, to stop at a pay phone minutes away from St. Cecilia's, where he dialed the rectory phone number only to be greeted by the early morning optimism of a church secretary. She informed the caller that Father Prio was gone for the day—no, not out of town—but off on church business.

Ingels was disturbed by this break in stride, but recomposing himself, decided it was best to use the intervening hours for sleep. He would, however, station one paramilitary at St. Cecilia's waiting on Father Prio, and the other two at the U.S. Attorney's office, in hopes of latching a tail onto Nicholas Plauche.

He had received from his Tasses network in Washington a photograph of Plauche and made sure his paramilitaries had noted Carlo's description of the priest; gray-black beard, wire glasses, receding hairline.

Ingels gave each of his men a handful of pills—uppers—to maintain them.

They dropped Thessalonian off at the swank Airport Hilton Hotel in Kenner, picked up another car, separated, and headed for their respective surveillance posts.

Just as Thessalonian/Ingels laid his old man's body to sleep, all hell, literally all hell, erupted in the world of Father Joseph Prio. It was the lead story on a local noon TV news program. Again Father Prio was fortunately in the right place at the right time.

He was in the rear altar relaxation area of St. Louis's Cathedral waiting for his visiting Parisian prelates to tour at their leisure the interior of the Cathedral. There was a TV softly playing in the corner of the back room, with two altar boys there for mid-day worship services, giving it their undivided attention. When Carlo Cefalu's dated mug shot flashed across the screen Father Joey Prio jumped. The priest felt his life—his peace within his cell—shatter.

The story indicated that reputed New Orleans Mafia boss, Carlo Cefalu had been found shot to death in the Broadwater Beach Hotel, Biloxi, Mississippi early that morning. It went on to say that law enforcement officials immediately classified it as a professional gangland murder because of Mr. Cefalu having been shot once in the head at close range by a silenced weapon. An investigation was continuing but there were at this time no suspects in custody. There was an afternote describing Mr. Cefalu as a reputed high-ranking member of the Nuccia/Sincelli organized crime family and that Mr. Cefalu was rumored to be heavily involved with loan sharking and prostitution. There was further speculation by the broadcasters as to whether or not this incident signaled the onset of another Mafia war like the one New Orleans had experienced in 1983.

Father Prio, dressed in standard cleric black, stroked his gray-black beard with nervous energy and pure tics of panic. The priest knew instinctively that Carlo had not been killed in a Mafia dispute. Carlo was too well respected for his money-making abilities, as evident by the royal treatment he had received from the staff at Mama Maria's.

"No," Joey decided, "Carlo's death is connected to Legerdemain. Supra powerful forces are at work here and what better way to eliminate the leak than to kill all of us—Carlo, me, whatever Federal investigator is involved, and Vince." Joey was in immediate danger. He knew it as sure as he knew his sacraments.

"What to do? What to do?" Father Prio's mind was spinning like a Mardi Gras cartwheel.

First, he had to lose today's assignment. Joey walked to a telephone sitting on a wall mount in the back of the relaxation area and called his Bishop. He lied to his superior about a family emergency—life or death—and asked for an immediate leave of absence. The Bishop was surprised by this, knowing full well that Joseph had no living family relatives, at least not in New Orleans. The Bishop knew that Salvatore "Toto" Prio, Father Prio's father, and Lucia Prio, his mother, had both passed away some years ago. Then again, Joseph had mentioned to the Bishop on occasion that he did have some still-living relatives in Alexandria and Torbert, Louisiana. Presuming that these were the relatives Father Prio was speaking of, the Bishop granted him immediate emergency leave.

Joey left the rear of St. Louis's Cathedral without even bidding farewell to his Parisian guests. He did not have time. He was a man—a priest—running for his life. His next move was to get out of his cleric outfit and buy a tourist T-shirt and a pair of gaudy tourist pants. This he did from a rather startled street market vendor.

In a fast trot, the priest began aimlessly walking in circles. Down Dumaine, down Madison, down St. Claude, down Claiborne, Father Prio's hypermotion began to finally take direction. He decided on his next move. He would call the U.S. Attorney's office and ask for the agent who was handling the

Carlo Cefalu investigation. He stopped at a pay phone somewhere on Conti Street. He dialed information, got the U.S. Attorney's office number, and rang it. He asked for whomever was handling the Carlo Cefalu case.

Nicholas Plauche, with cornpipe firmly gripped between his teeth, answered.

"This is Nick Plauche, Assistant U.S. Attorney. I'm in charge of the Cefalu investigation. Who's calling,. please?"

Joey Prio stammered foolishly for a syllable or two, stopped, collected himself, and answered, aware of the huge risk he was taking.

"I know Carlo was giving you information from tapes, tapes of Vince Angeletta's confession, recorded by a priest." Father Prio hesitated, then continued courageously, "I am that priest. My name is Father Joseph Prio. I heard about Carlo's murder. I'm sure it has to do with Vince's and my tape. It's time we met. But just you and I, Mr. Plauche. No one and I mean no other damned soul around."

Nick Plauche made a throaty cynical hmmph, then responded as casually as possible, "You're sort of rough for a priest, huh?"

"These are rough times, sir. When and where?"

"The Glass House Restaurant. It's very public. One hour. There'll be a briefcase by my chair in view of the entrance. And Prio—watch yourself."

"One hour. And, Mr. Plauche, don't be late. What I have to tell you could change the course of history."

"I'll be waiting."

In the Glass House Restaurant, New Orleans, Louisiana, USA

Nicholas Plauche, for the first time in many years, not only arrived on time, but ahead of time.

"That in itself would amaze Annie," he thought as he sat his briefcase on the floor entrance side, beside his chair. His wrist watch buzzer started buzzing noisily.

A man about five feet ten inches, one hundred seventy pounds, entered the posh restaurant. His attire was tourist tacky and the restaurant host was not about to allow him inside. He had a gray-black beard and glasses, but appeared, aside from his clothing, to be well-groomed. Nick walked up to him.

"Mr. Prio?"

"Yes," Joey answered.

Nick turned to the host, "It's all right, he's with me." The host turned his nose up at both men and walked away begrudgingly.

The priest and the prosecutor seated themselves. There was little time for posturing or game playing, so without preliminary Father Prio began. Nick dipped his pipe bowl into his leather tobacco pouch, lit it, and listened.

At every turn of the priest's story, from Whiskey Bay to Carlo to Vince's original confession to re-recording the tapes to Clemer Dodd to Plato, Mancus, SFG Team LED, White Star, Marsh, Taylor, Holt, Jimenez, Pluto, Mongoose, and Sosar Tomeen and Thessalonian, Nick found himself puffing hotter and hotter on his cognac and cherry tobacco bowl.

"Thus Charlie Nuccia, Vince Angeletta, Stefano Anacondini, and Gaetano Rossini were all manipulated by this CIA operative Thessalonian/Victor Ingels on orders of General Marion Armstrong—Intercept Eagle. Vince fired at Kennedy from behind the grassy knoll and escaped using his Secret Service identification. Captain Marsh fired from the floor below Oswald, and lastly, Oswald, an American intelligence agent himself packaged as a Cuban-connected nutcase, fired from the sixth floor of the Depository. Oswald, too, was set up to take the fall. Anacondini and Rossini, again manipulated by Thessalonian, arranged for Jack Ruby to dispose of Oswald. Now the clincher, Mr. Plauche, is that the Inter Inpetto Communications man—Clemer Dodd—figured all of this out and documented it ten years later. He was, however, leery of turning the information over to the U.S. government, knowing how entrenched IIPAC was. So instead he revealed it to Vince, probably hoping that Vince or Nuccia would have some underhanded or underworld way of turning it against Tomeen and Thessalonian. The thing was that neither Vince or Nuccia knew what to do with it. So they just stashed it in a Dallas safety deposit box; the same box in which Vince had stashed Thessalonian's final assassination plans for safekeeping in 1963."

Father Prio stopped, short of breath, grabbed the full water glass before him, and downed it impolitely.

Nicholas Plauche felt like Moses on the Mount after being delivered God's Ten Commandments. This story was enough to inspire not only one but several religious experiences. The prosecutor grappled to regain his grip on the English language. He couldn't. Joey continued.

"Furthermore, I am convinced, Mr. Plauche, that the surviving principle controllers of Legerdemain—Tomeen and Thessalonian—have somehow found out about your investigation and are out, at this very moment, to silence all of its participants. Carlo, I believe, was the first to go, then me, then you, then Vince, then Nuccia. I believe we are all in the gravest danger."

This logical assumption by the priest cleared Nick's mind and his manner. He realized now that this was no time to be dazzled. They had to act, to take the initiative. Nick's baby-blue eyes defogged.

"I agree with you, Father Prio," he blurted.

"Just call me Joey, Nick. I haven't felt much like a priest lately."

"Okay, then our only course available is to go legitimately public with all of this; to somehow get Vince, get to that safety deposit box in Dallas, examine the evidence, bring it before a grand jury, then issue an indictment, even if in absentia, on Tomeen and Ingels. My God, this whole thing could impact an entire generation—our generation!"

"Yes, it could, Nick," Father Prio agreed.

Nick tapped out his pipe bowl and leaned his six foot one inch frame towards the priest.

"Also, Joey, we mustn't separate until this is done—until we are all out of harm's way."

The priest agreed again and asked, "Do you have any clue as to how they found out about your investigation?"

Nick's thin mustache scowled downward at this, "Unfortunately I do. You see we queried the OCIC, the Organized Crime Information Center, after our first meeting with Cefalu. We referenced the words: Legerdemain, Thessalonian, Intercept Eagle. They must have had the OCIC monitored. The query was signed by me and my staff processor. All too easy for people as powerful as these."

"Do you trust your staffer?" Joey hated asking, but had to.

Nick scowled even more.

"Not really, Joey. I don't feel good about having to admit this, but I think he resents me. He could probably be gotten to."

"He may have been already, Nick. How else would they have known to find Carlo at the Broadwater Hotel last night?"

That hit Nick Plauche like a case of jungle rot. It seems Annie had been right all along about Mike McKinney.

"Let's get out of here. Now!" Nick insisted, stood, pocketed his pipe and pouch and grabbed his briefcase.

Father Prio seconded the prosecutor's motion, stood and began trailing Nicholas Plauche like a blind man being led to safety. The priest felt he could trust this roguish-looking man.

He wanted to bless him. Instead he silently begged God to.

In the Airport Hilton Hotel, Kenner, Louisiana, USA

"Burma, Burma ... this is Sumatra and Indonesia ... come in."

Ingels, waking quietly, feeling his age as he did, reached over next to the bed, to the nightstand and the radio transmitter sitting on it. He pulled the receiver unit out of its holder and replied, his voice especially husky.

"This is Burma ... come in."

"Burma, we have Plauche in our sights. Left the U.S. Attorney's office an hour and a half ago. Met an individual matching the description of Priest Prio—gray-black beard, wire-rimmed glasses, receding hairline—an hour ago at the Glass House Restaurant. They've exited the restaurant now and are heading north on Interstate 10 towards LaPlace or possibly Baton Rouge. Require instructions."

"Stay on them, Sumatra, all the way. Contact Triad. Instruct him to change surveillance location from Cecilia's Church to Interior Self Design Studios. Tell him to stay on Annie Plauche. She's tall, five feet eleven inches, brown hair, very attractive. Shouldn't be hard to spot."

"Received. Anything else?"

"Stay awake, all of you. This is escalating more rapidly than we had anticipated. No mistakes, men."

"Received ... no mistakes!"

In Annie Plauche's Interior Self Design Studios, New Orleans, Louisiana, USA

"Hello."

"Hi, honey."

"Hey, Nick, what's wrong? You sound a little strange."

"Annie, I want you to listen to me very closely—very, very closely. Something very bad is happening and I want you to do exactly what I say, okay?"

"Okay, kiddo, is this about that old man's confession?"

"Yes, Annie. Now this is what I want you to do, right now. You close up shop and you get in your car and drive to your parents' house in Chalmette. There may be some people looking to hurt you, so do not delay one minute. Any questions?"

"No, kiddo. Remember where we met now, in South Vietnam. I know all about this stuff."

"I know you do, honey. Once you get to your parents' house, stay inside. Wait for my call. Do not leave for any reason. It may be several days before I can contact you. Got it?"

"Nick, are you going to be all right?"

"I will, Annie, as long as I know you are where I'm telling you to be."

"We can't get any police protection, Nick?"

"No, this is all too big for that. These people are international, with wires everywhere. I don't know who we can trust yet. And, Annie, one last thing—do not, I repeat, do not communicate with Mike McKinney. Looks like you were probably right about him."

"I told you so."

"Yes, you did, Annie. I love you more than anything in the world. You remember that, honey."

"And you remember it, too, Nick. I love you, so much."

"We'll talk soon."

"Yes, we will."

Annie O'Merly, the Irish Protestant girl inside the mature adult woman of Annie Plauche, began crying like a young chickadee. She was just a girl. In love with love, cheerleading, stray dogs and Nicholas Plauche.

So very much.

IN RYAN AIRPORT TERMINAL, BATON ROUGE, LOUISIANA, USA

"We may need help where we're going, Joey. There's only one group of people I can trust at this point to help us get Vince out of Angola."

Father Prio was all ears, wondering why the prosecutor had stopped at the Baton Rouge Airport. The priest was worried. He had no love for planes.

"It will probably take me a few hours to reach them all, but we should be able to get them here within a day."

Father Prio couldn't help but express concern.

"But, Nick, do we have a day?"

"We'll have to make a day. Without help, getting Vince and getting him to Dallas will be impossible."

Father Prio assented, then asked two questions.

"I'm ashamed to ask this of you, Nick, but I am really craving a cigarette and have you noticed any surveillance?"

Nick smiled, "No problem. I'll get you a pack and, no, I haven't noticed any tails yet. But with people as professional as these I don't expect to. So look, come on inside the terminal with me. I'll get you some cigarettes. Stand right next to me. I'm going to find the busiest set of pay phones here and start calling. Remember under no circumstances do we separate. Let's go."

The priest, still dressed in his tourist tacky shirt, grabbed Nick's arm.

"Wait, Nick, I'd appreciate knowing who these fellows are you're calling."

Nick paused and apologized.

"I'm sorry, Joey. In Vietnam me and some other soldiers formed a little club. We called ourselves the "War Babies." Over the years we've attended a lot of Veteran conventions together, stayed in touch, grown together. There's an unwritten rule between us. If ever any of us is in deep trouble, all he has to do is call and our fellow War Babies will be there. That's what I'm going to do. Call everyone of them and cry help as loud as is possible over a commercial phone. I trust these men implicitly and I trust they'll be here."

Nick, having finished his explanation, became impatient to move.

"Now, let's get to it and get some help."

Chapter Thirty-Two

In the Interstate Hilton Hotel, Baton Rouge, Louisiana, USA

The six War Babies arrived at the Baton Rouge Interstate Hilton within twenty-four hours: Ray Parks, Jimmy Tortillino, Jeffrey Turner, Graham Mathew, Keith Vangels, and the ever-complaining D.D. Sebastian. An emergency planning session was in order, with Nick at the helm.

"Friends, this is Father Joseph Prio from New Orleans. Forgive us if we both look a little ragged, but yesterday we were thrown into a mind-boggling, death defying predicament, and we've been alternating two-hour sleeping routines since. I called you from a pay phone at the Baton Rouge Airport yesterday. This is one dangerous situation, fellows, and before I go any further I can't tell you how much I appreciate your bringing yourselves and your weapons, here. Thanks."

The bald-headed Keith Vangels piped up.

"Oh geez, Nicky, what could be so friggin' bad? What? Did Annie catch you with another woman?"

The men laughed. Even Nick and Father Prio tried to join in the camaraderie.

"I wish, Keith."

The room became quiet again.

"Brothers," Nick resumed, fidgeting with his short hair, sticking a pencil behind his ear. He reached for his empty corn pipe.

"There is a man I have to break out of prison."

The silence was deafening. None of the War Babies had expected this. They were unilaterally taken aback. Ray Parks shifted his impressive in-shape frame, Jimmy Tortillino shrugged, Jeffrey Turner's mouth dropped, Graham Matthew froze, and D.D. Sebastian wheezed.

Keith Vangels, with bald head bobbing, was the only man in the room to voice his surprise.

"Nick, aren't you still an assistant United States Attorney?

And aren't prison breaks in this country still illegal? So, what in the friggin' world is going on?"

Nick felt the walls contracting. He packed and lit a bowl of tobacco for good luck.

"The story I have to tell you guys is fantastic, undoubtedly the most fantastic story you'll ever hear in your lives."

"Go on," Keith prodded, sensitive to the obvious strain Nick and Father Prio were under. The priest was chain-smoking.

"Maybe it'll be easier if I explain, Nick," Joey offered. Nick gratefully accepted.

"A few weeks back I received a letter from an old acquaintance. You see, gentlemen, when I was young, before I became a priest, I ran with an Italian street gang down in the French Quarter. There was an incident involving me and a girl which resulted in her death. The leader of the gang covered up her death. I only aided him in this. Therefore, he's felt for over twenty-five years that I've owed him. By the way, after her death, I mended my ways and became a priest. Nonetheless, a few weeks ago he contacted me to collect on his debt. What he wanted was for me to tape record the confession of an old dying Mafioso here in Louisiana's Angola State Penitentiary. My old gang leader, being under federal investigation, thought that this old Mafioso's secrets would be valuable to the Feds, so he wanted them. Not knowing what to do at the moment, I went ahead and drove to Angola and heard the man's confession."

Father Prio lit another cigarette while the previous one still burned in the hotel ashtray.

"The man's confession was long and complex, but its essence wasn't. He, Vincenzo 'Angler' Angeletta, was one of three triggermen who assassinated President John F. Kennedy."

The effect of the priest's statement was palpable. Each of the six War Babies stiffened like bamboo stakes.

"Not only that, but Vince hid in a Dallas safety deposit box every detail of the assassination, including the names of the people who manipulated it, the details of that manipulation, and the outline of the entire covert operation."

Jimmy Tortillino couldn't help himself, "Holy Macaroni!"

"That's not all," Father Prio continued, "Vince is not without remorse over the whole thing. He feels he failed some of his people by allowing them to be used as they were. With that in mind, I made a strong appeal to him to go public with his information, made it part of his penance, convinced him that it was his only way to get even before dying. Finally he agreed, so we concocted a plan to funnel the information to the authorities—Mr. Plauche here—using my ex-gang boss as the conduit. We retaped Vince's confession onto a series of carefully worked out sampler tapes."

"Why the precaution, Father Prio? Why not just call the New York Times?" Jeff Turner asked.

"Because ... I'm sorry, I don't know all your names."

"Turner, Jeff."

"Because, Mr. Turner, the people responsible are extremely wealthy executives with one of the leading armament and defense contracting companies in the world. There is no way of knowing where or with whom they have influence. We, Vince and I, thought it best to first try and go through proper judicial channels quietly. Releasing it to the press would have been like disclosing a sealed indictment. It gives the accused time to cover their backs—time to destroy evidence—time to destroy unprotected witnesses."

Turner jerked his head in acknowledgment.

"What has happened now is that my ex-gang boss was murdered two nights ago. We have reason to believe that these same elements are out to murder both me and Mr. Plauche, and as soon as they can arrange it, Vince in prison."

"You're right," D.D. finally spoke, "this is utterly unbelievable! Nick, when you make a mess, you do make a mess!"

Father Prio disregarded Sebastian's negativity.

"One last note—in fact, probably the most important in relation to each of you—the armaments company had a sole, overriding motive in risking the murder of an American president. That was that this American president—John Fitzgerald Kennedy—was hesitant to commit U.S. conventional forces in Southeast Asia. This was unacceptable to these powers. With Kennedy dead, a hawk like Lyndon Johnson could be seated. Need I say that Johnson's outlook was much more in line with their thinking. In other words—yes, killing President Kennedy was a national tragedy that still haunts us, but wasn't killing over 50,000 young, courageous men, just like yourselves, in a manufactured, or at the very least, exploited confrontation with North Vietnam so much more horrible? Wasn't it?"

The priest was whispering now, nearly weeping.

"My new friends, Vince Angeletta knows the exact identities of these men and can prove their culpability in these acts beyond a shadow of a doubt in any court in the world. We must save him soon, before he is murdered in prison. And we must bring him to Dallas to retrieve his evidence. Mr. Plauche trusts you more than any other living souls and right now you may very well be the most important living souls on earth. I'll tell you what I told Vince. America has suffered enough. Close its wounds. Only with our help will Vince Angeletta be able to."

Best friends,
Best buddies,
War Babies.
Heroes all—were born.

In the Airport Hilton Hotel, Kenner, Louisiana, USA

"Sumatra and Indonesia, this is Burma—do you copy?"

A sputter could be heard emitting from Ingels radio set, still positioned on the hotel nightstand.

"This is Sumatra and Indonesia."

"Status?"

"Six men are in Plauche's and Prio's hotel room, no information on their identities. None have checked into individual rooms. No further movement on Plauche and Prio since yesterday's trip from Baton Rouge Airport terminal pay phone to Interstate Hilton here. Surveillance is muted. Have no idea what's going on."

Ingels's mind methodically, precisely, went through the motions.

"Could the visiting six men have been carrying weapons into the hotel when you saw them?"

"Possible. There was a ton of luggage between them."

It was time for Thessalonian to make a critical snap decision.

"Put a tracker on the Plauche-Prio vehicle. Then come back.

We'll have to pull Plauche and Prio out with a draw ... bait. They seem to have cocooned themselves for the time being."

"Clear, Burma, we're on our way."

"Clear."

Ingels/Thessalonian readjusted the radio knobs and spoke again into the unit calmly.

"Triad, this is Burma, do you copy?"

No sputter this time because of less distance.

"Triad here, over."

"Status?"

"No change. Lady Plauche indoors in parent's house in Chalmette. Hasn't left once."

"Stay put, Triad. Sumatra and Indonesia will be there late tonight to join you. Instructions will follow."

"Over, copy."

"Burma, clear."

Victor Ingels picked up the hotel telephone and dialed. A voice answered.

"U.S. Attorney's office."

"Mike McKinney, please."

"One moment, please."

A moment later.

"McKinney."

"McKinney, this is Thessalonian. Any word from Plauche?"

"None. The people here are concerned. His wife's out of touch, too."

"That's OK. We've got them all covered. I need to see you, Michael."

"When and where?"

"I'd rather not reveal my location on your line. Go to the Delta counter at Moisant. Be there in two and a half hours. You'll be met."

"Please trust me, Thessalonian."

"Oh, I do, Michael, especially after everything we've been through together. Two and a half hours—be there!"

Thessalonian was getting antsy. He slammed the phone down.

"I want you to die, Ghost Legerdemain, soon," he said in full voice to an empty hotel room. Then, coining one of Sosar's oft repeated slangs, "painfully, cockhumper!"

In the Interstate Hilton Hotel, Baton Rouge, Louisiana, USA

It had been decided. Vince's prison break would go down as follows:

Father Prio would visit Vince early tomorrow morning. Joey would obtain from Vince a layout of Angola's Satellite Camp H. The most suitable spot for a helicopter landing would be chosen. Father Prio would then travel to a pre-selected spot just outside the eighteen thousand acre prison property. There Jeff Turner, being the unit cartographer, would meet him and analyze and determine the exact landing logistics. He would telephone Vangels, Sebastian, Parks, and Mathew near Baton Rouge's Ryan Airport with the specifics. These four men would then lease a helicopter from a local aviation leasing service. With Vangels piloting and the rest posing as oil speculators they would fly to Angola. Vince would be waiting.

None of the men relished the thought of dealing with prison guard tower fire, but there was just no other way to get Vince out on such short notice. Besides guards seldom fired on helicopters during prison escapes in fear of possible pilot-hostage situations.

From Angola the chopper would carry the five men to the small community airstrip of Ferriday, a half hour away, where a leased Lear 35 jet would be fueled and readied. Nicholas Piauche, Father Prio, Jeff Turner and jet pilot Jimmy Tortillino would meet them there.

The four War Babies and Vince would desert the chopper, board the Lear and all nine men would fly to Dallas/Ft. Worth Airport. Prior to this Tortillino would have taken the precaution of altering or defacing the Lear 35's tail wing ID markers, so if the chopper to jet transfer were witnessed, the wing marks would be misread.

After landing in Dallas, Nick and Father Prio would change Vince's clothes, escort him to his safety deposit box, and help him excavate his assassination evidence. They would then reboard the Lear and all nine men would fly back to New Orleans.

During the return flight Nick would have an opportunity to examine the much heralded evidence of Vince Angeletta and

Father Prio and Vince would have the opportunity to contemplate their penance ... and their much prayed for—longed for—absolution."

IN THE AIRPORT HILTON HOTEL, KENNER, LOUISIANA, USA

The two paramilitaries walked beside Mike McKinney into Victor Ingels's posh hotel room. McKinney immediately began kissing Thessalonian's ass, verbally.

"Thessalonian, I told you you could trust me. I told you. What do you need? Anything, anything."

Ingels smiled, his high cheekbones elevating higher than usual.

"Michael, we have to move quickly. Sit down, please."

"What, what?" McKinney asked again and again. He brushed back his brown ducktail haircut.

"You've got to get Annie Plauche on the phone and get her out of her parents' house. We are going to have to grab her, Michael, to pull Plauche and Prio in."

"That's not going to be easy. Annie doesn't think much of me."

"I see," Ingels said, gesturing, "then get her on the phone and tell her you and some people have Nick. That unless she comes out, Nick will die."

"But, Thessalonian, what if Nick has called her in the last twenty-four hours?" McKinney asked, cowering.

"He hasn't, Michael. You see, we have Plauche's car bugged." Thessalonian demonstrated, pointing to a red blinking tracker. "And it's been on the move all evening. My guess is that he and the priest are heading toward Angola to get our dying Vince out tomorrow. Which is all the better for us. We grab Annie and demand the presence of Prio, Vince, and Plauche, or his lovely wife dies. One nice precise package."

The rattiness that was Mike McKinney spawned an idea.

"Thessalonian, why don't you just send your men into Annie's parents' house, tranquilize her family and abduct her."

The old man with "Gli occhi di un pugnale"—the eyes of a dagger—even though fatigued, yelled at McKinney.

"Because, you idiot, my men have to ration their energies!

They have been up for days and her parents' house is in a crowded neighborhood which makes the risks for local police intervention exceptional!"

McKinney lowered his head pitifully.

"Now," Ingels ordered Sumatra and Indonesia, "go to Triad and tell him I'll be in contact. Between me and our new buddy here we're going to figure out a way to pull Annie Plauche out. Here," he said, reaching into his coat pocket, "here's some more pills. Stay on your toes, men. We're going to conclude this within twenty-four hours—or else!"

Chapter Thirty-Three

In the Offices of Acra-Crow Aviation Leasing, Baton Rouge, Louisiana, USA

"Yes, sir, an Aerospatiale AS 350B-1 should do," Keith Vangels requested, "I'm sure you know how it is; these friggin' gents are picky about room and comfort."

"Of course." The leasing agent behind the counter could relate to the pilot's dilemma.

"I'll need to see your identification and license, and we'll need you to fill out this form on fuel requirements, duration of rental, method of payment; all the necessary information."

An hour into the escape and the vocal, bald-headed Vangels was busted. He had had no time to arrange for a fictitious license or credit card to lease the chopper, meaning that once the prison break was done and the machine deserted at the Ferriday airstrip it would take just hours for the authorities to trace the helicopter lessee.

"Man, I hope Nicky has this friggin' case put together by then or I'm going to be a wanted man," Keith worried.

Vangels, however, had implicit trust in Nick's integrity, intelligence, and balls. Back in Nam, in the 25th, Nicky had made an effort to be the epitome of cheerfulness, and considering that Keith's wife had divorced him a month into his Vietnam tour, those efforts had been damned appreciated.

Anyway, for now, the objective was to get this Angeletta out. Everything else would have to mend itself.

The priest had visited Vince an hour ago in Angola and had received from the Mafioso a detailed layout of Satellite Camp H. Father Prio had then left the prison and rendezvoused with Jeff Turner. Turner calculated the landing coordinates within the prison camp, then placed a call to Vangels and his three phony oil speculators. That was forty-five minutes ago. No hitches.

Even now the helicopter leasing company gladly accepted Keith's legitimate credentials and credit card.

An hour later pilot Vangels and phony oil speculators Sebastian, Matthew, and Parks were on their way to Angola Penitentiary.

Speculating, indeed. But not for oil.

En Route To and In the Offices of Executive Jet Leasing, Lafayette, Louisiana, USA

Nick Plauche had let Father Prio and Jeff Turner drive his monitored vehicle to Angola, Louisiana last night. Therefore, the car Nick was driving in now with Jimmy Tortillino was unmonitored by Thessalonian's tracking device.

There was only one Lear Jet leasing company in South Louisiana. It was located about 80 miles west of Baton Rouge in Lafayette, Louisiana. The prosecutor sensed that dealing with them was going to be a hassle. The company had been rude and unhelpful on the phone; like who cares, we've got all the business we can handle. Jimmy Tortillino, though, was an experienced private jet pilot. Nick believed if anyone could get them a Lear, Jimmy could.

After stopping once in the city of Lafayette for guidance, they pulled into the hangar offices of Executive Jet Leasing.

Jimmy was a terrific negotiator, a talent attributable to his having lived in New York City for twenty years. Jimmy had been the resident War Baby host at the recent Veterans convention there. He had showed everyone a great time, especially Nick and Annie. The poor attitude of the agent for Executive Jet Leasing was subdued by Jimmy's hip, big city persuasiveness.

"Listen, I pilot for New York Private AT three to four days a week. I handle everything from Citations to Falcons to Gulfstreams to Lears."

"Yes, Mr. Tortillino, your credentials indicate that, but are you acting in capacity for your firm or is this a private leasing?"

Jimmy was becoming irritated.

"Private."

"Then I'm afraid, sir, that one of our pilots will have to accompany you. As I'm sure you are aware of, you must have two pilots in the cockpit of a Lear 35 at all times."

Jimmy looked to Nick who was sitting in the corner of the waiting room. Nick nodded a reluctant okay.

"Fine," Jimmy conceded, "Fine."

Time was running short.

Fifty minutes later Jimmy, Nick, and Reginald, a co-pilot from Executive Jet Leasing were airborne. Reginald, innocent, unsuspecting, was in for the ride of his life.

IN ANGOLA STATE PENITENTIARY, ANGOLA, LOUISIANA, USA

The helicopter passed over the heavily wooded Tunican Hills surrounding Angola. It skipped over the outer Mississippi River prison perimeter

Vince's housing unit, Satellite Camp H, was less guarded than the main Angola compound. Waiting for freedom, Vince stood now in the largest open yard of the camp.

The Aerospatiale AS 350B-1, piloted by War Baby Keith Vangels rose above the horizon. Due to a mid-day overcast, the few prison guards that were on duty heard the cutting blades of the chopper before actually spotting it.

Vangels masterfully brought the craft down in the yard as close to Vince as possible. At least he assumed it was Vince. The man was old, emaciated, and waving his arms frantically. Matthew and Parks disembarked with synchronous efficiency and ran to get Vince. Graham Matthew and Ray Parks were both athletes, in the health club business together in Kansas City.

The Satellite Camp H tower guards, few that they were, couldn't have cared less. They opened fire. The possibility of a pilot-hostage situation obviously meant nothing to them.

Vince made a zigzag dash for the chopper. Matthew and Parks met him and nearly lifted him off the ground. Bullets were hitting within inches of the three men. Only by the grace of a just God did they make it to the helicopter unscathed.

D.D. Sebastian helped the three men into the open passenger door, cackling, "I can't believe Nick got me into this—I can't believe I'm into this!"

Vangels had them lifted in fifteen seconds. Weapons fire from the prison guard towers continued to zing by, some passing as close as a pine needle to the aircraft. But after more than a decade of incarceration Vince wasn't noticing.

Only freedom and vendetta were on his mind.

En Route To and At the Ferriday Town Airport, Ferriday, Louisiana, USA

Nick Plauche was holding Reginald at gunpoint.

Minutes after taking off from Lafayette, Nick had entered the Lear Jet cockpit with a .32 caliber pistol Tortillino had given him. Nick, a man of law and strict conscience, then forced himself to draw down on the co-pilot.

"Reginald, don't be alarmed. Please. I am an Assistant United States Attorney and the trip we are on is most definitely official business. It will all be explained to you as soon as possible. Until then, just relax and don't do anything stupid. I'm sorry."

Reginald's black face registered shock, then skepticism, then acceptance. He would cause no trouble.

Ten minutes later the Lear 35 landed at Shreveport. Tortillino explained to Shreveport Control that he was having a problem with his tail wing ID markers, and that he needed to take a look at them. Even though an unusual problem, Shreveport cleared him for landing.

It took Tortillino fifteen minutes to alter and deface the jet's markers. They took off once more and landed at the Ferriday Airport fifteen minutes later.

Nick and Jimmy directed their senses towards the overcast sky, all ears alert for the swosh, swosh of helicopter blades. All eyes alert for the sight.

Outside the O'Merly Residence, Chalmette, Louisiana, USA

"Triad, Sumatra, and Indonesia ... this is Burma."

"We read you, Burma. This is Triad. Over."

"Triad, this is where we are at. McKinney's going to call Lady Plauche. Will advise her that unless she appears within thirty seconds outside her parent's house, you three will enter and pull her out—hurting her parents if necessary. You will not actually do this. What you will do is park and wait where Lady Plauche can see you. Wait one minute. Then stand outside the car as if about to pounce. Stand there for another minute. Get back in the car. Wait for one last minute. If she doesn't come out, leave. We'll regroup at the Airport Hilton here. McKinney will be calling her in thirty seconds. Copy?"

"Copy."

Mike McKinney, seated on the edge of Thessalonian's bed, picked the telephone receiver off the telephone sitting there. He dialed Annie's parents' number. The phone rang.

Annie answered.

Probably anticipating Nick's call, McKinney thought.

"Annie, this is Mike."

"What do you want, Mike?"

"Annie, you've got thirty seconds to walk out your parents' front door and come with some friends of mine. If you don't they're going to come in on your parents and grab you. They're armed, so I wouldn't try to resist."

Even Annie couldn't believe that Mike McKinney would stoop this low.

"Look out your front window now," McKinney continued. "You'll see them—three men dressed in black."

Annie left, then returned.

"Yes, I see them, Mike. Why are you doing this? Why? Hasn't Nick always been good to you?"

"FUCK NICK AND FUCK YOU! You stuck-up bitch! You've only got a couple of seconds left. And, Annie, when you leave, tell your parents to tell Nick when he calls next that you left with McKinney and for him to call McKinney at the office as soon as possible."

"Okay, Mike. I'm walking out."

McKinney hung up the phone. A long forty seconds passed.

"Burma, Burma, this is Triad. We've got her. She's sitting right here."

"Very good, men. Blindfold her. Over."

"Over, Burma."

Victor Ingels looked at Michael McKinney with appreciation.

"Now who says you can't do something once you put your mind to it, Michael? You're growing up, my young Georgetown friend. Very fast!"

At the Ferriday Town Airport, Ferriday, Louisiana, USA

Everyone's senses were being invaded. Nick's, Jimmy's, Reginald's, and the senses of two new passengers who had met the Lear shortly after it landed: Father Prio, who despised planes, and Jeffrey Turner.

The Angola escape helicopter, the Aerospatiale 350 B-1, containing Vangels, Parks, Matthew, Sebastian and Angeletta was making its approach.

It landed on the tarmac twenty yards away from the jet. Its passenger door slid open and the four War Babies and Angeletta exited.

The four men dressed like executive oilmen and Vince still dressed in Angola gray ran towards the Lear 35. The plane stairwell was let down for them and they climbed up it rapidly into the jet cabin. Tortillino lifted the stairwell behind them while Plauche still held Reginald at gunpoint in the cockpit.

Jimmy maneuvered himself back into the nose of the Lear, revved it, radioed Control and raised it aloft within minutes.

Next scheduled stop—Dallas/Ft. Worth—or be damned!

At Dallas/Ft. Worth Airport, Dallas, Texas, USA

"D/FW Approach Control, this is Lear A47. I'm five miles east of you. Winds are southerly at 20 miles an hour. Heading six zero. Request clearance for landing."

"Lear A47, this is D/FW Control. You're clear at present heading of six zero. Over. Runway Eight Eight. Clear for landing."

Vince Angeletta feebly turned to Keith Vangels behind him. "I used to be a pilot."

Vangels feigned interest out of politeness.

"No friggin' ... really, Vince?"

"Yea, I told Father Prio all about it," Vince said to both Vangels and the priest.

Father Prio smiled, then remembered Vince's clothes.

"Okay now, Vince, as soon as we touch down you're going to have to change clothes."

The once five foot eleven inch frame of the "Angler" diminished now with cancer said he understood and that he was ready

The priest added, "You know, Vince, I never have asked, but how are you so sure the safety deposit box is still secure and how, without any identification, are you going to be able to get into it?"

Vince's tongue lapped his mouth.

"I paid in advance a lifetime rental on the box, so I know it's secure. And I put in place code words instead of personal identification for authorized entry, not knowing who would be opening it or when. Only two people know the code words—me and Charlie."

Father Prio nodded in wordless appreciation of Vince's Sicilian sense of precaution.

The Lear 35 buckled, bounced, jerked, jerked-bounced, buckled. The Avenging Angler had arrived.

IN THE HANOVERS TRUST BANK BUILDING, DALLAS, TEXAS, USA

"Authorized entry to safety deposit box 108552/63. Bearer entry code—Rosalie, Mona, Mario, Spalloni, Don Vito Cascioferro."

Vince could have been anyone's charming grandfather. Accompanied by Nicholas Plauche and Father Joey Prio, Vincenzo had come alive, the idea of blessed freedom taking hold in his mind, as well as the cherished notion of vendetta. The character lines in his face had once again become striking, his nose defiant, his silvery-brown-blue eyes watchful, and his sunken cheeks pinchable. Nick and Father Prio had dressed him in a beige turtleneck sweater, brown corduroy sport coat and half-top cowboy boots.

The bank officer left the three men alone in a deposit box examining room. There were four bundles of documents; three bundles labeled: "The Property of Clemer Dodd," and one bundle, obviously some sort of government pouch, labeled with the rear seal of the United States and its ANNUIT COEPTIS inscription on its front.

That old rush of deep-seated reserve that Vince hadn't felt since 1963 blistered through him as he turned to Father Prio and the Assistant U.S. Attorney.

"They're all yours, Joey, Mr. Plauche. Three contain documentation from Dodd's investigation; the other one contains the final assassination plans that were given to me by Dan Carthage. Get Thessalonian or Victor Ingels or whatever the fuck his name is, and get Sosar Tomeen. That, besides my freedom on some fucking desert island, is all I ask for. Let's get out of here."

It wasn't until Nick actually began leafing through the documents on the trip back to D/FW Airport that he realized the volatility of what he was in possession of. The information was remarkably detailed and unmercifully incriminating.

"This will take days to unravel," he decided. "I best call Annie and tell her to hold tight."

He dialed Chalmette from the nearest available pay phone. Annie didn't answer. Instead, her mother did.

"Oh, hi, Nickie. Annie's gone. Told me to tell you she left with that McKinney fellow who works with you and for you to call him at the office as soon as possible."

Paralyzed, Nick grunted a thanks to his mother-in-law, and dialed his office in New Orleans.

"U.S. Attorney's office."

"Hey, this is Nick."

"Why, hello, Mr. Plauche, we've all been concerned about you. Where have you been?"

"I'm okay. Don't worry, be back in a few days. But I need to speak to Michael."

"Sure, Mr. Plauche, one moment."

"Hello."

"McKinney, this is Nick. Listen to me, you mangy—"

"Whoa, whoa, before you start, Nick boy, God's gift to the United States Justice Department—"

"What have you done with her?"

"I personally have done nothing."

"Except change sides!"

"Player cards change all the time, Mr. Plauche, in the big leagues."

"Since when have you been big league material, Mike? Don't you know that these people are going to kill you when they're finished with you? For God's sake, don't you realize that they've been covering their tracks for almost three decades? You think they are going to stop now?"

"You through, Nick? I asked you if you're finished."

"I'm finished, Mike, unfortunately so are you."

"Whatever ... this is the deal. An exchange you, the priest and Angeletta for Annie. She lives."

"But we die?"

"Look, these people only want to come to some accommodation."

"Yea, like they did with Carlo Cefalu? Let me ask you, Mike. Were you there when they blew the fat man's brains out?"

"Nick, I'm about to hang up. You want to listen or not?"

Nick backed off.

"I'm listening."

"In exactly six hours you, the priest and Angeletta be at the main launch of Whiskey Bay. Prio should know exactly where that is. There will be a man in a small boat waiting for you there. That man will know nothing about anything—just a local we hired to handle the boat. Somebody will be watching you at all times. One crazy move and Annie dies and gets sunk into the swamp.

"Again the priest can tell you how easily that's done."

"Then you're a wanted man, Mike."

"No, Nick, then I'm a man with plastic surgery and a new identity working for some of the richest people in the world. I know that pales in comparison to working for the likes of you, Mr. Fantastic, but I think I can adjust."

"Six hours, Mike, no funny shit."

"You, the priest and Angeletta for Annie. Six hours—absolutely no funny shit. See you then, Nick. Have a safe journey."

It would have been easy for Nicholas to indulge in some slaughterous imaginings over McKinney, but he knew that with Annie's life in the balance he couldn't afford them. He headed to the Lear, more frightened than he had ever been in his life. He and the War Babies had six hours to devise a strategy to save the woman he loved, the most beautiful woman in his universe ... his wife.

En Route to Whiskey Bay, Louisiana, USA

Victor Thomas Ingels/Thessalonian enjoyed looking at Annie Plauche. Even blindfolded she was beautiful. Five-feet-eleven inches tall barefoot, sensuous mouth, shoulder length fox-brown hair. Annie's hair reminded him of Margareta Jimenez. Of course, Margareta had been petite whereas Annie was tall; both women bright, emotional, determined but sadly aligned with the losing faction. Margareta with her father Juan and his Cuban Revolutionary Directorate, Annie with her husband Nicholas and his U.S. Attorney's office in the Eastern District of nowhere.

The paramilitaries, Sumatra and Indonesia, were seated in the freshly rented Dodge Van Cabin Cruiser seats nearest Annie. Thessalonian and McKinney were seated in its mid-section. Triad was at its wheel. South Louisiana was nearing dusk.

The IIPAC van was nearing Whiskey Bay. Thessalonian had chosen Whiskey Bay to conclude in, because of its dense isolation and inaccessibility. It was an appropriate place for him to asphyxiate at long last the experience of Legerdemain.

The deaths of Captain Marsh, General Mancus, Juan, going to work for IIPAC and Sosar in December 1963, Dan Carthage and his look-like suicide, being introduced by Sosar to George Whitten, the architect of Legerdemain, for the first time on June 8, 1968, investigating the Robert Kennedy assassination, the deaths of Clemer Dodd, General Armstrong and his aide Corporal Forrestol, Plato Smith, and ultimately George Whitten himself, then Stefano, "Mr. A" Anacondini, Gaetano Rossini, and Carlo Cefalu.

So much blood and treachery. And now more.

Legerdemain ... Operation Legerdemain.

Unavoidable, just as Sosar had admitted privately in 1980. If it hadn't been for Lyndon Johnson's conventional forces defense spending in Vietnam, IIPAC would not have survived, much less flourished to become the third largest armaments conglomerate in the world today.

Sosar ... Sosar ... his bent, crippled six foot three inch frame, warped with age, still having to murder over this, his phenomenally understated, "lifelong pain in the ass."

Sosar, missing Rocknawell, his childhood headmaster, still hearing the man's voice espouse capitalism and free markets ... the symmetry of Whiskey Bay.

Domino time!

EN ROUTE TO AND AT RYAN AIRPORT, BATON ROUGE, LOUISIANA, USA

They had kidnapped Annie, and each War Baby, even the ever-whining D.D. Sebastian, loved Annie. Father Prio and Vince, too, were outraged.

Nick, even though still struggling to contain his slaughterous imaginings, became a model of decisiveness. He had noted that McKinney had not asked him to bring along any Legerdemain documentation, which meant that McKinney and his group were unaware Angeletta possessed any, so even if he, Prio and Angeletta were killed, Ingels and Tomeen could still be prosecuted.

Therefore, Nick's first instructions were to Jimmy Tortillino. Nick explained to Jimmy that he was going to leave all the Legerdemain evidence with him. Jimmy would keep Reginald in custody inside the jet at the Baton Rouge Airport until exactly eight hours from now. They synchronized their watches. If, in eight hours, no one had contacted Jimmy, then he would assume everyone had been killed at Whiskey Bay. He would then release Reginald and fly to New Orleans. It would then be up to Jimmy to use his considerable New York persuasiveness to explain the historical events of the last few days to Nick's boss, the U.S. Attorney for the Eastern District of Louisiana, and to pass on to him the Legerdemain information. Jimmy would then be responsible for organizing a search team to recover the bodies from the Whiskey Bay bayou scuz.

At that point Reginald spoke up in a convincing baritone over the engine rumble of the Lear.

"Mr. Assistant U.S. Attorney, this is not wise."

"What's not wise, Reginald?" Nick rebutted.

"Listen, I believe I can be of some help if you'll trust me."

"How, Reginald?"

"For starters, I live in Lafayette, which ain't far from Whiskey Bay. I go fishing there a lot. I know my way around there like a swamp hoot, plus I've got a brother who's a sheriff's deputy in Krotz Springs, which is a small town not too far up the Atchafalya from Whiskey. I take it you're not too trusting of cops because whoever it is you're dealing with is powerful. Well, listen, my brother is the most uncorruptible son of a gun you'll ever meet. If I ask him to help me private-like, he'll help, and he knows Whiskey Bay even better than I do. This way, at least, you've got the law—somebody with a badge—on your side and as a witness. Trust me."

Nick made his second major decision. He lowered Tortillino's .32 caliber pistol. Reginald was right. It was unwise to continue holding the black man prisoner, especially if he could contribute, which it most definitely sounded like he could.

Ten minutes before touching down at Ryan Airport in Baton Rouge, D.D. Sebastian had a brainstorm, with pieces of Clemer Dodd's investigation scattered at his feet.

"Nick, now look, I care for Annie as much as anybody. I really do. And I'm willing to go in and get her out 'Nam style if necessary. But, hey, why don't we back ourselves up a tad by offering these papers as an extra to these guys. That way there will be no reason for them to kill anybody. I mean, you've got to admit without these papers there is no proof of anything. Legerdemain becomes just hearsay and 30-year-old hearsay at that."

Hearing this, Nick's pressure gauge broke. He ducked and slid as fast as an eel in the cramped aircraft cabin towards Sebastian. Sebastian weaved in his chair but not before Nick had grabbed him by his neck collar. Nick's baby-blue eyes were screaming.

"You do care for Annie, you fucking jerk, I know you do. It's me and my work you don't give a shit about. That, too, everybody knows! I've been truly surprised that you've gone this far with your big mouth pretty well shut. Now there's something you'd best understand. It's my wife out there whose life is in peril, but still I cannot—will not—throw this case away. Nor would my wife want me to!"

"But, Nick, these people didn't actually start the Vietnam War. Hell, Eisenhower had people in there supporting the French. We'd been fucking around there forever."

"No, D.D., these people didn't start the Vietnam War, but they did manipulate this country's commitment to it, and they did make a timely rearrangement of this country's political landscape to influence the extent of that commitment. They murdered, through an agent provocateur, a young president who was probably a better man than both of us put together, scarred the psyche of the American people and American history in doing so, then proceeded to make sure we were catapulted into an insane military involvement—one in which a quick victory could have been accomplished but never was because it was never intended. Their purposes were served by what happened; a long drawn-out escalation! And you, you fucking mealy-mouthed sack of shit, when we land you can walk, as far as I'm concerned. But, if you stay, you'd better put a lid on the negative comments! So help me God, D.D., just shut the fuck up and act like you're one of us instead of against us!"

If it had been possible, the other War Babies would have stood and applauded. Plauche had finally given D.D. Sebastian the twin barrels of verbal scattershot that he deserved. Finally. Bravo!

The Lear 35 hit the runway fast. Tortillino reeled it in skillfully. As the jet taxied a subdued Nicholas Plauche turned to Jeff Turner.

"Now, Jeff, since you haven't leased anything illegally today or run around any prisons today dodging bullets, go ahead and exit and rent us three solid, preferably all-terrain type, vehicles."

"Okay, Nick," Jeff complied.

Nick turned to the cockpit.

"Jimmy, be sure and park us as far away from—" Nick looked to Vangels.

"Acra Crow Aviation," Keith provided.

"Right, Acra Crow. So our bogus helicopter oil speculators here won't be spotted."

"Gotcha," Tortillino responded. Then added, "Yep, I can see the Acra Crow building now. Must be at least a dozen police cars parked around it. Holy Macaroni!"

"Looks like I'm busted, Nick," Keith remarked.

Nick turned back to Joey, Vince, Reginald, and the other

War Babies and proceeded to talk strategy. He purposely ignored D.D.

"As soon as Jeff returns with the vehicles we are all going to drive to the Interstate Hilton and retrieve our weapons there."

The jet came to a stop.

"Go to it, Jeff," Nick said. Jeff Turner exited, headed for the Ryan Airport terminal and vehicle rental.

Nick continued, "By the way, I appreciate the fact that you all agreed to carry just one sidearm apiece during the prison break today. But now it's full scale. The Angola Prison tower guards were not the bad guys. McKinney and his bunch are." Nick paused and focused on Reginald.

"Reginald, after we get the weapons from the hotel you need to call your brother in Krotz Springs. You're going to have to let me speak to him."

Reginald nodded. Nick went on.

"We've still got about three and a half hours till meeting time, but we can assume that they've already got Annie in place. So we are going to have to move fast. Reginald, where is Whiskey Bay's main launch located?"

"Off its southern side," the baritone said.

"Okay then, is it possible to get to Whiskey Bay from Krotz Springs by boat down the Atchafalaya through some northern inlet?"

"Very possible."

"How long would that take?"

"About an hour and thirty minutes."

"Okay. That means we've got thirty minutes to get the vehicles, thirty minutes to retrieve the weapons and make the call to Reginald's brother. From there we'll head straight to Krotz Springs. How long will that take?"

"Forty minutes," Reginald offered.

"Forty minutes," Nick repeated, "so that's one hour and forty minutes to get to Krotz Springs. One hour and thirty minutes to get to Whiskey Bay from there. That's three hours and ten minutes. Close, real close. Now, me, Vince and Father Joey are going to have to drive from Krotz Springs to the southern side launch of Whiskey Bay. Is that possible, Reginald?"

"Yes, there's a levee road and it should take about as long to drive it as it'll take by boat; an hour and a half."

"That works—barely."

Nick Plauche sat back, reached into his leather pouch for his corncob pipe, lifted it out, put it in his mouth like a teething ring, and chewed ... for luck ... good, good luck.

Twenty minutes later a cream-colored Bronco jeep drove up next to the jet. It was Jeff Turner. Two other Broncos followed. Jeff had apparently enlisted two drivers from the rental agency to drive the jeeps out onto the runway.

By now Vince had disguised Vangels, Matthew, Parks, and himself, remembering Thessalonian's lesson in Honduras so many years ago: the least disguise is the best disguise. D.D. Sebastian moved closer to where Nick was sitting and spoke as softly and as unobnoxiously as he was capable of.

"Nick, I'm sorry. Very few of us get an opportunity in our lives to right a wrong and we War Babies have that opportunity now. I'm sorry. I'm really sorry. For so much wasted time. I always knew you were a bigger man than I am. Let's be friends."

He offered his hand and Nick accepted it. Nick's baby-blue eyes were easy now.

"As long as we stay the same size, D.D."

Vince put Father Prio's wire-rimmed glasses on D.D. for disguise. Everyone climbed down the jet stairwell except Jimmy Tortillino.

"Good luck, brothers. Good luck!" he yelled.

"Eight hours, Jimmy," Nick yelled back, "and good luck to you, brother!"

IN THE INTERSTATE HILTON HOTEL, BATON ROUGE, LOUISIANA, USA

"Charleston, this is Reginald."

"Why hey, brother! How's the life in the jet set?"

"Not meaning to interrupt, Charlie, but I've got an emergency on my hands."

"What's wrong, Reg?"

"A client I was flying today, his wife's been kidnapped. But there's a lot more to it than that. I trust him, Charlie. They're holding her in Whiskey Bay. They want some things in exchange for her."

"Hell, bro, shouldn't we call the FBI?"

"No. Listen, Charlie, it's involving some big time corruption in New Orleans. This client is an Assistant U.S. Attorney there."

"Shit!"

"And, Charlie, we've got just a couple of hours to do the exchange or she's dead."

"Christ!"

"We need your help—but just you—you can't even tell your boss man."

"You got it. What do I do?"

"Here, I'm putting the man on, Charlie. Remember now I trust him. He's for real."

"Then I trust him, too. Put him on."

"Charlie?"

"Hello."

"Charlie, my name is Nicholas Plauche. This is where we are at."

"I'm with you."

"There are probably at least five to ten men holding my wife somewhere in Whiskey Bay. They are real pros, Charlie. They want me and two other men in exchange for her. You see, Charlie, we are in possession of some very valuable information that they want buried."

"Which means they want you buried, too."

"Right. But listen, we're not alone. I've got five men, old war buddies, with me plus Reginald. And plenty of weapons, too. This is my plan. We meet you in Krotz Springs in forty minutes. You get me a wire to wear, okay?"

"I got you."

"And get a boat. One that can hold everyone and the weapons, but streamlined enough to navigate well in the dark."

"I can do that."

"You'll have to take my five men and Reginald in from the north of Whiskey Bay. Me and the other two they want will have to meet them at the main launch on the south side of Whiskey Bay in a few hours. Reginald tells me there's a levee road we can drive down on."

"That's right."

"Okay. They said somebody regular is going to meet us at

the launch, but that they will be watching our every move. So no one else can be seen. What I'm hoping is that the John Doe boatman will be a Cajun. I was raised by a Cajun, so I'm going to try to get him to tell us where we're going. Maybe tell him what's really happening. God willing, he tells me. Then I'll tell you through the microphone wire. Then you and the others will carefully enclose the area and do whatever's necessary to get my wife out."

"A wire mic and a boat—forty minutes. I've got plenty of weapons, too. Get a move on then, Mr. Plauche. We don't want your wife to catch cold now, do we?"

"I like you already, Charlie. We're on the way!"

ON THE ATCHAFALAYA RIVER, KROTZ SPRINGS, LOUISIANA, USA

Father Prio had been strangely quiet on the drive from Baton Rouge to Krotz Springs. For Joey the thought of revisiting Whiskey Bay was a painful one. The tragedy of Whiskey Bay—1963—the memory that had mutilated his senses again and again, lay on his shoulders like a cross. His spirits lifted though standing beside Vince, watching Reginald's brother, Charleston, and Nicholas Plauche in action. With Reginald, Vangels, Parks, Matthew, Sebastian, and Turner they were efficiently loading the mass of War Baby weapons retrieved from the Baton Rouge Hilton and the extra arms of the Krotz Springs Sheriff's Department onto the sheriff's boat. Included in the arsenal werethree G11 serial launch salvo rifles with night scopes, eight 5.56 mm MKA2 machine guns, six M-11 semi-automatics and a dozen Mac-10 machine pistols. The boat was a Starcraft tri-hull sloop equipped with a 350 horsepower motor and two 30-gallon tanks.

Afterwards, Charleston, who resembled Reginald, both men resembling muscle-bound Sidney Poitiers, proficiently attached a small wire microphone to Nick's chest.

The Krotz spring night had become dense with river gases and Charleston suggested that they attach a power foglight to the Starcraft. Nick, looking more Barateria pirate-like and more ferocious than ever, agreed. He began a final review of the night's war plan.

"D.D., you, Ray and Jeff being the best marksmen, work

the rifles with the night scopes. Keith, you, Graham, Reginald, and Charlie stay with the larger stuff. Needless to say, this will require perfect timing and perfect setup. Charlie, that's where you come in. You must stay behind your night glasses every step of the way. It'll be your decision when to open fire after you've spotted Annie. Remember now that me and Annie met in Nam. She's no stranger to gun play. She'll know right off when the shooting starts to hit the deck. D.D., Ray and Jeff, you must take whoever's beside her out first. I'd assume these guys will be in a couple of boats, so be sure to open fire simultaneously, taking their attention away from Annie back to protecting themselves. I think we'll have the element of surprise on our side. Just by them wanting to do the exchange in Whiskey Bay says to me that they're thinking massacre. They've obviously been told how much of a wilderness it is and I'm sure McKinney has told them how close me and Annie are. So they are probably expecting no resistance—and certainly no counterattack from me."

"Who's McKinney?" Charlie threw out.

"He was part of the staff at the U.S. Attorney's office. But he's with them now. In truth, he's a mutt, but a dangerous mutt," Nick replied.

"Should we hesitate on him?" Reginald asked.

"Absolutely not. We hesitate on none of them," Nick emphatically ordered. "Now one part of this I can't figure out is how they are going to check me and Father Joey and Vince for weapons. I know they will. Again, I don't know how. Having a civilian at the helm of the launch boat leads me to believe that we will be dropped off on the bank somewhere. Which means I'll have to give you our location before that happens. Then I'll have to ditch the mic. From that point on us four—me, Annie, Vince, and Joey—will be wholly dependent on you."

"And, Nick, we are going to be wholly dependent on you and that mic. But better yet," Charlie reached for an item in the sheriff's department supply case. "Here is a compass for backup. It'll give you your location coordinates. If all else fails, you can transmit them. At least, that way, I know without a doubt I can find you. Otherwise it will be next to impossible, especially in this murk." He handed Nick the compass and pointed to the encroaching river gases.

Nick nodded and concluded.

"That's it then," he paused, his six foot one inch frame puffed and alert, "I can't tell you—every one of you—how much I appreciate this. Never in a billion years."

Keith Vangels cut him short.

"Just next time, Nick, try not to let Annie catch you with that other woman ... okay?"

Like mirrors reflecting one another's hell, they laughed!

In Whiskey Bay, Louisiana, USA

Laughing Mirror, laugh—laugh at my ugliness
Laughing Mirror, laugh—laugh if you must
Pretty Angels love me—they swallow me sweet
So laugh, Mirror, laugh—in hell we will meet.
In hell we will meet.

Whiskey Bay looked like hell to Vince Angeletta. But it was in this hell where Vince felt certain he would meet Thessalonian/Miles Barker/Victor Thomas Ingels for a final time. Looking around it was impossible for the Angler to imagine four kids, Father Prio amongst them, a generation ago coming to this surreal, haunting, vaporous quagmire to have fun—to have sex.

Thinking of this he turned sideways in his front window seat towards Joey. Nick had flipped the Bronco's internal cab light on so that the IIPAC kidnappers, wherever they were watching from, could confirm the three of them. The jeep light glow, however, cast a putrid tint on the priest's complexion. Vince couldn't help thinking that Joey looked now just as he had at Angola a few weeks back, when he had confessed to Vince his tragedy of Whiskey Bay 1963.

"We all have our demons," Vince thought, "like me, and my promise—questo te prometto—to make it up to the man who had put wings on my soul and taught it to fly—Charlie Nuccia. And my failure, by allowing him to be manipulated by Thessalonian/Ingels and Sosar Tomeen."

Vince's face, though, in contrast to the priest's, was beaming as it had for hours. Full of blood and excitement, knowing in his guts that Thessalonian was waiting for him here. The prospect of freedom diminished now in comparison with the opportunity—an unheard of third chance—to settle old scores and make things right for his Don Nuccia.

Approximately sixty yards away, concealed on a stretch of protruding bank, across from the main launch, paramilitary Triad sighted his night vision binoculars. Through a gap in the fog he confirmed the presence of Angeletta and the priest in the cab of the jeep. Plauche was talking to the civilian boatman on the pier; the one Thessalonian had hired hours ago to transport the three men.

That accomplished, Triad ran swiftly through the shore overgrowth to a parallel inlet unseeable from the main launch. There Thessalonian, Sumatra, McKinney, Indonesia, and Annie waited in two flatbottom skiffs.

Sumatra and McKinney were in the boat with Thessalonian. Triad ran up to it and gave it the "go-ahead" in military sign language. He then jumped into the other boat with Indonesia and Annie. Both boats quietly pulled away and disappeared into the thickening morass.

Thessalonian scratched his throat. The swamp mist was making his scars itch. Or was it just nervousness?

Sosar Tomeen's master spy was uneasy. There were creatures here, in this place. He was sure of it. Creatures lurking—crying for release!

Nick Plauche waved to Vince and Father Prio, "Let's go. C'mon!"

The old Mafioso and the middle-aged priest made quite an unusual sight as they stepped out of the Bronco cab. Vince was moving faster and lighter on his feet than Joey.

The Assistant U.S. Attorney turned back to the Whiskey Bay boatman. Nick's attempts at getting the short, stocky, weatherworn bograt to disclose their destination had been futile. The man had simply nodded once at the name of Nicholas Plauche, spit a chaw of tobacco, and readied his laketrotter for a trip. Nick even tried speaking Cajun to him. No response. The bograt boatman, though uninvolved in the larger scheme of tonight's events, had evidently been well paid for his services by someone on McKinney's crew. Thus, he was not really an innocent.

"Look, I don't know whether you are listening to me or not, but I have to know where we are going. Do you understand? I have to know. Man, please, please, listen to me! It's a matter of life or death!"

No response. Nick tried a different approach.

"I was raised in Cameron. My step-daddy was a fisherman just like you. I know he skirted the law. But I also know he'd never fuck over a man who was down. He'd always do the honorable thing."

"That's why I got nuthin' to say. I been paid, buddy," the bograt countered.

Nick was tired of begging the man. He needed to conserve his energy. Besides he did have the compass Charlie had given him.

The laketrotter they were in was flying across the water dangerously fast. The swamp spray was stinging their faces.

Nick showed his anger.

"Yea, well, fuck you, too, bloke!" Nick screamed over the accelerated boat engine. "If you ever hear the name of Marlow Hebert, I'd advise you to avoid him. He'd spit you out like that fucking pig slop you got in your mouth!"

With that Nick settled back.

Father Prio's manner, however, was becoming increasingly furtive, as if he expected the skeleton of Scarlet Leblanc to reach out from the depths of Whiskey Bay and pull him asunder. His color resembled the cypress on the banks; green—cypress green.

Vince was the only one of the three men who had noticed the boatman jerk at the mention of Nick's stepfather: Marlow Hebert. Vince's deep-seated reserve was motivating like a spacecraft. He felt sharp, strong, and ready. His old romantic lips were lapping the bay spray; as vital and as potent as a Tyrannosaurus Rex resisting extinction. He looked down at his hands—the hands of a good Sicilian solidato—and that was enough. No hero, no patriot, no god, just a good Sicilian soldier. Yes!

Fucking Mirror ... laugh!

The boatman throttled back the laketrotter. It slowed. It stopped. The weatherworn man turned to Nick. He leaned overboard and spewed out the tobacco he had been chomping. Nick prepared himself for a fight.

"You say your daddy's Marlow, buddy?" the bograt asked.

Nick hesitated, surprised.

"Yea, he's my stepdaddy. You know him?"

"Known him for years. Look, I don't know what's going on here and I don't want to know, but for Marlow's son I'll tell you where they told me to take you and that's all. The old man paid me a lot of money."

Vince shot back

"Old man with scars on his throat, his arms, funny eyes, high cheekbones?"

The boatman nodded and took another dip of tobacco.

Nick searched Vince's face, expectant.

"It's Thessalonian, Nick, in the flesh."

The boatman continued.

"He told me to drop you at Flukers Spill. We'll be there in five minutes. That's it."

He turned back to his controls and throttled to speed.

Nick feverishly yelled, "It's Flukers Spill," into the wire mic ten times.

Just as feverishly he ripped the wire microphone off his chest, reached for the police compass and threw them both as far back into the deluge as he could, hoping like he had never hoped for anything in his life that somewhere out in the glade a Krotz Springs sheriff's deputy had heard his transmission.

Five minutes later the bograt boatman, Marlow Hebert's friend, deposited the three men on the shore of Flukers Spill. He turned his laketrotter around and without looking back faded into the billow.

"This is it—Vince, Joey—you ready?"

"Fuck, yes," was Vince's instant reply.

"Yes," Father Joey Prio answered, still cypress green but with a bit of hurricane returning to his voice.

Like a nightmare the two boats appeared, riding on the wisp and tension of an Atchafalaya back canal splinter. The bullfrogs ceased to bellow, the snakes slithered beyond, and Nick Plauche was horror stricken. His beautiful wife was standing in the boat, most visible, with two men dressed in black and heavily armed standing beside her. She was blindfolded.

The haze parted to the left and the other craft drifted closer. A .50 caliber Browning machine gun was mounted near the aft of this vessel and a man was standing behind it. Next to him was what looked to be an older man seated, with a black long coat draped over his shoulders, European style. There was movement in this boat—a splash—and Nick recognized the ducktail haircut of Michael McKinney, wading knee-deep toward them. There was a pistol in his hand.

"On the ground! Face down! All three of you!" McKinney ordered in a weak, unconvincing voice. Nick's slaughterous imaginings about McKinney came alive again as he, Vince, and Joey dropped to their knees, then to their faces.

"So this is the big league, huh, Mike? In the swamp, in the middle of the night, holding an innocent woman hostage, threatening an old man dying of cancer, and his priest ... "

"You think you're so fucking brill—"

"Shut up, Michael. Just search them!" Thessalonian snapped.

McKinney searched the men lying in the wet gunk. Across their backs, then rolled them onto their sides, then their chests.

"They're clean," McKinney said, backing away.

"Vincenzo, stand up," Thessalonian ordered from across the watery muck.

Vince stood, every cancerous capillary burning with vendetta. Thessalonian's thin lips contorted.

"Hello, Angler, you dago bastard punk! Long time no see. Ha!"

"Yea, long time, Thessalonian."

Vince was careful not to provoke or say too much to Ingels. The Mafioso did not want to reveal just how much he knew about this intelligent, ex-intelligence bitch-turd or his boss Tomeen.

"I understand you are dying of cancer, Mafia man."

Vince answered, again selectively.

"We all have to die sometime, somewhere, Thessalonian," Vince paused, stalling. "By the way, Thessalonian, since it appears you've got the upper hand here, do you mind answering a question for me?"

"For you? The Top Man's top man. I hear that Napoleon fuck is in prison now, talking to the walls."

Vince disregarded the insult to Charlie. In the old days he would have killed over it.

"That's right. How about that question?"

Thessalonian gave a husky snort.

"Sure, my old chum, I'd think you'd have lots of questions."

Vince proceeded to ask Ingels a question that he, Vince, already knew the answer to, thanks to Clemer Dodd.

"How did it go down with Mario and Mona, Thessalonian? How? I know you were responsible."

Thessalonian scratched his throat.

"Oh, Vince, you are such a dumb fuck! That's the thing with you Sicilians. People think you are so smart. If they only knew, huh, poor, dumb Vince ... huh?"

Vince hearing this, partially agreed. He and Charlie should have taken offensive action against Ingels and Tomeen immediately after Clemer Dodd came to them in '73.

"I called Anacondini in Chicago the day of our meet at Lafitte's, told him he had till midnight to find his leak and remove it. So he found Mario and removed him. Mona, too. I guess your little bimbo was in a bad place, hanging out with Mario. That's that! Who do you think supplied Ruby? It was Anacondini and Rossini. And who do you think had them killed years later? Me! Me! Are you following, dago?" Thessalonian hesitated. "Now, what I want to know from you, Vince, is why did you let this Fed and this priest bring you out here tonight? You must be losing it, too, like Charlie. What do you care about his wife?" Thessalonian pointed to Plauche with his cane. "Or the priest? Why give a shit about what happens to him? If I was dying of cancer and had been locked up thirteen some odd years, I'd boogie as fast as a Cuban crab to the Riviera."

Vince managed to smile. A handsome smile. A Sicilian Adonis to the end.

"Well, it's like this, Thessalonian," Vince said as he straightened his soiled turtleneck sweater shirt. Mike McKinney, pistol in hand, was standing five feet to the side of him.

"I intended to boogie, but when I found out you had the man's wife," he said, pointing to Nick, "I couldn't. Now, don't look so startled, Thessalonian. You know I'm a loyal fellow. After all you manipulated my loyalty to Charlie. You see, I come from the old school just like Charlie. When someone does right by me, I do right by them. Our cosches, our families, are our lives. This Fed got me out of Angola."

Thessalonian interrupted.

"You are one idiot, dago! Don't you know that he only got

you out because of your role in Legerdemain. He didn't get you out because he's your friend."

"That's all right, Mr. Bible man, whatever the reasons, he did get me out! And he's treated me with decency since. That goes a long way with a lot of us in my world. The misfits like Cefalu, unfortunately, make me out to be a liar when I say that but then again the Cefalus never do last long."

"And you call living in Angola Penitentiary all these years having lasted, Vince?"

"I call it having survived; having survived a mistake."

Vince gasped. He could see the outline of another boat, barely cloaked, far in the background, like an alligator silently converging, jaws open. He could see several light-colored oars, water-blinking in and out, in and out.

Vince became flustered.

"A mistake—survived a mistake. You know, Bible man, we all make mistakes."

Vince, his silvery brown-blue eyes as big as pancakes, tried to get Nick's attention.

"Some mistakes are diversions though."

Vince looked again at Nick who was still face down. Vince's eyes were bigger now than one of Charlie's bocci balls.

Unexpectedly—insanely—Vince began singing like Pavarotti, "Laughhinng Mirror, laugh—at my oogliness—Gli occhi di un pugnale—it's your mistttakkee now!"

Suddenly a shrill creature's howl invaded the night. Thessalonian, alarmed by the noise and Vince's behavior, shouted to McKinney, "What is that? What is he doing? What did he say?"

McKinney ran towards Plauche and the sound emanating from him.

"It's just his wrist wa—"

McKinney's new life expectations ended with the word watch.

A round from D.D. Sebastian's G11 Salvo rifle with night scope crashed into McKinney's patella, bludgeoning the mutt's knee first, then pulverizing his deltoid, his shoulder, finally the aortic valve of his heart and—death.

Nick and Joey jumped up.

Rapid-fire weapons fire was coming from all directions.

Nick couldn't see Annie. He hoped she had hit the deck. The power fog light coming from the War Babies boat not only illuminated their two targets but also blinded Thessalonian's men. More rapid-fire everywhere.

The man behind the .50 caliber machine gun, Sumatra, was spraying the swamp wildly with rounds, but none were hitting close to the foglight. Within seconds though, Sumatra was sprayed, from his clavicle to his pelvis, out from behind his weapon by Turner and Parks.

Vince, who had squatted and had remained stationary, made his move. He leaped into the shallow water, running for Thessalonian's boat. Nick and Father Prio dashed in, too, headed for Annie's boat. Joey had grabbed McKinney's pistol.

Indonesia and Triad—the IIPAC paramilitaries in the flatbottom with Annie—were returning fire effectively, but were unprepared for an onslaught from the shore.

The soulful, basic Father Joseph Prio, without glasses, up to his thighs in water, stopped, aimed and fired. Miraculously, Triad dropped.

Indonesia spun around and fired a ludicrous pattern into the glade. Father Prio crumpled.

Thessalonian had commandeered Summatra's .50 caliber machine gun like a much younger man, but his dead-fish gray eyes were straining to find their target.

He triggered in all directions. And triggered! And triggered!

The bullet entered Vince's left tricep with the force of a Luigi Bertucci. The Angler stumbled, but kept on—splashing water into his arm wound—unrelenting.

He reached Thessalonian's boat, lifted himself over its edge, and grabbed the ex-CIA man's legs with both arms. Ingels, off balance, let go of the machine gun for a second, clasped both hands together, and brought them down squarely on the top of Vince's head. The Angler, true to his name, yanked and yanked—a final life-depleting yank—just as Charlie, Reginald, Matthew, and Vangels unloaded.

The face of Thessalonian burst, the scars on his throat became bluish popping veins, the scars on his arms, after lifting to his face, were sliced away.

He fell. And with him fell Burma, Miles Barker, and Victor Thomas Ingels. All overboard. All mortally wounded. Into the surreal, haunting, vaporous quagmire of Whiskey Bay.

Never lonely—
Never now—
The Ghost of Scarlet Leblanc
Rejoiced.

Epilogue

THREE MONTHS LATER

"Share with us, Mr. Plauche, please, one more time, your proposed press conference layout. Please."

Nick was agitated. He had had enough of these Justice Department analysts and their condescending politeness.

"Please, Mr. Plauche, please bear with us. We have after all been required to assimilate a great deal of information in a short period of time," the chief analyst pleaded, somehow artificially.

"Fine," Nick thought, "but after this, no more." He was suffocating. It was as if the analysts crowded around him were trying to hoard for themselves, in an inhuman way, the room's oxygen. Nick gasped slightly, then began, "The U.S. Attorney for the Eastern District of Louisiana will chair the conference. Seated to the left of his speaker's podium will be Father Joseph Prio."

"And what's his status again?" another analyst asked.

Nick sighed, frustrated with having to repeat himself—over and over.

"Father Prio was wounded in the shoulder. He is still recovering, but will never regain full use of his upper body."

"And the unresolved matter concerning Father Prio and the disappearance of Scarlet Leblanc in 1963?"

"The Louisiana Attorney General's office has agreed to no further action in the case. Father Prio will not be prosecuted."

"But wasn't Father Prio showing signs of mental instability in the hospital?" asked yet another analyst.

"No, he was not. The nurses reported only that in the initial days following he would pray out loud."

"That prayer being," the analyst shot up, "Peace within the cell, fierce warfare without. Hear all, believe a few. Honor all. Do not believe everything you hear. Do not judge everything you see. Do not do everything you can. Do not give everything you have. Do not say everything you know. Pray, read, withdraw, be silent, be at peace. Quite an unusual prayer, don't you think, Mr. Plauche?"

"No, I do not. What I think is unusual is that someone was monitoring Father Prio close enough to make a copy of it."

"Go on, Mr. Plauche," the chief analyst requested.

"Seated next to Father Prio will be Anthony Bartello of Bartello and Jacobs Law Firm representing Calogera 'Charlie' Nuccia."

"And what is Mr. Nuccia's status?"

"Mr. Nuccia was given an early release from federal prison—credit for time served—on the condition that he give his full testimony with immunity on Legerdemain to a secretly convened federal grand jury, and that he be represented publicly at this press conference to help substantiate our claims concerning his involvement, and then that he retire."

"And how sick is Charlie Nuccia? How bad is his Alzheimer's disease?"

"It is bad, very bad, but oddly enough when we explained to him that Vince, with his dying breath, had been responsible for Thessalonian's death, he became almost fully coherent, and agreed to our conditions. I'm sure only because of his long-standing friendship with Vince. Vince was like a son to him."

"Please continue, Mr. Plauche."

"Seated next to Bartello will be Keith Vangels, representing the group of men who rescued my wife."

"Why none of the others?" the analyst so familiar with Father Prio's prayers asked.

Nick could no longer contain his aggravation.

"Look, I can get them all—Sebastian, Matthew, Parks, Turner, Tortillino, Reginald, Charlie, even my wife Annie if need be—I just thought it best not to confuse the public with too many players at once."

The chief analyst used Nick's verbal slip as an excuse to suddenly drop his facade of civility.

"Players? Players, Mr. Plauche, like play-acting?"

"I didn't mean it like that," Nick said angrily, "it's just a figure of speech."

The chief analyst persisted.

"Have you ever considered, Mr. Plauche, that maybe this

entire investigation has been just a figment of your imagination?"

Nick bolted up from his chair, outraged.

"What in the world are you talking about? You've seen Clemer Dodd's documentation. You've seen the assassination plans that were given to Vince in '63. What in the world are you talking about?!"

The chief analyst stood, too, shaking like a ninny in the face of Nick's intimidating physical presence.

"What we are talking about, Mr. Plauche, is national security and a law passed in 1980 called the Classified Information Procedures Act which governs the use of secret information in criminal trials, and the fact that up until now all the critical data pertaining to Kennedy's assassination and subsequent related events has been vaulted in the National Archives."

Nick exploded.

"I KNEW IT! I KNEW IT! So this is what all this redundant questioning has been about. Vault it! The American people can't handle it! They're not sophisticated enough to absorb it! Just keep them fed and fat and they'll buy any sack of shit they're sold! Leave the wound open! Leave them questioning! Besides, we need the Sosar Tomeens of the world for our defense! For protection! Without stopping to think what that says about the state of our society—being in a position to need—to need the likes of him!" Nick waved his arms in semicircles. "Or is it that, maybe, you're all working for Tomeen? That you all belong to him, too? Is that it?" Nick gasped deeply now. "Well, hear this and hear it clear, my little pieces of afterbirth!" Nick lowered his voice to a solid rumble and stopped moving his arms. "I suspected that this might happen as far back as three months ago. Even before my clothes had dried off the water of Whiskey Bay. So I made arrangements. I told a story to a gentleman. I copied evidence and showed it to him. I presented to him sworn affidavits. And do you know what the gentleman said? He said that it was the scoop of the century! Scoop—get it? That means press—media."

Nick paused, almost winded from his tirade.

"And understand this, piss ants! My story has a face—and it's your face—all of yours. The face of American political, industrial, military hypocrisy and corruption! And I named names like Sosar Tomeen. And I explained just why and how John Fitzgerald Kennedy was brutally murdered. And why and how over 50,000 American boys died as brutally as Kennedy in a war that should never have been—a war that they were never meant to win! So, if by some sinister machination of yours this press conference is not held and Sosar Tomeen is not prosecuted, my story will go public. In fact, you're very fortunate it hasn't already. It took a lot of persuasion to hold my gentleman friend of the press back."

The chief analyst shrugged.

"Mr. Plauche, no one will believe you. And whatever evidence you've kept from us or made a record of, I assure you will be discredited, as you personally will be. Why throw your life away? With Vince dead your story will sound like a fairy tale. Think about it, Mr. Plauche. Think about it!"

Nick smiled, then without hesitation gathered up his tobacco pouch, corncob pipe, paperwork, and overcoat, and walked to the door.

"See you in the headlines, fellows. You think about that!"

Nicholas Plauche walked away laughing; a Cameron, Louisiana boy gone mad.

"How are you?"

"So, so, not bad, not near as bad as everyone thinks. Have you heard from him?"

"Yes, he was in Washington yesterday. He called me. Told me to do it; to run his story. He said Washington wanted to blanket it. He sounded kind of crazy, very stressed out."

"He still doesn't know that me and you have a relationship?"

"No. Let me explain something. Nick came to me after Whiskey Bay for the same reason you did later. Because I'm the best investigative journalist in this part of the country and I keep commitments. When Nick gave his story to me three months ago I made no guarantees to him in what form it would be released. But I did agree, reluctantly, to not release it until I received his go-ahead. Just as I promised you no release without your okay. Anyway, with Nick's story that worked out fine since a week later you approached me about officially co-writing but in reality writing your autobiography. So by combining the two under the heading of your life story our words have twice the believability."

"I'm holding the manuscript in my hands now. You've done a good job. I like the way you laid it out with Legerdemain but talked around the rest of my life without admitting anything."

"I wanted to be careful. Anything admitted in the government's eye would be indictable. As it is, you've admitted nothing specific but your role in Operation Legerdemain. That alone will generate a lot of trouble for you and your family."

"Trouble? I'm fast on my way ta that big house in the sky anyway, remember? And as far as my family is concerned, they've diversified and legitimized ta the point where they're three-quarters legal anyway. They'll survive it. And I do intend to bring Tomeen down. He was just as responsible as Thessalonian, if not more so, for Vince's death. And no one is going ta hurt me or my family like that without repercussion. No one!"

"I can appreciate your determination, sir."

"And I can appreciate your talent. Especially the way you described Vince. As a man who lived and died by his code—a code nonexistent today even amongst his own. A man ... a triggerman."

Silence followed respectfully.

Then Calogera "Charlie" "Top Man" Nuccia uttered the two words that both men knew would alter the course of history.

"Print it."

[illegible]

you are a reality [illegible] So [illegible] the [illegible] make the [illegible] of [illegible] [illegible]

I'm holding the [illegible] in the [illegible] [illegible] the way you [illegible] [illegible] [illegible]

[illegible] to the [illegible] [illegible] you [illegible] [illegible] that [illegible] and you [illegible]

[illegible] in this [illegible] [illegible] as far as [illegible] they [illegible] [illegible] the [illegible] where they [illegible] [illegible] [illegible] was [illegible] as [illegible] death. And [illegible] going to [illegible] No one!"

[illegible]

"And I [illegible] your [illegible] [illegible] the way you described [illegible] a man who [illegible] his life [illegible]

[illegible]

[illegible]

[illegible] and [illegible] would [illegible] the [illegible]

[illegible]

Political Current Events from SPI Books

[illegible] **Compromised: Clinton, Bush and the** [illegible] [illegible] [illegible] [illegible] Governor of Arkansas [illegible] CIA [illegible] [illegible] Vice-President [illegible] [illegible] the presidency [illegible]

[illegible] **Terror** [illegible] **U.S. Today** [illegible] [illegible] [illegible] Task Force on Terrorism [illegible] [illegible] and Canada. [illegible]

[illegible] SPI Books [illegible] New York, NY [illegible]

[illegible]

[illegible]

Name

Address

☐ [illegible] The Story Of A [illegible]

[illegible]

ISBN 1-56171-[illegible]

☐ They Died [illegible]

[illegible]

ISBN 1-56171-[illegible]

☐ [illegible] Official Rules and [illegible] Book [illegible] the reader [illegible] the rules and regulations [illegible] poker [illegible] to improve your game. [illegible] illustrate the various points.

ISBN 1-56171-[illegible]

[illegible]

S.P.I. Books • 136 W. 22nd St. • New York, NY 10011

Tel: 212/633-2022 • Fax: 212/633-2123

[illegible]

[illegible]

Name

Address